ENCYCLOPAEDIA OF INDIA, PAKISTAN AND BANGLADESH

ENCYCLOPAEDIA OF

INDIA, PAKISTAN AND BANGLADESH

(In 9 Volumes)

(Volume 6)

OM GUPTA

ISHA

ISHA BOOKS

Delhi-110033

Encyclopaedia of India, Pakistan and Bangladesh
(In 9 Volumes)

ISBN : 81-8205-389-7 (Set)
ISBN : 81-8205-395-1 (Vol. 6)

Rs. 6300 (Set)

Published in 2006 in India by
Isha Books
D-43, Prithviraj Road,
Adarsh Nagar, Delhi - 110033
e-mail : ishabooks@hotmail.com

Laser Typesetting : Vinayak Printers, Delhi
Printed at : Salasar Imaging Systam, Delhi

Preface

According to Oxford dictionary Encyclopaedia is a book or aset of books that gives information on many subjects or many aspect of one subject. This encyclopaedia does that on India, Pakistan and Bangladesh. It is the first work of its kind. There have been anthologies on India but there is no compendium of information in an alphabetical order. Even Britannica could go as far as four-volume encyclopaedia on Indian history.

Encyclopaedia is an extension of a dictionary. The latter gives you meanings of words while the former gives facts about people, places and events. No one can claim to compile all the facts and that of a sub-continent called India. But then it is the prerogative of the editor to pick up his entries that he considers would be useful to his reader. Generally we soon find our comfort levels in a language. And rarely consults a dictionary and lesser an encyclopaedia. But those who dare, find the experience worth it. It can be easily compared to a human body. In our daily life we tend to be our own quacks and medicate on the basis of common sense. If we refer to a doctor we come to know the actual cause of the symptom and get relieved on knowing the gravity of the situation or the absence of it. One would realize that encyclopaedia reveals the fundamentals of any situation, person or the event and we feel at home with that information.

A dictionary and an encyclopaedia can easily enlarge the process of learning even to an uninitiated person. It is truer in case of humanities. Popular myth about encyclopaedia is that it is meant to be referred to in a library only. The librarians, the world over keep encyclopaedia in such zealously guarded protection that the generally refrain from asking for it. Since the advent of internet in our life, the bulkiness of encyclopaedias has disappeared. That is why we have divided this enterprise in nine volumes. Encyclopaedias are generally global in its expanse. Even subject-related encyclopaedias give the global perspective.That is why country-specific encylopaedias have never been seriousy attempted. We hope that this effort will fill that volume. Traditionally encyclopaedias don't deal with factual data e.g. Indian exports, population figures, GDP. That is the job of annual reference books. They are also different from alamans in as much as that they don't give dated entries. That will become texts on history. Encyclopaedias need to be updated. A country is alive and kicking. People and events continue to play role in various aspects of life. Hence they need to be added. That is why either annual supplements or updation needs to be done in encyclopaedias. We would strive for that.

Regarding its contents only those entries have been included that continue to influence the life of a nation. There are historical figures who might have played a significant role in their times but if those deeds have no relevance to the present they have been excluded. Another example is literary awards. They always create controversies because their selection at times is subjective. Hence only universally accepted meritorious work has found place in these volumes. In this context a debatable point need to be stated. Who is more important book or the author. Conventionally work is an end product and only that is a measure of the author's importance but then a prolic writer might have produced a large body of creations. Hence to save space the author is entered with all his important work.That is also an international practice.

Lastly, why India, Pakistan and Bangladesh have been clubbed together. Before India's independence they were one nation. They share a common heritage and composite culture. Their post-independence history is different but 22their foundation is undivided. In order to appreciate the historical context better it is necessary to cross-refer and that was possible when they are juxtaposed.

Om Gupta

L

Laad Bazaar : Laad Bazaar is a locale in the Indian city of Hyderabad. Standing on one of the four main roads that branch out from the Charminar, it is located in a very old area of Hyderabad."Laad" is a term in Hindi and Urdu. While it is difficult to fully translate to English, its meaning can be approximated to indicate "to love" or "to pamper" – and a more appropriate name would be difficult to bestow upon it. In this gently sloping, roughly kilometre-long strip, one finds a number of stores selling articles primarily targeted towards women. A vast and colourful array of stores selling bangles, saris, wedding clothes and items, jewellery and other such items present themselves here.

Shopkeepers may "set" prices which seem outlandish, however, they do so in anticipation of the haggling known to take place in the bazaar as prices are in actuality rather arbitrary. Some shopkeepers also employ "beckoning" tactics, positioning an employee at the entrance of the store beckoning passers-by to enter and peruse their selection. While they are generally brushed off and considered a nuisance by shoppers, they occaisionally draw a client in, and thus justify the tactic in the shop owner's eyes. Many of the stores selling clothing and related items are furnished with a clean, softly padded floor. The philosophy behind this is that to conserve space in a cramped store, the floor becomes in a sense, everything. The customer sits down on the soft floor having removed her shoes, leans against a wall against a pillow and the employee presents different items to her, right there on the floor. All business is conducted on this floor and often other employees use the padded area in the back, as they may be sorting or sewing something. Autorickshaws and cars are barred entrance from the Charminar end(the preferred entrance) of the strip due to the narrow street being quite crowded, and as such only pedestrians, bicycles, motorcycles and scooters, and perhaps cycle-rickshaws are permitted to enter.

Lachen River : Lachen River is a tributary of the River Teesta.

Ladainha : Ladainha or Ladin is a thanksgiving ritual among the Christians of Goa. The Ladin which literally means a litany to the Virgin Mary, is a religious function of thanksgiving to god for material and spiritual benefits that have accrued or are sought for, by the persons sponsoring the Ladin. Preparations for Ladin would begin with the purchase of grams, branco wine, candles, coloured tinsel paper in the local market. The family altar is bedecked with flowers, creepers, crotons laid out in vases. The gram soaked in water since morning is then put on the fire to be boiled and coconut chips are sliced to be mixed with the boiled grams.

The Ladin consists of a litany sung by every one present, to the accompaniment of the violin, singing of hymns and prayers. The village choirmaster or a local violinist conducts the show involved in the singing of the litany. Muharram, Bakrid and Ramzan are the festivals celebrated by the Muslims in Goa.

Ladakh : Ladakh is the largest district of the Indian state of Jammu and Kashmir, covering more than half the area of the state (of which it is the eastern part). Nevertheless Ladakh is one of the least populated districts in India. It is renowned for its remote mountain beauty and Tibetan Buddhist culture; it is sometimes called "Little Tibet". The capital is Leh. Recent protests by the people of Ladakh have called to make the Kashmiri district a new Indian union territory because of its difference from predominantly Sunni Islamic Kashmir.

Ladakh Scouts : Ladakh Scouts is an infantry regiment of the Indian Army. It was raised on 1 June 1963, following the 1962 Indo-China War, with just eight companies taken from the 7th and 14th Battalions of the Jammu & Kashmir Militia; the regiment's main task at its inception was to guard India's borders in the high altitude areas of the Ladakh region. Also known as the Snow Warriors, the Regiment has taken part, and proved itself, in various operations since the 1965 Indo-Pak War. The Regiment was one of the first units to take part in Operation Vijay—the 1999 Kargil Conflict—and covered itself with glory during the conflict. Major Sonam Wangchuk, was the most recent recipient of the MVC for the Regiment in the Kargil Conflict.

Laddu : Laddu or Ladoo is a popular Indian sweet. It is made of flour and other ingredients formed into balls that are dipped in sugar syrup. The popularity of Laddu is due to its ease of preparation. In fact, Laddu is so popular that any chubby kid in India is affectionately called 'Laddu.'

Variations in the preparation of Laddu result in different tastes. Laddu is often made to celebrate festivals or household events such as weddings. 'Tirupati Laddu', the most famous laddu made at Tirumala in Andhra Pradesh, is immensely popular for its taste.

Lagaan : Lagaan, is an award winning movie made in India, released on June 1, 2001 and nominated for the

Academy Award for Best Foreign Language Film (the award actually went to No Man's Land that year). Unusually widely distributed throughout the world, this was for many Westerners the first opportunity to see a genuine Bollywood film in their own movie theaters.

Lahiri Mahasaya : Shyama Charan Lahiri, best known as Lahiri Mahasaya (September 30, 1828 - September 26, 1895) was an Indian yogi and the guru of Sri Yukteswar Giri. Mahasaya is a Sanskrit religious title. He was unusual among Indian holy men in that he was a householder. Lahiri lived with his family in Benares rather than in a temple or monastery apart from family life. Nonetheless, he achieved a substantial reputation among 19th century Hindu religionists.

Lahiri was an office worker until the age of about 30, when he met his own guru, Mahavatar Babaji. Lahiri was said to have been chosen by his semi-legendary guru to reintroduce the lost practise of Kriya Yoga to the phenomenal world. Lahiri's disciples included both Yogananda's parents as well as Yogananda's own guru Sri Yukteswar. Lahiri Mahasaya is said to have prophesied that the infant Yogananda would become a great yogi.

Lahoor : This dance is generally performed by women during the Spring season when work in the fields is over.

Lahore : Lahore is a major city in Pakistan and is the capital of the province of Punjab. A native of Lahore is called a Lahori. It is located near the river Ravi and the Indian border, at 31°34'N 74°20'E. Lahore is estimated to have approximately 8.5 million people residing in it. This makes it the second largest city in Pakistan. It is considered to be the 24th largest city of the world. Punjabi is the language of the province, and is the most widely spoken language in Lahore. Punjabi spoken by the people of Lahore is known as Lahori Punjabi due to a mixture of Punjabi and colloquial Urdu spoken in Lahore.

Lahore is largely thought of as the cultural centre of Pakistan ever since its accession by the Mughal Empire since the 16th century A.D.This is apparent by the vast array of historic buildings, architecture from pre-Mughal, Mughal and British periods, and cultural events held throughout the year. The recently renovated Data Durbar is perhaps the most famous example of architecture from pre-Mughal times. Mughal architecture can be seen in the Badshahi Mosque, Lahore Fort and Shalimar Gardens. Various buildings originally built by the British still retain their Mughal-Gothic style.

Location of Lahore city is bounded on the north and west by the Sheikhupura district, on the east by India and on the south Kasur district. The Ravi river flows on the northern side of Lahore. Lahore covers a total land area of the city is 404 sq. Km, but the city is still growing at a considerable rate. The altitude of the city lies between 31-15 and 31-45 North, latitudes and 74-01 and 74-39 East longitude. The ever increasing population of the city is approximetely seven million, in which many languages are spoken which include Punjabi, Urdu and English.

Lahore Ahmadiyya Movement : The Lahore Ahmadiyya Movement, Ahmadiyya Anjuman Ishaat-i-Islam (not to be confused with the Ahmadiyya Muslim Association), formed as a result of an ideological differences between the Ahmadiyya Community after the demise Maulawi Nur 'ud-Din in 1914, the first Khalifa of its founder, Mirza Ghulam Ahmad. The dispute was based on differing interpretations of a verse (33:40) in the Qur'an related to the finality of prophethood, other issues of contention were the Kalima, funeral prayers, and the suitability of the elected Khalifa (2nd successor) Mirza Bashir-ud-Din Mahmood Ahmad (the son of the Founder).

The Ahmadiyya Anjuman Ishaat-i-Islam is led by a President or Amir.

Lahore District : Lahore District is a district in the Punjab province of Pakistan that contains the city of Lahore, the capital of the province.

Lahore Fort : The Lahore Fort, locally referred to as Shahi Qila is the citadel of the city of Lahore, in modern day Pakistan. It is located in the northwestern corner of Lahore, adjacent to the Walled City. Some of the famous sites within the fort are: Sheesh Mahal, Alamgiri Gate, Naulakha pavilion, and Moti Masjid. The fort is 1400 feet long and 1115 feet wide.

According to available historical information, the origin of Lahore Fort is obscure. Traditionally the foundation of Lahore and its fort is attributed to Loh, the son of Rama, Avatara of Lord Vishnu of Hinduism, and hero of the Ramayana of epic age (1200-800 B.C.). However, during the execution done in the year 1959 A.D. by the Department of Archaelogy, in front of Diwan-e-Am, a gold coin of Mahmood of Ghazni dated A.H. 146 (1025 A.D.) was found at a depth of 25 feet from the level of the lawns.

Cultural layers continued to a further depth of 15 feet, giving strong indications that people had lived here, long before the conquest of Lahore by Mahmud in 1021 A.D. Further mention of the fort is traceable in connection with Shahab-ud-Din Ghori's successive invasions of Lahore from 1180 to 1186 A.D.

Lahore Museum : Lahore Museum, was established in 1894 in Lahore, Pakistan, and it is a major museum of the South Asia. Lahore Museum is also known as Central Museum. The museum has on display a number of objects including Greco-Buddhist sculptures, Mughal and Pahari paintings. The Fasting Buddha is one of the unique collections of this museum.

Lahore Resolution : The Lahore Resolution is a political statement adopted by the All India Muslim League on 23 March 1940.

Although the idea of founding the state Pakistan had been introduced as early as 1930, very few had responded to it. However, the volatile political climate and hostilities between the Hindus and Muslims in British India gave the idea stronger backing. The division of India into two separate sovereign states is sometimes referred as Two Nation Theory.

In 1939, the Viceroy Lord Linlithgow declared India's entrance into World War II without consulting provincial governments. In protest, the Indian National Congress asked all of its elected representatives to resign from the government. In 1940, Mohammad Ali Jinnah called a general session of the All India Muslim League in Lahore to discuss the situation. The meeting was also aimed at analyzing the reasons that led to the defeat of the Muslim League in the Indian general election of 1937 in the Muslim majority provinces. Jinnah, in his speech, criticised the Congress and the nationalist Muslims, and espoused the Two-Nation Theory and the reasons for the demand for separate Muslim homelands. Sikandar Hayat Khan, the Chief Minister of the Punjab, drafted the original Lahore Resolution, which was placed before the Subject Committee of the All India Muslim League for discussion and amendments. The resolution, radically amended by the subject committee, was moved in the general session by Shere-Bangla A.K. Fazlul Huq, the Chief Minister of Bengal, on 23 March and was supported by Choudhury Khaliquzzaman and other Muslim leaders. The Lahore Resolution ran as follows:

That the areas where the Muslims are numerically in a majority as in the Northwestern and Eastern zones of India should be grouped to constitute 'independent states' in which the constituent units shall be autonomous and sovereign.

Lahore Stock Exchange : Lahore Stock Exchange (Guarantee) Limited came into existence in October 1970, under the Securities and Exchange Ordinance, 1969, of the Government of Pakistan in response to the needs of the provincial metropolis of the Punjab. It initially had only 83 members and it was housed in a rented building in the crowded area of Bank Square in exotic city of Lahore. The number of members has increased from 83 to 650 over a period of 25 years. Lahore Stock Exchange has opened its branches in Faisalabad and Sialkot (2 industrial Cities of Pakistan) for trading.

Lahul and Spiti : The district of Lahul and Spiti in the Indian state of Himachal Pradesh consists of the two formerly separate districts of Lahul and Spiti. The present capital is Keylong in Lahul. Before the two districts were merged, Kardang was the capital of Lahul, and Dankar the capital of Spiti. Lahul and Spiti are cut off from the rest of the world by high mountain ranges. The Rohtang Pass, at 3,978 metres, separates Lahul and Spiti from the Kullu Valley. The district borders Tibet to the east, the Ladakh region (within the state of Jammu and Kashmir) to the north, and Kinnaur and Kullu to the south. The Lahul sub-division consists of the Rangoli, Bhaga, Pattan, and Lingti valleys; while the Spiti sub-division consists of the Sham, Pin, Bhar, and Tud valleys.

Lai - Haraoba : The Manipuris believe that this dance represents the concept of the beginning of the world. There is a legend that in the beginning there was only Guru Sidaba, the highest Lord, existing in the dark vacuum. Once the brilliant hues of the rainbow shot into this dark space, the beams of lights motivated the Guru to witness the world with flora and fauna. He sent Atiya Guru Sidaba along with a creature to create the world. This creature spun a web-like frame work on which the human inhabitation was to be initiated. Atiya Guru desired to solidify the framework. He went again to Guru Sidaba. The Guru offered him some dirt from his navel and he also created nine men from right side and seven women from his left side to assist Atiya Guru. The dirt was to be applied to the framework to solidify it. The Atiya Guru along with the team of men and women sat down to work. Their attempt was foiled twice by one Harba. Guru Sidaba then sent the goddess of lightning to assist Atiya Guru. With the graceful beauty and charm the goddess could entice Harba away. The framework was then solidified and declared fit for human habitation. On its completion the occasion was celebrated as Lai-Haraoba. Twelve main sequences which part by part depict each process in the creation.

Laiharaoba Dance : It is an ancient village dance, which is the fountainhead of the modern Manipuri dance form.

Lake Manasarovar : Lake Manasarovar (also known as Lake Manasarowar or Mapam Yumco Lake) is a lake on the Tibetan Plateau near Mount Kailash and Lake Rakshastal. It is considered to be the highest freshwater lake in the world. The Brahmaputra River (the Tsangpo), the Indus River, the Sutlej River and the Karnali River all trace their sources to this lake. Manasarovar is very holy to Hindus in India and some make the pilgrimage every year to visit this lake.

According to Hindu mythology, the lake was first created in the mind of the Lord Brahma. Hence, in Sanskrit it is called "Manasarovar", which is a combination of the words Manas (mind) and Sarovar (lake). Lake

Manasarowar is relatively round in shape, and has a few monastaries on its shores. The most notable of which is the ancient Chew Monastary, which has been built right onto a steep hill. It looks as if it has been carved right out of the rock.

Lakhon Puza : It is a dance of the Lalung tribe.

Lakhueen-jo-daro : Lakhueen-jo-daro is a archaeological site located in Sindh, Pakistan. The site of Lakhueen-jo-daro, near Sukkur, belongs to the Matura Harappan Civilization as indicated by the characteristics of the structural remains, material culture finds and one radiocarbon date, covers a wide area, from which a few mounds emerge. The site indicates that the origins of Sukkur are to be referred to a much older period than previously suspected.

Lakki Marwat : Lakki Marwat is a district of North-West Frontier Province in Pakistan. It was created as an administrative district on July 1st 1992, prior to which it was part of Bannu district. The district derives its name from the district headquarters town. The word Lakki derives from Lakai which means tail in the local dialect, referring to the location of the town at the tail of the area which inhabited by the Marwat tribe - hence the name Lakki Marwat.

Lakki Marwat district had a population of 490,025 at the 1998 census of which only 46,878 people or 9.6% of the population live in urban areas, while 443,147 persons or 90.4% of the population lives in the rural areas.

Lakkidi : Lakkidi is the gateway of Wayanad district of Kerala state, south India. It gets the second highest degree of rainfall in the world. Lakkidi is one of the highest locations in Wayanad. It is situated 700 m above mean sea level, atop Thamarassery ghat pass. Vythiri is the nearest town, just 5 km from Lakkidi. Chain tree, Pookot Lake, Sight seeing point on ghat road and number of tourist resorts are within 5 km from Lakkidi.

Lakshadweep : Lakshadweep is the smallest Union Territory of India. It consists of 12 coral atolls, three coral reefs, and five banks. The total land area of the territory is 32 km^2. The islands are located in the Arabian Sea, between 200 to 300 km off the coast of Kerala. Eleven of the islands are inhabited. There are numerous islets which are not counted in this number. Lakshadweep is the northern part of Old Lakshadweepa.

The main islands are Kavaratti (where the capital city, Kavaratti, is located), Agatti, Minicoy, and Amini. The total population of the territory was 60,595 according to the 2001 census. Agatti has an airport where there are direct flights from Cochin. Tourists may need a permit to visit the islands; foreign nationals are not permitted to visit some islands.

The name of the archipelago literally means hundred thousand islands (laksha = one hundred thousand, dweep = island). Until 1973, the island group was known by the Anglicized name Laccadives (compare to Maldives and Suvadives) although the term Laccadives strictly only applies to central Lakshdweep with the northern Amindivi Islands and Minicoy to the south considered separate. This is reflected in the pre-1973 name of the union territory, Laccadive, Minicoy, and Amindivi Islands.

Lakshmi : Lakshmi is commonly represented as Vishnu's wife. Lakshmi is widely represented as the goddess of wealth. Being, the power and consort of Vishnu, the preserver, she is represented as the power of multiplicity and the goddess of fortune.

Lakshmi is usually described as enchantingly beautiful and standing on a lotus and holding a lotus in each of her two hands. It is because of this perhaps that she is named as Padma or Kamala. She is also adorned with a lotus garland. Very often elephants are shown on either side, emptying pitchers of water over her, the pitchers being held by celestial maidens. Her colour is variously described as dark, pink, golden yellow or white. While in the company of Vishnu, she is shown with two hands only. When worshipped in a temple, she is shown seated on a lotus throne, with four hands holding Padma (lotus) Sankha (conch) Amrtakalasa (a pot of ambrosia) and Bilvafruit.

If Lakshmi is pictured as dark in complexion, it is to show that she is the consort of Vishnu, the dark god. If golden yellow, that shows her as the source of all wealth. If white, she represents the purest form of prakti (nature) form which the Universe had developed. The pinkish complexion which is more common, reflects her compassion for creatures, since she is is the mother of all.

Her four hands signify her power to grand the four Purusharthas (ends of human life), Dharma (righteousness), Artha (wealth), Kama (pleasures of the flesh) and Moksa (freedom).

Lakshmi Mittal : Steel tycoon Lakshmi Mittal, the 55 year old non resident Indian living in Britain, rose into focus this year when he was named the third richest person in the world by the Forbes Magazine after Microsoft chief Bill Gates and US investment guru Warren Buffett. He was also listed as the richest person in Britain in the Sunday Times Rich list 2005. Mittal heads the multi national Steel Company Mittal Steel, the largest producer of steel in the world.

Lakshmi Narayan Mittal alias Lakshmi Niwas Mittal was born on June 15th, 1950, in Sadulpur, in Rajasthan, India. After finishing his Bachelor of Commerce degree in business and accounting with first class, Mittal began his career in his father's steel firm in the early seventies. His success has largely been built on buying up loss-making state-owned mills and quickly turning them around. He had one of his most notable successes in the late 1989, when he turned around a loss-making government-founded steel firm in Trinidad and Tobago which was losing $1 million a day. Within a year, Mittal had doubled the output and made the business profitable where US consultants and German experts failed to find a solution.

In 1992, he went to Mexico and bought the country's third largest steel producer, Sicartsa for $220 million. This was followed by an acquisition of Siderurgica del Balsas SA at Lazaro Cardenas in Mexico and then more companies in Canada, Germany, Ireland etc. Mittal followed the same strategy in former Soviet republic of Kazakhstan, and took over the state-owned blast furnace steel plant in 1995, renaming it Ispat Karmet. It was a risky proposition even by Mittal's standards, workers had not been paid for six months. But within a year it was profitable and production has doubled from 120,000 tons a month to 250,000. In 1995, two new companies Ispat International Ltd. and Ispat Shipping were formed to provide technical and commercial services to the Group and to meet its growing shipping needs. The same year, he entered into Europe by acquiring a steel plant in Hamburg, Germany. With this, the capacity of the group reached to 11.2 million tonnes. Meanwhile in 1994, a partition in the family business group, transferred all the foreign business into Ispat International, under the control of Lakshmi Mittal. The Indian operations remained with his younger brothers P K Mittal and V K Mittal. In 1997, Ispat International, the company that controlled the Group's steel making operations in Mexico, Trinidad and Tobago, Canada and Germany went for listing in 1997 on the New York and Amsterdam stock exchanges. The Ispat group went on making major acquisitions.

In 2004, Mittal Steel was formed through the merger of Ispat International and LNM Holdings, at the same time Ispat International merged with International Steel Group Inc. (ISG) an Ohio based company, becoming the world's most global steel producer with a net worth of over $22 billion. Mittal's industrial empire has steel making facilities in 14 countries and stretches from Indonesia to Poland, via Mexico, US, South Africa and Trinidad, North America, Africa, Asia and many European countries.

Mittal has received accolades for his achievements. In 1996, he was awarded the title 'Steel maker of the Year' by New Steel Magazine in the USA, and he received the Eighth Honorary Willy Korf Steel Vision Award, the highest recognition for world wide achievement in the steel industry in June 1998. The award was presented by the American Metal Market, a specialised publication, and Paine Weber's World Steel Dynamics in New York., for outstanding vision, entrepreneurship, leadership and success in global steel development, from the American Metal Market and Paine Weber's World Steel Dynamics. In 2004, he was awarded the 'European Business man of the year' by Fortune Magazine.

Lal Baag Palace : Lal Baag palace lies on the south-west of the city, surrounded by gardens in Madhya Pradesh. It was built between 1886 and 1921. Currently this is the residence of Usha Raje, direct descendent of the Holkars, whose ancestral palace it used to be. It is one of the grandest monuments of the Holkar dynasty. The rooms have been restored and furnished to pleasing effect. Much of the furniture and ornamentation is in the late Regency, early Georgian style. It's Italian marble columns, grand chandeliers, rich Persian carpets, flying nymphs on the ceiling, Belgium stained glass windows, Greek mythological relief's, Italian style wall paintings, a wooden ballroom floor mounted on springs, stuffed leopards and tigers are magnificent. The whole complex has a total area of 28 acres and at one time had one of the best rose gardens of the country.

Lal Bahadur Shastri : He (October 2, 1904—January 11, 1966) was the second permanent Prime Minister of independent India and a significant figure in the struggle for independence.

Lal Bahadur was born in Moghalsarai, also spelt as Mughalsarai. To take part in the non-cooperation movement of Mahatma Gandhi in 1921, he began studying at the nationalist, non-government university in Kashi, and upon completion was given the title Shastri, or Scholar, Doctor at Kashi Vidya Peetha in 1926. He spent almost nine years in jail in total, mostly after the start of the Satyagraha movement in 1940, he was imprisoned until 1946.

Following India's independence, he was Home Minister under Chief Minister Govind Vallabh Pant of Uttar Pradesh. In 1951, he was appointed General Secretary of the Lok Sabha before re-gaining a ministerial post as Railways Minister. He resigned as Minister following a rail disaster near Ariyalur, Tamil Nadu. He returned to the Cabinet following the General Elections, first as Minister for Transport, in 1961, he became Home Minister.

Jawaharlal Nehru died in office on May 27, 1964 and left something of a vacuum. The major figures of the Congress Party were unable to find enough support which allowed the lesser regarded Shastri to come through as the compromise candidate, becoming Prime Minister on June 9. Shastri, though mild-mannered and soft-spoken, was a Nehruvian socialist and thus held appeal to those wishing to prevent the ascent of conservative right-winger Morarji Desai.

In January 1966 Shastri and Pakistani President Muhammad Ayub Khan attended a summit in Tashkent (former USSR), organised by Kosygin. Shastri signed a treaty with Pakistan on January 10, the Tashkent Declaration, but the next day he was dead of a heart attack. He is the only Indian Prime Minister to have died in office overseas, and indeed probably one of the few heads of government in history to do so. All his lifetime, he was known for his honesty and humbleness. He was the first person to be posthumously awarded the Bharat Ratna and a memorial "Vijay Ghat" was built for him in Delhi. The slogan Jai Jawan, Jai Kisan (Hindi for "Hail the soldier, Hail the farmer") is attributed to Shastri.

Lal Kot : Lal Kot was an 8th century fortress in the Kingdom of Delhi. Anangpal, often described as the founder of Delhi, built the citadel some 10 kilometres from Suraj Kund around 731. Lal Kot was later used as a grand fort built by Anang Pal Tomar. The kingdom of Delhi was captured by the Chauhan Rajputs in the 12th century, and Prithviraj III built massive ramparts around the area and called it Qila Rai Pithora. The ramparts were later demolished by the slave kings and Lal Kot became the site of the first mosque in India, Quwwat-ul-Islam Masjid.

Archaeological excavations uncovered the earliest of proper settlements in Delhi. Only ramparts of the city, dating back to the 11th century remain. Heavy encroachment by population is endangering the historic saga of the site.

Lal Krishna Advani : Lal Krishna Advani also known as Lal Kishenchand Advani was the President of the Bharatiya Janata Party (BJP) until year-end 2005 and is Leader of the Opposition in the 14th Lok Sabha. He is a prominent figure in his party and was the Deputy Prime Minister and Home Minister in the Indian government (1998-2004). He is considered to be the most influential leader in his party. He was conferred the Outstanding Parliamentarian Award for the year 1999.

Advani was born on November 8, 1929 in Karachi (now in Pakistan) to Kishichand D. Advani. His early schooling was at St.Patrick's school in Karachi. He later joined the D.G. National College in Hyderabad, Sindh (now in Pakistan). He later on graduated in Law from the Government Law College Bombay University.

The BJP launched a decade-long movement led by Advani on the issue of the Ram Temple. The BJP demanded that a temple dedicated to Lord Rama be created on the spot where (according to their claim) a temple stood till Babar's invasion of India. The Ayodhya site is claimed by both Hindus and Muslims. A mosque there was torn down by Hindu activists in 1992, sparking riots nationwide that cost 2,000 lives. Hindus consider Ayodhya a very sacred place since Lord Ram was born there. The disputed mosque was built on the site of an earlier grand temple dedicated to Lord Ram. Speaking to correspondents on his appointment as President of BJP, Advani said: "We must be candid enough to recognise the Hindu anger that exploded on the streets in the early 1990s has given way to a patient wait for the new temple whose construction, I feel is inevitable.". A promise which he failed to keep even after being elected to the post of deputy prime minister. In appearances before the Liberhan Commission, a judicial body set up to investigate the Babri incident, Advani claimed that the demolition was the most agonising moment of his life.

Lal Suhanra Nartional park : Lal Suhanra Nartional park was declared a national park on 26 October 1972, following recommendations made by the Wildlife Enquiry Committee in 1971. Originally, the park comprised an area of 31,355ha, of which 20,932ha were desert, 8,488ha irrigated forest plantation and 1,934ha reservoir; it was due to be enlarged by 22,680ha. It is crossed by the dried-up bed of the Hakra River and features an important wetland, Patisar Lake. Pakistan Tourism Development

Corporation(PTDC) has 6 A/C bedroom resorts in the park. Beside this camping can also be done in selected campsites.

Lala Amarnath : Nanik Amarnath Bhardwaj (commonly known as Lala Amarnath; September 11, 1911 – August 5, 2000) was an Indian Test cricketer. He was the first cricketer to score a Test century for the Indian cricket team, which he achieved in his debut Test. He was also Independent India's first Test captain, leading the team to a tour of Australia in 1947-1948. He is widely regarded as one of the earliest Indian legends of cricket, alongside with Ranjitsinhji and Duleepsinhji.

Amarnath was born in Kapurthala, Punjab, and was raised in Lahore. He played his debut match against England in 1933 on the Bombay Gymkhana grounds in South Bombay. Amarnath also played for the Hindus in the Bombay Quadrangular. Along with being a tenacious batsman, Lala Amarnath was also a bowler of some repute and is the only bowler to have got Donald Bradman out hit wicket.

When the Partition of India took place in August 1947, Amarnath and his family had to flee the city to escape the Muslim mobs that looted his house and almost killed him. Amarnath lived in Patiala in the Indian state of Punjab till 1957, when he moved to the capital, Delhi. However to this day, he remains a legend and an adored figure in Pakistan, with many friends of the era before partition, like Pakistani legends Fazal Mahmood. Amarnath is widely respected for reaching out to bridge the divide between players and fans of India and Pakistan, caused by political tensions between the two countries.

Amarnath as captain was complimented for being straightforward, aggressive and possessing a tactical genius. Under him, India won the first-ever Test against the Pakistan cricket team in Delhi in 1952, and won the series 2-1. Amarnath also managed the team when it toured Pakistan in 1954-55. His sons Mohinder Amarnath and Surinder Amarnath, the latter of which also scored a century on his debut, also played cricket for India. Mohinder was considered one of the best Indian all-rounders ever, and along with captain Kapil Dev, the hero of the Indian victory in the 1983 Cricket World Cup.

Lala Jagat Narain : Lala Jagat Narain was the founder of the Hind Samachar group. An Arya Samaji, he was a prominent opponent of Bhindranwale. He was murdered on September 9, 1981. He was shot dead on September 9, 1981, near Amaltas Motel on the national highway while returning to Jalandhar from Patiala. Bhindranwale barricaded himself inside the fortified Gurudwara Gurdarshan Parkash at Mehta Chowk, but was pursuaded to surrender on September 20, 1981. For 25 days, violence exploded all over [[Punjab, while Bhindranwale was jailed in a Circuit House.

During the eighties, sikh extremists killed anyone who sold their papers. Hind Samachar Group of Newspapers had initiated a fund for helping victims of terrorism and that of natural calamities. His family had not only lost two of its members — Lala Jagat Narain and Ramesh Chander, but the newspaper lost 62 of its editorial staff A chair in the name of Lala Jagat Narain was established at Kurukshetra University in 1998.

Lala Lajpat Rai : Lala Lajpat Rai was an Indian political leader who is chiefly known for leading movements against British Raj in India. The freedom fighter was popularly known as Punjab Kesari (The Lion of Punjab). Rai was born on January 28, 1865 in village Dhudi Ke, in present day Moga district of Punjab, India. He was the eldest son of Munshi Radha Kishan Azad and Gulab Devi.

He was one of the famous three Extremist leaders of the Indian National Congress who had fought and given their lives during the Indian independence movement in the first half of the twentieth century. The other two were Bal Gangadhar Tilak of Maharashtra and Bipin Chandra Pal of Bengal. Collectively, they were dubbed Lal-Bal-Pal.

It was the Partition of Bengal in 1905 that aroused their robust nationalism and set them firmly on the path to fighting for freedom. The repressive measures of the British Government against the growing nationalist movement inspired them to infuse greater national pride and self-respect into the populace. The trio wanted a degree of self-government that was considered radical at the time. They were the first Indian leaders to demand complete political independence.

Rai presided over the first session of the All India Trade Union Congress in 1920. He also went to Geneva to attend the eighth International Labour Conference in 1926 as a representative of Indian labour. He had an opportunity to watch the labour movement in the USA and England where he was required to prolong his stay for political reasons.

Rai led the Punjab protests against the Amritsar Massacre (1919) and the Non-Cooperation Movement (1919 - 1922). He was repeatedly arrested. Rai however disagreed with Mohandas Gandhi's suspension of the movement due to the Chauri Chaura incident, and formed the Congress Independence Party, which was particularly pro-Hindu in voice and policy.

He was not only a good orator but also a prolific and versatile writer. His journal Arya Gazette concentrated mainly on subjects related to the Arya Samaj. Bande Mataram and People, contained his inspiring speeches to end oppression by the foreign rulers. He founded the

Servants of the People Society, which worked for the freedom movement as well as for social reform in the country. He also wrote an autobiography in English titled The Story of My Life.

A strong believer in leading by example, he himself led a procession to demonstrate against the Simon Commission, which was to prove fatal for him. He was made the target of a brutal lathi charge in which he was injured badly. A meeting was held the same evening where he spoke with such vigour that his words, "Every blow aimed at me is a nail in the coffin of British imperialism", became historic. Though he recovered from the fever and pain within three days yet his health had received a permanent setback and on November 17, 1928, he succumbed to the fatal injuries.

Lalbagh Botanical Gardens : This garden is at Lal Bagh Fort Road in Karnataka. The pleasant and supereb 100 ha Botanical garden were laid out by Hyderali in 1760 while his son Tippu Sultan added a wealth of plants and trees from many countries. It was originally called Lalbagh because the garden had profusion of red roses. It has a very good collection of tropical and sub tropical and medicinal plants.

The galss house, based on London Crystal Palace, is the main attraction in this huge park. It is built in 1881. There are major flower displays here in the week preceding Republic day and the week before Independence day. The gardens are open daily from sunrise to sunset. Entry free during flower shows. The 'Bal Bhavan is a children park with pony rides, boat rides, toy train rides and other attractions. It open on Sunday 09.30—18.00, public holidays 09.30 -20.00. Closed on Monday and second Tuesday of the month. The Rose garden is another attraction at Lal Bagh garden. It is placed at the heart of the Lal Bagh, near to north gate entrance. 150 different kinds of roses are grown here.

Lalbagh Fort : Lalbagh Fort (also known as "Fort Aurangabad") is an incomplete Mughal palace fortress at the Buriganga River in the southwestern part of Dhaka, Bangladesh. Construction was commenced in 1678 by Prince Muhammad Azam during his 15-month long vice-royalty of Bengal, but before the work could complete, he was recalled by Aurangzeb. His successor, Shaista Khan, did not continue the work, though he stayed in Dhaka up to 1688.

For long, the fort was considered to be a combination of three buildings: the mosque; the tomb of Bibi Pari; and the Diwan-i-Aam, comprising two gateways and a portion of the partly damaged fortification wall. Recent excavations carried out by the Department of Archaeology of Bangladesh, however, have revealed the existence of other structures, and it is now possible to have a more or less complete picture of the fort.

In the present fort area of 18 acres (73,000 m^2), excavations have revealed the remains of either 26 or 27 structures, with elaborate arrangements for water supply, sewerage, roof gardens, and fountains. Renovation work by the Archaeology Department has now put Lalbagh Fort in a much-improved shape, and it has now become an interesting spot for tourists and visitors.

Lalgudi Jayaraman : Sri Lalgudi Jayaraman (born 1930, India) is a legendary violinist performing Carnatic music. In his own lifetime he has gained the title with his spellbinding technique and mastery over the instrument. In the sphere of Carnatic music, Sri Lalgudi Jayaraman is a name that is instantly associated with musical excellence in melody, rhythm, style and technique.

Born in the lineage of an illustrious disciple of the great saint musician Thyagaraja, Sri Lalgudi Jayaraman inherited the essence of Carnatic music from his versatile father late V R Gopala Iyer who trained him meticulously. At the early age of 12 he started his musical career as an accompanying violinist. Being endowed with rich imagination, quick grasp and an ability to adapt easily to the individual styles of the leading maestros in Carnatic music while accompanying them in their concerts, he reached the forefront in rapid strides. The rich concert experience he thus gained, coupled with sheer hard work and perseverance and the strong urge to give original expression to the musical ideas surging in him, he emerged as a solo violinist of rare brilliance.

He revolutionised the style of violin playing by inventing a whole new technique that is designed to best suit the needs of Indian Classical Music and establishing a unique style that came to be known as 'Lalgudi Bani'. His flawless and fascinating style, graceful and original, yet not divorced from traditional roots gained him numerous fans. This multi dimensional personality have to his credit composed several 'Krithis', 'Thillanas' and 'Varnams' and dance compositions, which are a scintillating blend of raga, bhava, rhythm and lyrical beauty. The unique feature about Lalgudi is that his music is very expressive. Lalgudi's instrumental genius comes to the fore in the form of lyrical excellence.

The genius has earned several titles like 'Nada Vidya Tilaka' by Music Lovers' Association of Lalgudi in 1963, 'Padma Shri' by the Government of India in 1972, 'Nada Vidya Rathnakara' by East West Exchange in New York, 'Vadya Sangeetha Kalaratna' by Bharathi Society, New York; 'Sangeetha Choodamani' by Federation of Music Sabhas, Madras in 1971 and in 1972; State Vidwan of Tamil Nadu by the Government of Tamil Nadu and Sangeetha

Natak Academy award in 1979 etc. The First Chowdaiah Memorial National-Level award was given to Sri Jayaraman by the Chief Minister of Karnataka. He has also received honorary citizenship of Maryland, USA in 1994.

Lalon Fokir : Lalon Fokir, also known as Lalon Shah (1774–1890), was born in a village in the district of Kushtia, now in Bangladesh. Lalon was one of the greatest mystic-singers the Indian subcontinent has ever produced, and also a radical and secular voice in India during British colonial rule, which also witnessed increased miscommunication between Hindus and Muslims. He is often referred to as Baulsamrat (The emperor of the Bauls).

Lalon had no formal education and lived in extreme poverty. Tradition has it that the Hindu family he was born to abandoned him when he was suffering from smallpox. Shiraj Shai, a Baul of Muslim background saved him from death and took him under his wing. Following the Baul tradition, Lalon started to write songs to communicate his ideas. Writing in nineteenth-century lyrical Bengali, Lalon composed numerous songs which still provide spiritual and political inspiration to the Bengali rural peasant, a class from which Lalon himself came. The religious message in his songs are often obscure; however, a basic humanist element can be seen underlying his work. Lalon's songs oppose religious intolerance, casteism, sectarianism, and colonialism.

Lalon Geeti : Lalon geeti is the work of composer and philosopher, Lalon Shah (Lalon Fokir). Most of his songs are extensions of Baul geeti. However, his songs are always more philosophical in nature, involving greater thought about abstract themes. Lalon geeti originated in Kushtia and has been popularised throughout the two Bengals (West Bengal and Bangladesh) by various artists. Among the proponents of Lalon geeti, Farida Parveen is particularly worth mentioning for her extensive work in modernising tunes.

Lalon Shah Bridge : Lalon Shah Bridge is a recently made road bridge in Bangladesh over the Padma. It was completed in 2004 and is one of the larger bridges of the country.

Lalu Prasad Yadav : Lalu Prasad Yadav (officially born on 1947-06-112) is the president of the Rashtriya Janata Dal, a political party of India. He is often referred to as Lalu. As of December 2005, he is the Minister for Railways in the Manmohan Singh government. Formerly, he was also the Chief Minister of Bihar.

Lalu was born to Late Kundana Raiye at Phulwaria, Dist, Gopalganj, Bihar. His first political step was involvement in the elections of the Patna University students union. Later he joined the student movement led by Jai Prakash Narayan in the 1970s. Lalu is one of India's most maverick politicians and is a formidable force in Indian state of Bihar, which his Rashtriya Janata Dal has governed for 15 years.

Lama Devil Dance : It is one of the most attractive dances of the Kinnauri tribals, where the dancers are masked. Two of them are dressed as lions. The dance depicts the taming of the lion that represents evil spirits.

Laman : Laman singing is popular in the Kulu valley in Himachal. These songs sing of the romantic love between men and women. The first line is only for rhyming with the second and it is the second line which furthers the theme. Syllables like Oa, Aa form the 'Tek' or the note which is prolonged at the end of the line. These syllables help the singers establish a certain resonance and a definite rhythmic pattern.

Lambadi Dances : Lambadi is the semi—nomadic tribe that is spread all over Andhra. They are also known as Banjaras or Sugalis. Their dances are inspired by the movements associated with daily tasks like harvesting, planting and sowing. The costumes, embroidered with glass-beads and shining discs are picturesque; matched by the abundance of ornate jewellery worn by them. The jingling brass anklets, the hanging cowry bunches and the ivory bangles from wrists to elbows provide a natural rhythm to their dances.

Dussehra, Deepavali and Holi are the festive occasions when the Banjaras go from house to house dancing and receiving alms. Twenty to thirty Banjara women dressed in colourful costumes with shining brass vessels filled with water either on heads or waists present a group dance. The graceful movements of their waving hands and supple waists provide a feast to the onlookers.

Lance Naik Muhammad Mahfooz : Born 25 October 1944 in Pind Malikan (now Mahfuzabad), Rawalpindi district. Enlisted in the Army on 25 October 1962. Serving in 'A' Company of 15 Punjab Regiment when war broke out in 1971, Lance Naik Mohammad Mahfuz was deployed on the Wagha-Attari Sector in East Pakistan where his company was pinned down by unceasing frontal and crossfire from automatic weapons.

Although his machine gun was destroyed by an enemy shell, Mahfuz advanced towards an enemy bunker whose automatic fire had inflicted heavy casualties. Even though wounded in both legs by shell splinters, when he reached the bunker he stood up and pounced on the enemy, but was hit. Although unarmed, he caught hold of one enemy was slowly strangling him when another bayoneted him to death during the night on 17 December 1971. He was 27 years old.

Landhi Town : Landhi Town is a large industrial town in the eastern part of Karachi, Pakistan. It is bordered by the Faisal Cantonment and Shah Faisal Town to the north across the Malir River, Bin Qasim Town to the south and east, and Korangi Town to the west. The population of Landhi Town was estimated to be over 660,000 at the 1998 census, of which 99% are Muslim. There are several ethnic groups including Urdu speakers, Punjabis, Sindhis, Kashmiris, Seraikis, Pakhtuns, Balochis, Memons, Bohras, Ismailis.

Landi Kotal : Landi Kotal in Pakistan is the highest point on the celebrated Khyber Pass, a prominent route across the mountains from the near-border city, Peshawar. Landi Kotal is quite a popular tourist destination, often traveled by train, to or from Afghanistan.

It is the living place for clans of the Afridi tribe, namely Zakha khel (as common) Wali Khel, Sultan Khel, etc. Its people live totally in villages built on mountains. Two large villages are Zintara (Chinar Kaley)—which is famous for a very long and tall wall built for ensuring its safety—and Ayub Kale, famous in the region for its modernity. It was constructed by a billionaire of Khyber Agency.

Language Martyrs' Day : Language Movement Day or Language Revolution Day, which is also referred to as Language Martyrs' Day or Martyrs' Day, is a national day of Bangladesh to commemorate protests and sacrifices to protect Bengali as a national language during the Pakistani regime in 1952. Around 1950-52, the emerging middle classes of East Bengal underwent an uprising known later as the Language Movement. Bangladeshis (then East Pakistanis) were initially agitated by a decision by Central Pakistan Government to establish Urdu, a minority language spoken only by the supposed elite class of West Pakistan, as the sole national language for all of Pakistan.

The situation was worsened by an open declaration that "Urdu and only Urdu will be the national language of Pakistan" by the governor, Khawaja Nazimuddin.

Police declared Section 144 which banned any sort of meeting. Defying this, the students of University of Dhaka and Dhaka Medical College and other political activists started a procession in February 21, 1952. Near the current Dhaka Medical College Hospital, police fired on the protesters and numerous people, including Abdus Salam, Rafique, Barkat, Jabbar died. The movement spread to the whole of East Pakistan and the whole province came to a standstill. Afterwards, the Government of Pakistan relented and gave Bengali equal status as a national language. This movement is thought to have sown the seeds for the independence movement which resulted in the liberation of Bangladesh in 1971.

Language Movement : The Language Movement was a cultural and political movement in the erstwhile East Pakistan (now Bangladesh) in 1952. After the formation of Pakistan in 1947, the West Pakistani rulers, who dominated the Government, intended to make Urdu (spoken mostly in West Pakistan) the national language of the whole Pakistan. The Bengali population, which was an ethnic majority in erstwhile Pakistan, was not in agreement with this and started a movement to provide equal status for their own language, Bangla. The matter worsened in February, 1952 when Khawaja Nazimuddin, governor of East Pakistan, reiterated the government position on the national language.

Police declared Section 144 which banned any sort of meeting. Defying this, the students of Dhaka University and other political activists started a procession in February 21, 1952. Near the current Dhaka Medical College Hospital, police fired on the protesters and numerous people, including Abdus Salam, Rafique, Barkat, Jabbar died. The movement spread to the whole of East Pakistan and the whole province came to a standstill. Afterwards, the Government of Pakistan relented and gave equal status to Bangla.

This movement is thought to sow the seeds for the independence movement which resulted in the liberation of Bangladesh in 1971. To commemorate this movement, Shaheed Minar, a solemn and symbolic sculpture, was erected in the place of the massacre. The day is remembered as the Language Movement Day in Bangladesh and is a national holiday. Recently, February 21 has also been declared as the International Mother Language Day by the United Nations.

Language Movement Day : Language Movement Day or Language Revolution Day, which is also referred to as Language Martyrs' Day or Martyrs' Day, is a national day of Bangladesh to commemorate protests and sacrifices to protect Bengali as a national language during the Pakistani regime in 1952.

Laokhowa Wildlife Sancuary : This sanctuary is situated in the Nagaon District of Assam covering an area of 60 Sq. Kms. It harbours wildlife species like the Great Indian one-horned rhinoceros, Wild Buffalo, Swamp Deer, Duck, Cormorant, etc. It is only 15 Kms. from Nagaon Town.

Lara Dutta : Lara Dutta, the first Miss Universe of the new millennium was born in Ghaziabad, India on April 16,1978. She was the youngest of three children born to Wg.Cdr. L.K. Dutta and Jennifer Dutta. She completed her high school in Bangalore scoring the highest marks in English in the National Board Exams. She later joined Bombay University and did her degree in Economics.

Lara is a model by profession. She was first discovered by Gladrags' annual modelling competition.

After winning Miss Intercontinental in Germany, she started to build up a very successful modelling career on a national scale. She appeared in ads. for Synergie, Ceat, Coke and Sprite which made her popular. She participated in the Miss Femina India contest and won the title which paved her way to the Miss Universe Crown in 2000. A mix between Punjabi and Scottish parents this stunning beauty always emerged a winner. She started her acting career with the film 'ArasaktchiI' (Tamil) with Arjun. But her entry to the bollywood film industry is the movie 'Andaaz' and she got the film fare award for Andaaz as a new comer. Her other films are 'Mumbai Se Aya Mera Dost' 'Masti' 'Aan' and currently 'Ab-bas'. She looks ahead to many more and her steely determination lead her to win.

Apart from these she participated in various AIDS related events and worked along with the UNFPA. Adventurous by nature her hobbies include bungee-jumping, para-gliding, white water rafting etc. She also has a flair for cooking. Her ambition was to study Media Marketing or be a journalist to uphold the truth. Her confidence, elegance and exotic looks made her stand far above the other contestants and clinched the crown.

Lasbela : Lasbela is one of oldest districts of Balochistan province of Pakistan. It was notified on 30 June 1954. Lasbela became a separate district in Kalat division. The district of Lasbela derives its name from the words LAS which signifies a plain, the greater part of the area being a flat plain, and Bela, the principle town of the district. Uthal is the district headquarters. Alexander the Great passed through Lasbela on his way back to Babylon after conquering Pakistan. In 711 AD, Arab general, Muhammad-Bin-Qasim, who passed through Makran on his way to Sindh. The population os Lasbela is estimated to be over 700,000 in 2005. More than 97% of the population is Muslim with small Hindu minority. The majority of population speaks Balochi and there is a large Sindhi speaking minority.

Lashkar : Lashkar is a city in Madhya Pradesh, India. It serves as a local commercial and rail centre. Its 1960 population was roughly 115,000. It was formerly the capital of Madhya Bharat state. but is now part of the Gwalior municipality, a modern commercial center and transportation hub. Sites of interest include Victoria College, the palace of the maharaja of Gwalior, and a state-run museum.

Lassi : Lassi is a traditional South Asian beverage, originally from Punjab, made by blending yogurt with water, salt, and spices until frothy. Lassis are enjoyed chilled as a hot-weather refreshment. Traditional lassi is salty and sometimes flavored with ground roasted cumin.

Sweet lassi is a more recent invention, flavored with sugar, rosewater and/or lemon, mango, strawberry or other fruit juice. Saffron lassis, which are particularly rich, are a specialty of Sindh and Jodhpur, Rajasthanin India. Another popular variation on the Lassi is the Mango Lassi, which is orange in color and mango flavored. The Lassi-like Ayran is also popular on hot summer days in Turkey, where it typically contains only water, salt, yoghurt and sometimes lemon. In areas of the Middle East including Iran and Lebanon, a similar salty yogurt beverage, named doogh, is popular.

Lata Mangeshkar : Lata Mangeshkar is the melody Queen of India. Lata Mangeshkar has ruled over the hearts of millions of music lovers throughout the world for the last forty years by the magic of her melodious voice.

She was born on 29th September 1928, in Indore (Madhya Pradesh) in a family of musicians. She took to singing at the age of 13. She has sung songs based on classical Indian music and ragas, bhajans or devotional songs, romantic and melancholic songs and so on.

Lata's name has come in the Guinness Book of Records as the singer of the highest number of songs. She has already sung over 30,000 songs in a variety of languages. She is recipient of many awards and honours both within the country and abroad. The Government of India has conferred on her the title of 'Padma Shri'. The Government of Madhya Pradesh has instituted an annual award of Rs. 1 Lakh in her name. She has also received the prestigious 'Filmfare Award' for best singer many times. 'Dadasaheb Phalke Award' was conferred upon her in the year 1989 and 'Rajiv Gandhi Sadhbhavana Award' in 1997. Her hit songs of the films Anarkali, Mughul-E-Azam, Bees Saal Baad, Amar Prem, Mehbooba, Sangam, Jurmana, Arpan, Ek Duje Ke Liya, Ram Teri Ganga Maili etc. are worth mentioning. The songs sung by Lata in the recent films '1942- a Love Story, Dilwale Dulhanya Le Jayenge, Dil To Pagal Hai etc, ' have become enormously popular and shows that Lata's voice has improved further in spite of her age.

Lavani : Lavani is a musical discussion. It has something in common with the bow-song. It is performed in the months of April-May to herald the coming of spring chiefly in Thanjavur district, the culturally important areas in Tiruchirappalli district and in Madurai district. One team argues that Manmatha or Kaman, the god of love was burnt to death by lord Shiva and that it was a physical act reducing him to ashes. The other team argues that it was an allegory. What was burnt was Kama or Carnal desire and maintains that Kaman never died and that he has ingrained himself in the heart of countless souls. In counter-arguments and rebuttals, ideas or religion and ethics are put forward to the accompaniment of drum music provided by each of the singers in the group.

Lawrence Garden : Lawrence Garden or Bagh-e-Jinnah is a beautiful historical garden in the city of Lahore, Pakistan. It is a botanical garden but also serves as an entertainment venue with an open-air theatre, mosque, library, restaurant, tennis courts and the Gymkhana Cricket Ground. It is located on Lawrence Road next to Lahore Zoo, directly across from the Governor's House on Mall Road.

Layyah District : Layyah District is a district in the Punjab Province in Pakistan. It is located in the southern part of the province. The capital is Layyah. It is a very historical city. District Layyah is bounded to the North by district Bhakkar, to East by district Jhang. River Indus flows to its Western side across which lies district D.G.Khan and to the South district Muzaffargarh.

Leander Peas : Leander Paes, India's Tennis pride, was born in Goa on June 17,1973 and brought up in Kolkata. Born into a family of sportsmen; His father, Vece was a member of the Indian field hockey team which won a bronze medal in the 1972 Munich Olympic Games and mother, Jennifer a member of the basketball team; Leander began playing tennis at the age of 5.

He captured the 1990 Wimbledon Junior title and was ranked as the No.1 junior player in the world at one time. Since then he has been representing India at various international events winning matches bringing glory to the country. He is also a member of the Davis Cup squad since 1990, compiling a 32-19 career record (21-12 in singles). In 1996 Atlanta Olympics, he won the bronze medal in the Tennis event and made India proud with this individual medal won after a long gap of 44 years. The last individual medal being the wrestling medal won by K.D Jadhav in1952 Helsinki Olympics.

He teamed up with Mahesh Bhupathi to form the Indian doubles team and the duo in 1999, showed their class by winning the French Open and Wimbledon and entering the finals of the two other Grand Slam Tournaments; the Australian and US Opens. But the dream team separated soon after, due to mutual misunderstanding. They came together again in time for the Sydney Olympics and started regaining their lost prestige at the end of 2000, winning the Men's Double title in Japan Open 2000 followed by Worlds Doubles Championship in Bangalore, Verizon Atlanta Challenge, US Clay court Championship in Houston and at Roland Garros defeating the Czech pair of Petr Pala and Pavel Vizner, ranked no. 2 in the world.

Lebang Boomani Dance : After the Garia festival is over, the Tripuris have a time to rest awaiting the monsoon. During this period, folks of charming colorful insects called 'Lebang' use to visit hill slopes in search of seeds sewn on it. The annual visit of the insects renders the tribal youths to indulge in merry-making. While the men-folk make a peculiar rhythmic sound with the help of two bamboo chips in their hand, the women folk run tottering the hill slopes to catch hold of these insects called 'Lebang'.

The rhythm of the sound made by the bamboo chips attracts the insects from their hiding places and the women in-groups catch them. With the change of time jhuming on hill slopes are gradually diminishing. But the cultural life that developed centering round the jhum delved deep into the society. It still exists in the state's hills and dales as a reminiscence of the life, which the tribal of today cherish in memory, and preserve as treasure.

Leh : Leh is the capital of the former Himalayan kingdom of Ladakh, which is now Leh District in the state of Jammu and Kashmir, India. The town is still dominated by the now derelict Royal Palace, which resembles a mini-

Potala Palace. Approximately 81% of Leh's population are Buddhist, 15% of Leh's population are Muslim, mainly Sunni. The Muslim presence dates back to the annexation of Ladakh by Kashmir, after the Fifth Dalai Lama attempted to invade Ladakh from Tibet. Since then, there has been further migration from the Kashmir Valley due firstly to trade and latterly with the transfer of tourism from the Kashmir Valley to Ladakh. Leh was an important stopover on trade routes along the Indus Valley between Tibet to the east, Kashmir to the west and ultimately between India and China.

Lepcha : The Lepcha (population: 50,000) are the aboriginal inhabitants of present day Sikkim. Many Lepcha are also found in western and southwestern Bhutan, the Ilam district of eastern Nepal and even the hills of West Bengal. They are also known as the Rong, Rongke, or Rongpa.

The origin of the Lepcha is obscure. They speak a Tibeto-Burman language which some classify as Himalayish. Based on this some anthropologists suggest they emigrated directly from Tibet to the north, while others suggest a more complex migration that started in southeast Tibet, migrated to either Thailand or Burma, then navigated the Ayeyarwady River and Chindwin rivers, crossed the mighty Patkoi range coming back west, and finally entered into ancient India. While migrating westward through India the are surmised to have passed through southern Bhutan before reaching their final destination near Kanchenjunga.

The Lepcha have their own language, also called Lepcha. It belongs to the Tibeto-Kanauri group of the Tibeto-Burman languages. The Lepcha write their language in their own script, called Róng, which is derived from the Tibetan script. It was developed between the 17th and 18th century by a Lepcha scholar named Thikúng Men

Salóng. The world's largest collection of old Lepcha manuscripts is found with the Himalayan Languages Project in Leiden, The Netherlands with over 180 Lepcha books. Most Lepchas are Tibetan Buddhist by religion, which was brought by the Bhutias from the north, although a few have also adopted Christianity. However, the Lepcha have not give up their shamanistic religion which is known as Mun. In actual practice, rituals from Mun and Buddhism are frequently practiced alongside.

Liaqat Baloch : Liaqat Baloch (born December 9, 1952) is a political leader in Pakistan. He is originally from Muzaffargarh, a remote area of southern Punjab. He played an active role in student politics in the late 1970s at the University of the Punjab where he was twice elected president of the Islami Jamiat-e-Talaba. He holds an MSc (Mass Communication} and LLB degree from the University of the Punjab. He was a member of the Pakistani parliament in 1985 and 1991. Critics accuse him of encouraging gun culture and terrorism in educational institutions. He allegedly tortured and killed some of his student-leader opponents. His brother Sadaqat Baloch, a Physician, died in 2001. Today, Mr Baloch lives in Lahore and is the vice president of Jamaat-e-Islami, Pakistan's hardline Islamic religio-political party. He is also the secretary-general of the Muttahida Majlis-e-Amal (MMA) and the deputy leader of the opposition in the National Assembly.

Liaquat Ali Khan : Nawabzaada Khan Liaquat Ali Khan (October 1, 1896 – October 16, 1951) was the first Prime Minister of Pakistan. He was born in the town of Karnal in present-day Haryana to a land-holding family. Khan completed his early education at Aligarh University, and obtained a law degree from Oxford University in 1921. Upon his return to India in 1923, Khan devoted himself to the Indian nationalist cause, and increasingly began to work for a Muslim state due to the injustices he felt were leveled upon Muslims by the British. In April 1933, he was married to Begum Ra'Ana Liaquat Ali Khan. He was invited to join the Indian National Congress, but refused, forming his own party. He joined the legislative council of Uttar Pradesh, and served there until 1940, when he was elevated to the central legislative assembly.

During this time, Muhammed Ali Jinnah had moved to the United Kingdom, where he was disinvolved from Indian politics. Khan was instrumental in getting Jinnah back to the subcontinent, and Jinnah made Khan the secretary of the Muslim League. Thus in the 1940s, Khan was heavily involved in convincing the British of the need for a separate Muslim homeland in India. His primary emphasis was on separation from "Hindu" India, rather than on freedom from British colonialism. This work helped lead to the formation of Pakistan in 1947, and Liaquat Ali Khan was made the first Prime Minister. Liaquat Ali Khan was given the the title of "Quaid-e-Millat" (Leader of the Nation) by Muslim League for his great leadership and contribution to the cause of Pakistan. During his time in office, he had to deal with the setup of a new government that was plunged into a war with neighboring India, and that faced a refugee crisis after the independence. Quaid-e-Azam Muhammed Ali Jinnah died in 1948, leaving Khan at the helm of Pakistan, he began to work on a constitution, and began building foreign relations with western nations, culminating with a trip to the United States. In 1950, he worked out an agreement with Nehru that sought to ease tensions between India and Pakistan. He also managed to quell the 1st coup attempt in Pakistan to overthrow his Government by Major General Akbar Khan in the famous or rather infamous Rawalpindi Conspiracy Case 1951.

Khan's time as Prime Minister was cut short by an assassin's bullet. On October 16, 1951, he had been scheduled to make an important announcement in a public meeting of Muslim City League at Municipal Park, Rawalpindi. Khan was shot twice in the chest during that meeting by a man sitting in the audience's only fifteen yards away, and the security forces immediately shot the assassin, who was later identified as Saad Akbar. Killing the assassin erased all clues to the identity of the real culprit behind the murder. Upon his death, Liaquat Ali Khan was given the honorific title of "Shaheed-i-Millat", or "Martyr of the Nation".

Liaquatabad Town : Liaquatabad Town is a town in the central part of Karachi, Pakistan and is named after Liaquat Ali Khan who was the first Prime Minister of Pakistan. It is bordered by the towns of North Nazimabad to the north, Gulberg and Gulshan to the east, Jamshed to the south across the Lyari River, and SITE Town to the west across the Orangi Nala stream. The population of Liaquatabad Town was estimated to be about 650,000 at the 1998 census, of which 99% are Muslim. There are several ethnic groups including Urdu speakers, Punjabis, Sindhis, Kashmiris, Seraikis, Pakhtuns, Balochis, Memons, Bohras, Ismailis.

Liberal Party of India : The Liberal Party of India was an organization espousing the liberal, pro-British point of view in the politics of India under the British Raj. The Liberals at various points backed British rule in India, and virtually never supported India's exit from the British Empire. These stances rotated around the idea that Indians must petition and conduct a dialogue with the British to obtain more self-government and political freedoms. They also espoused the British system of education and cultural influences on Indian life. Although initially members of the Indian National Congress which had been formed to create a mature political dialogue with the British government, liberal Indians left the Congress with the rise of Indian nationalism, and leaders like Bipin Chandra Pal, Lala Lajpat Rai and Bal Gangadhar Tilak.

The Liberal party was formed about 1910, and British intellectuals and British officials were often participating members of its committees. Its most prominent leaders were Tej Bahadur Sapru and M.S. Jayakar. The Liberal party opposed Mahatma Gandhi and the Non-Cooperation Movement (1919-1922), the Salt Satyagraha (1930-31), and the Quit India Movement (1942-1945). Liberals also participated in the legislative councils and assemblies at the town, provincial and central levels. Up till the Government of India Act 1935, most Indians and the Congress Party rejected the councils and hardly voted. They were seen as rubber stamps of the viceroy, and stacked with un-elected British officials, pro-British princes and members of religious minorities represented beyond reasonable proportions. Up till 1935's legislation, only a few seats were up for popular election. The Liberal party was never popular with common Indians, and distrusted intensely by Indian nationalists. With the British decision to grant independence to India, the party disappeared from existence.

Liberation War Museum : The Liberation War Museum (called Muktijuddho Jadughar in Bangla) is a museum in Segunbagicha, Dhaka, the capital of Bangladesh. The museum is dedicated to all freedom loving people of the world, and celebrate the sacrifices of martyrs of Bangladesh Liberation War.

Liddar Valley : In the Liddar Valley, large glaciers are observed in Himachal. On the mountain range of this Valley, the glaciers are found in Kolahoi. According to Dr. Neve "one glacier is about five miles in length and comes down as low as 11,000 feet" From here to the cast on the way to Amar Nath cave lies the famous Shesh Nag at an elevation of 14,000 feet. Glaciers are prominent in this area.

Coming into the Valley proper, we find the frozen lake of Alapathar or Apharwat, well over Khilanmarg. Flowers of rainbow colors are found in wild profusion here. The mountain tarn stands at the height of about 12,500 feet. It is said to be 500 yards long and 150 yards wide. The surroundings are austere and wild. It is popular haunt of tourists.

The nearest tarn to the city is that of Harwan on the slopes of Mahadev Mountain about a mile and a half further away from the Moghul garden –Shalimar. The source of its fresh water is Tarsar, a lake on the Amar Nath Mountain. Harwan looks beautiful in its sylvan surroundings. This tarn is the chief source of water supply to the city. Besides the above enumerated lakes and lakelets, there are scores of tarns and glaciers found in the mountain ranges around the Gurais valley, Ladakh and Karakorams.

Kashmir is rich in forests. A variety of spruce, stately trees some of which are towering masses, grow in them such as Blue Pine, silver Fir, Himalayan spruce, Birch, Maple, Beech, Hazel, wild Oak. Almost all the mountains are coated with dense forests, which, besides lending charm and healthful fragrance to the atmosphere, are a great factor of revenue to the country. The best varieties of pine and Deodar are found in the dense forests of Kishtwar and Bhaderwah.

Likir : Likir is a small town located in Ladakh, which is part of the state of Jammu and Kashmir in India. It is perhaps most famous for the nearby Klu-kkhyil (meaning "water spirits") Gompa. The monastery was first built in the 14th century and was rebuilt in the 18th century, and currently has a twenty-five foot tall gold-covered Buddha statue. It is occupied by monks of the Gelupka order.

Lingaraj Temple : This temple is dedicated to Shiva as Lord Lingaraj. Lingaraja Temple represents the peak of achievement in Orissas middle period. The 54m spire of the temple dominates the Bhubaneswar landscape. Set in a walled compound, the Lingaraj is surrounded by many smaller shrines. The Lingaraj compound has another outstanding temple, dedicated to Parvati. Open only to Hindus, the Lingaraj temple is the site of a major Shivaratri festival in February-March, On the night preceding the new moon thousands of pilgrims light lamps in a nightlong ceremony of devotion.

Lion Capital of Ashoka : The Lion Capital of Ashoka is a sculpture of four lions standing back to back. It was originally placed atop the Ashoka pillar at Sarnath, now in the state of Uttar Pradesh, India. The pillar, sometimes called the Ashoka Column is still in its original location, but the Lion Capital is now in the Sarnath Museum. The Lion Capital is the national emblem of India.

The capital contains four lions, standing back to back, mounted on an abacus, with a frieze carrying sculptures in high relief of an elephant, a galloping horse, a bull, and a lion, separated by intervening spoked chariot-wheels over a bell-shaped lotus. Carved out of a single block of polished sandstone, the capital was believed to be crowned by a 'Wheel of the Law' (Dharma Chakra), which has now been lost.

The Asoka Column, standing at its original location since the 3rd century BC, is believed to be the same spot where the Buddha first proclaimed his gospel of peace and emancipation to the four quarters of the Universe; This is represented by the four lions pointing to the four cardinal directions. The four small animals girding the abacus represent the four cardinal directions. The lotus in full bloom, which also acts as the base of the abacus, represents the fountainhead of life and creative inspiration.

In the emblem adopted by the Government of India on January 26, 1950, only three lions are visible, the fourth being hidden from view. The wheel appears in relief in the centre of the abacus with a bull on the right and a horse on the left and the outlines of other wheels on the extreme right and left. The bell-shaped lotus has been omitted. The words Satyameva Jayate from the Mundaka Upanishad, meaning 'Truth Alone Triumphs', are inscribed below the abacus in Devanagari script. These words are the official motto of the Indian Republic.

Lion-tailed Macaque : The Lion-tailed Macaque (Macaca silenus) is an Old World monkey that lives only in southwest India. The skin of the Lion-tailed Macaque is dark-brown or black, and its most outstanding characteristic is the silver-white mane which surrounds the head from the cheeks down to its chin, which gives this monkey its German name of "Beard Ape". The hairless face is black colored. With a head-to-tail length of 45 to 60 cm and a weight of 3 to 10 kg it ranks among the smaller macaques. The tail is medium length with a length of approximately 25 cm and is a black tuft at the end, similar to a lion's tail.

The Lion-tailed Macaque primarily eats fruits, but also eats leaves, buds, insects and small vertebrates. The Lion-tailed Macaque ranks among the rarest and most threatened primates. According to estimations of the IUCN, only approximately 2,500 of these animals lives scattered over several areas in southwest India. The destruction of their habitat and the fact that they avoid human proximity, has led to the drastic decrease of their population. Many zoos take part in breeding programs which help to secure the survival of this species.

Lipu-Lekh Pass : Lipu-Lekh pass is a Himalayan pass in the Pithoragarh District of Uttaranchal state, India. Situated at 5,350 M AMSL, the Vyans valley ends at this pass. The pass links India with Tibet, and forms the last territorial point in Indian territory. The famous Hindu pilgrimage tour Kailash Mansarovar yatra (that is, the journey to the Mansarovar) traverses this pass. Lipu-lekh pass is connected to Chang Lobochahela, near the old trading town of Taklakot (Purang), on the Chinese side.

LOC : Specifically, the term "LOC" refers to the military control line between India and Pakistan, in the province of Kashmir. Originally known as the "Ceasefire Line", it was redesignated the "Line of Control" after the Simla Agreement, which was formalized in December 1972. The Indians refer to their portion of the territory as Jammu and Kashmir, while the Pakistanis refer to the Indian portion as Indian Occupied Kashmir (IOK). The Pakistanis refer to their portion of the territory as Azad (Free)Jammu and Kashmir; in turn, the Indians refer to Pakistani Occupied Kashmir (POK). The cease-fire line between India and People's Republic of China in the Aksai Chin is known as the "Line of Actual Control" (LAC). There have been proposals in the Indian press to regularize the LOC as the international boundary between India and Pakistan; this, however, is against official Indian government policy. Pakistan also desires sovereignty over the entire area. The LoC has seen various Indo-Pakistani Wars, the latest one being in 1999 when both India and Pakistan fought in the Kargil War. There have been frequent artillery duels between India and Pakistan along the LOC. Portions of the LOC have been fenced in.

Lodhi Gardens : Lodhi Gardens is a little oasis in the middle of Delhi. The gardens are situated between Khan Market and Safdarjang's Tomb on Lodhi Road. Lodhi Gardens was originally a village surrounding monuments surviving from the Sayyid and Lodhi dynasties, but the villagers were relocated in 1936 in order to create the gardens.

As there is little architecture from these two periods left, Lodhi Gardens is an important place of preservation.

The tomb of Mohammed Shah (1944) is visible from the road, and is the earliest structure in the gardens. The architecture is characterised by the octagonal chamber, with stone chhajjas on the roof and guldastas on the corners.

In the middle of the gardens is the Bara Gumbad and Sheesh Gumbad. The Bara Gambad (Big Dome) consists of a large rubble-construct dome, a three domed masjid (mosque) and a residence surrounding a central courtyard, where the remains of a water tank can be seen. Opposite the Bara Gambad is the Sheesh Gambad, which contains the remains of some unknown family. Further into the gardens you can travel across what used to be a watercourse connected to the Yamuna River to Sikander Lodhi's tomb. This tomb still has the battlements enclosing it. Nearby to Sikander's tomb is the Athpula (Eight Piered) Bridge, which was built during Akbar's reign.

Lodi Dynasty : The Lodi Dynasty (1451 to 1526), belonged to the Pashtun Ghilzai tribe of Afghans and ruled over the Delhi Sultanate during its last phase. *Bahlul Lodi* : After the last Sayyid ruler of Delhi, Mohammed-bin-Farid, died in 1451, Bahlul Khan Lodi, a warrior and governor of Punjab, took the throne of the Delhi sultanate. He quelled uprisings in the provinces and garnered political support by granting extensive lands to his native Afghan nobles. *Sikandar Lodi*: Bahlul nominated his second son, Sikandar Lodi (born Nizam Khan) to succeed him. However, nobles backed the rule of Barbak Shah, his elder son, who had been appointed viceroy of Jaunpur. A power struggle ensued; Sikandar eventually won the struggle against Barbak and his ally, Hussain Shah of Jaunpur. He proved to be a capable ruler, and was somewhat merciful to his opponents. He allowed Barbak the governship of Jaunpur and also resolved differences with an uncle, Alam Khan, who had conspired to overthrow him. Sikandar also brought many Afghan nobles under his control, conquered

Gwalior and Bihar, and encouraged trade across his holdings. He was a kind ruler and founded the present-day city of Agra in 1503. *Ibrahim Lodi*: Sikandar's son Ibrahim Lodi took the throne in 1517. His rule began on a problematic note; in an attempt to divide his kingdom, the nobles recognized his break-away brother Jalal Khan as independent ruler over Jaunpur. Ibrahim had his brother assassinated in an attempt to consolidate power. However, he never really gained the support of his nobles, as he ruled by fear. He was very strict and disrespectful to his nobles.

Ibrahim retook Gwalior in a military campaign and then menaced Mewar, then ruled by Rana Sanga. Under the premise that Ibrahim threatened to expand the Delhi Sultanate into the desert regions of Rajasthan, which had largely been left alone by previous sultans, Rana Sanga was able to unite the rajput chieftains of the desert into a shortlived military alliance. This alliancemade common cause with discontented muslim nobles of the sultanate to invite Babur, the ruler of Kabul, to overthrow the Lodi dynasty.

Babur was officially invited to take India by Daulat Khan Lodi, a governor in Lahore, and by Alam Khan, an uncle of Sultan Ibrahim Lodi. Babur was able to defeat the Lodis at the Battle of Panipat in 1526. His army's use of artillery, plus the desertion of many nobles and soldiers from Ibrahim Lodi's forces, led to victory despite being Babar being heavily outnumbered. This victory caused the Delhi sultanate to be supplanted by the Mughal Dynasty founded by Babar.

Lohit : Lohit is an administrative district in the state of Arunachal Pradesh in India. The district headquarters are located at Tezu. The district occupies an area of 11,402 km^2 and has a population of 143,478 (as of 2001). This area was one of the last territories to be brought under British control after the punitive Abor and Mishmi Expedition in the first decade of the 20th Century, and was known earlier as the Mishmi Hills. The district is named after the Lohit River, from the Sanskrit Louhitya, reddish- or rust-coloured, and consists of the river valley and hills/ mountains to the North and South.

The area is highly inaccessible, and it is only in 2004 that a permanent bridge has been made operational across the Lohit at the holy site of Parashuram Kund, giving round-the-year connection to Tezu. East of Tezu (about 100 km.) lies the small town of Hayuliang, and this is slated to become the headquarters of a new district. The road along the Lohit runs right up to the small garrison town of Walong just South of the China border, site of the famous Battle of Walong in 1962.

Lohit is the home of the Zekhring, Khampti, Singpho and Mishmi tribes. A small group of Tibetan refugees have settled in Lohit since the 1960s. The Zekhring are Tibetan Buddhists; the Khampti and Singpho are Theravada Buddhists, and the Mishmi are mainly Animists.

Lohri Festival : Lohri marks the culmination of winter, and is celebrated on the 13 Jan a day before Makar Sankranti. For Panjabis, this is an important festival. Lohri celebrates fertility and the spark of life. People gather round the bonfires, throw sweets, puffed rice and popcorn into the flames, sing songs and exchange greetings. The *prasad* comprises of things like til, gazak, gur, moongphali, phuliya and popcorn. There is *puja*, involving *parikrama* around the fire and distribution of *prasad*. This symbolizes a prayer to *Agni*, the spark of life, for abundant crops and prosperity. The first Lohri of a bride is extremely important. The first Lohri of a newborn baby, whether a girl or a boy, is also equally important. Children go from door to door singing and asking for the Lohri *prasad*.

Lok Jan Shakti Party : The Lok Jan Shakti Party is a political party in India. It is led by Ram Vilas Paswan. The party was formed in 2000 when Paswan split from Janata Dal (United). The party has considerable following amongst Dalits in Bihar. The 2004 Lok Sabha elections marked a major break-through for the party.It contested the polls in alliance with Congress and RJD and won 4 Lok Shabha seats. Ramvilas Paswan became the minister of Steel and Fertilizers. In 2005 Bihar assembly poll the party contested in alliance with Congress and against RJD and won 29 assembly seats. It has the key to form the next government in Bihar. After no group was able to form a coalition Presidents rule was imposed. After a few months Bihar's state assembly was dissolved because no group could form a coalition and fresh elections returned NDA supported Nitish Kumar as Chief Minister. This has been a major setback for Paswan.

Lok Sabha : The Lok Sabha is also known as House of People or the lower house. Almost all of its members are directly elected by citizens of India. It is the more powerful of the two houses since it can precede or overrule the upper house in many matters. The Lok Sabha has 552 members as of now. The number of members in Lok Sabha is regulated by Article 81 of the Constitution of India. It has a term of 5 years (it may be dissolved earlier by the President in the event of no party getting a majority). The representatives from States and Union Territories are directly elected by the people on the basis of universal adult suffrage. Every citizen who is over 18 years of age is eligible to vote. There is reservation of some seats for members of Scheduled Castes and Scheduled Tribes but not for members of any other community.

Loktak Lake : Loktak Lake is the largest freshwater lake in northeastern India. It is located near Moirang in

Manipur state. It was designated as a wetland of international importance under the Ramsar Convention on March 23, 1990. It is an ancient lake and plays an important role in the economy of Manipur. It serves as a source of water for hydropower generation, irrigation and drinking water supply. The lake is also a source of livelihood for the rural fisherman who live in the surrounding areas and on Phumdis - floating islands, which are actually heterogeneous mass of vegetation, soil, and organic matters at various stages of decomposition.

The Keibul Lamjao National Park, which is the last natural refuge of the Manipur brow-antlered deer (Cervus eldi eldi), is situated in the southeastern region of this lake. It is also the home of other endangered species including a species of python (Python molurus molurus). Human activities have led to severe pressure on the lake ecosystem. The lake is managed by the Loktak Development Authority (LDA), which was established in 1987. The LDA produced a management plan in 1993, which emphasized the development of fisheries, agriculture, and tourism.

Lolab Valley : The Lolab valley too is thick with them in Himachal. These forests are regular haunt of lovers of sports. Ibex, Snow Leopard, Musk Deer, Wolves, red Bear, Markhor, Backbear, Barasingha etc can be found in these forests. Ibex is a wild goat with very long horns. Snow leopards are found in high forests. The country also holds a variety of winged game, such as duck, goose, chakor, monal pheasant, Patridge and Snipe. These are found in low forests, in swamps and on banks of the lakes. Kashmir is pre- eminently the land of forests which stately among othet things are the mainstay of its economy. These are thus guarded against erosion and other losses so as to yield Maple, more and more income. It was not until 1891 that a separate forest department was formed under Mr. MacDonell – first conservative of forests.

He organized the department, marked out the forest areas and made a plan for the control of felling of forests. Export began to increase until timber become a major state industry. By 1924 it had grown to such proportions that the forest department had to be reorganized and a uniform system of working was introduced in the Lolab area and later extended to the other forest ranges.

Belladonna grows well among the firs, and its roots and leaves which are used in pharmaceutical processes yield about 500 maunds a year, the price being between Rs 150 and Rs 200 a maund. The Drug Research Laboratory makes considerable use of Bella Donna. The scattered wild growth of this plant is being framed out on a larger scale at Tangmarg with considerable success.

The blue pine is one of the most useful trees. Its wood makes excellent charcoal, its resin is used for medicinal purposes, and in the mountain villages pine chips are used as lights and torches. The silver fur has durable wood, free from knots and consequently easy to work. This tree grows to great size, reaching in some cases to one hundred and fifty feet in length and sixteen feet in girth. The elm is a dine tree and is used for ploughs and buildings. The young shoots are fed to the buffaloes Boatmen like the ash tree for the paddles it produces, and walnut is priced for the making of furniture and spinning, wheels, but its growth and has not yet been fully developed.

The most magnificent tree of Kashmir, and one of the most splendid in the world, is the Chinar. Sir Walter Lawrence states that he once measured one, which was sixty feet in girth. It is a beautiful tree, majestic, and giver of perfect shade from the sun and of protection from the rain. In the autumn, its reddening leaves are one of the sights, which the visitors to Kashmir can never forget. Its Timber is used for making oil-presses, boxes of all kinds and furniture. The Moghuls, it is said, introduced the

Chinar, and the poplar, into kashmir. The Chinar is splendid monument to them.

Lollywood : Lollywood refers to the Pakistani film industry, based in the city of Lahore. The name is a conflation of "Lahore" and "Hollywood".

Loralai : Loralai is a district in the center of Balochistan province of Pakistan. Loralai district was created in October, 1903. Loralai town is the district headquarters. Previously it consisted of Loralai, Barkhan and Musakhail Sub-Division. Musakhail and Barkhan were separated from Loralai and given the status of independent districts in 1992. The present boundaries of Loralai district contain two sub-divisions namely sub-division Duki and sub-division Bori. Duki sub-division is further divided into Tehsil Duki and Sub-Tehsil Sinjavi. Sub-division Bori consists of tehsil Bori and sub-tehsil Makhter. The district is controlled by a Deputy Commissioner.

Losar Festival—Monpa Festival : Losar is one of the important festival of Monpas. The festival is celebrated to commemorate the advent of new year. Before the commencement of Losar, they make arrangement for a feast with local drinks where all the relatives and friends are entertained and wish each other happy New Year (Tashi Delek) of the 15th day of the same month they bid good bye to Losar festival with merry making.

Losar Shona Chuksam : This is an agricultural dance of Kinnaur that takes its name from losar or the Tibetan New Year. This dance is held in the months of April/May.

Lothal : Lothal was one of the most prominent cities of the ancient Indus valley civilization. Located in the modern state of Gujarat and dating from 2400 BCE, it is India's most important archaeological site that dates from that era. Lothal's dock—the world's earliest—connected the city to an ancient course of the Sabarmati river on the trade route between Harappan cities in Sindh and the peninsula of Saurashtra when the surrounding Kutch desert was a part of the Arabian Sea. It was a vital and thriving trade centre in the ancient times, with its trade of beads, gems and valuable ornaments reaching the far corners of West Asia and Africa. Discovered in 1954, Lothal was excavated from February 1955 to May 1960 by the Archaeological Survey of India. A major part of the township and dockyard were surfaced. Resuming excavation in 1961, archaeologists surfaced trenches sunk on the northern, eastern and western flanks of the mound, bringing to light the inlet channels and nullah ("ravine", or "gully") connecting the dock with the river. The findings consist proper of a mound, a township, a marketplace and the dock. Adjacent to the excavated areas stands the Archaeological Museum, where some of the most prominent collections of Indus-era antiquities in modern India are displayed.

Lotus Temple : Lotus Temple is the Bahá'í temple in New Delhi, India. It was completed in 1986. It has won numerous architectural awards and been featured in hundreds of newspaper and magazine articles. Inspired by the lotus flower, its design is composed of 27 free-standing marble clad "petals" arranged in clusters of three to form nine sides. Nine doors open onto a central hall, capable of holding up to 2,500 people. Slightly more than 40 meters tall, its surface luminous, the temple at times seems to float above its 26 acre (105,000 m^2) site on the outskirts of the Indian capital.

Since its inauguration to public worship in December 1986, the Bahá'í House of Worship in New Delhi has, as of late 2002, attracted more than 50 million visitors, making it the most visited edifice in the world. Its numbers of visitors during those years surpassed those of the Eiffel

Tower and the Taj Mahal. On Hindu holy days, it has drawn as many as 150,000 people.

The Indian Bahá'í National Spiritual Assembly reports that many Indian visitors expressed perplexity at the absence of any idols. The Bahá'í guides have a hard task explaining to them their belief that the all-pervasive Almighty cannot be put in any limited form. Often the visitors ask the guides where the object of adoration is. Some have placed flowers before the lectern used during regular prayer services.

This temple is generally referred to as the "Lotus Temple" by Bahá'ís and non-Bahá'ís alike.

Lowarai Pass : Lowarai Pass is located between the Panjkora and Chitral valleys in North-West Frontier Province of Pakistan. The pass is at 10,450 ft. elevation.

Lowari : Lowari Top is a pass that connects Chitral with Dir in Pakistan. Lowari Top is a relatively low pass, only 10,230 feet high, which makes it by far the lowest pass to enter Chitral, the rest all being 12,000 to 15,000 feet high. Lowari Top is closed by snow from late November to late May every year. During this time, jeeps cannot cross so men must travel by foot. This is dangerous, as there are high mountains on each side of Lowari Top, and a deadly avalanche can come at any moment without warning. Every winter a few men are killed by avalanche while crossing Lowari Top. Their bodies are buried under the snow and it is only when the Summer comes and the snow melts that their bodies are found and their fate learned.

Lower Gangetic Plains Moist Deciduous Forests : The Lower Gangetic plains moist deciduous forests is a tropical moist broadleaf forest ecoregion of Bangladesh and eastern India. The ecoregion covers an area of 254,100 square kilometers (98,100 square miles), covering most of Bangladesh and the Indian states of West Bengal, Bihar, and Tripura, and extending into adjacent portions of Assam, Uttar Pradesh, and Orissa states.

The Lower Gangetic plains moist deciduous forests extends across the alluvial plain of the lower Ganges and Brahmaputra rivers, which form the world's largest river delta. The ecoregion is currently one of the most densely-populated regions on earth, and the forests have largely been replaced with intensive agriculture.

The ecoregion is bounded on the east and northeast by montane tropical rain forests; the Mizoram-Manipur-Kachin rain forests lie in the Chin Hills and Chittagong Hills to the east, and the Meghalaya subtropical forests lie in the Khasi Hills and Garo Hills to the northeast. To the north, the ecoregion extends to the base of the Himalayas, where it is bounded by the Terai-Duar savanna and grasslands. The upper portion of the Brahmaputra valley in Assam is home to the humid lowland Brahmaputra Valley semi-evergreen forests. To the northwest, the forests are bounded by the Upper Gangetic plains moist deciduous forests, and the dry Chota Nagpur dry deciduous forests lie on the Chota Nagpur Plateau to the northwest. The Sundarbans freshwater swamp forests and Sundarbans mangroves ecoregions lie in the swampy, semi-brackish and brackish southern reaches of the Ganges-Brahmaputra Delta bordering the Bay of Bengal.

L Subramaniam : Doctor Subramaniam, gave up his medical practice to devote all his attention to music. He began playing violin professionally, as a six year old boy. He took his masters degree in Western Music from California Institute of Arts. He and his wife Viji, who was a singer, popularised Karnatic music in the West. But in 1996 Viji died.

This violinist has more than 100 recordings to his credit and has performed with the world's major orchestras. Dr. L. Subramaniam's performance with its unique blend of the east and west has music lovers always eager to hear this violin virtuoso perform on stage. Bolshoi Theatre, the Lincoln centre, the Royal Albert Hall, the Champs Elysses Theatre are the famous theaters where he brings out his enchanting charisma enthralling his fans. Legendary musicians like Sir Yehudi Menuhin, Zubin Mehta and Stephane Grappelli have made music with him. In 1999, this California-based violinist married the well known Hindi play back singer Kavitha Krishnamurthy setting the foundation of a harmonious partnership. They organised the Global Fusion Music Concert in Delhi.

Lubna Agha : Lubna Agha is a renowned Pakistani painter who is very much at the forefront of modern Islamic art and contemporary Asian art. She has exhibited in art museums and galleries throughout the world, in her homeland, Pakistan, as well as Britain, Japan, Jordan, Switzerland, and the United States. Where revival of miniature paintings and calligraphy characterizes much of modern Asian and Islamic art, the artist's latest paintings draw inspiration from Asian and Islamic architecture and from traditional Muslim crafts such as woodcarving, metalworking, and textile-production.

Lucknow : Lucknow is the capital city of the state of Uttar Pradesh, India. It had a population of 2,207,340 in 2001. Lucknow is also the administrative headquarters of Lucknow District and Lucknow Division. The name is derived from the name of the brother of the Lord Rama, Lakshmana in Hinduism who stayed here for a period of time.

Lucknow Pact : Lucknow Pact refers to an agreement between Indian National Congress and Muslim League. In 1916, Mohammed Ali Jinnah, a member of the Indian

National Congress, negotiated with the Muslim League to reach an agreement to pressurise British Government to have a more liberal approach to India and give Indians more authority to run their country. This was a considerable change of policy for Muslim League as it was established to preserve Muslim interests in India, and for this, they needed to support British rule in India. After the unpopular partition of Bengal, Muslim League was confused about its stand and it was this time that Jinnah approached League. Jinnah was the mastermind and architect of the pact. Even though Jinnah was a member of Indian National Congress then, he later went to become the leader of Muslim League.

The Lucknow Pact also marked the establishment of cordial relations between the two prominent groups of the Indian National Congress - the extremists or the garam dal led by Bal Gangadhar Tilak, and the moderates or the naram dal led by Gopal Krishna Gokhale.

Luddi : Luddi is a victory-dance having vigorous swaying movements of the head. Its costume is a simple loose shirt.

Ludhiana : Ludhiana in India is the largest city in Punjab. It is situated on the banks of the Sutlej River. The city's population is 2,500,000 (2001 estimate). It is a major industrial centre of northern India. Famous for its hosiery, textiles and bicycle industries, Ludhiana is also sometimes called the "Manchester of India".

Hero Cycles is largest producer of bicycles in the world and was first established in Ludhiana. Through its collaboration with Honda, Hero Cycles also produces Hero Honda motorcycles.Kular cycle etc are also there.

Ludhiana is also home to the largest agricultural university in India, Punjab Agricultural University (PAU).

Guru Nanak Dev Engineering College is one of the most respected engineering colleges in the region. The college has produced engineers in the field of civil, mechanical, electrical, computer, IT, electronics and production engineering who are working all over the world. A number of spinning mills and hosiery units exist in and around Ludhiana.

Ludhiana also has major medical institutions like the Christian Medical College (C.M.C.), Dayanand Medical College (D.M.C.) and Apollo Hospitals.

A number of 'freedom fighters' that championed an independent India originate from Ludhiana. The most prominent of them being Bhagat Singh, who was hanged by the British along with Kartar Singh Sarabha, Sukhdev Thapur and Rajguru. Apart from this Ludhiana has been done proud by Sahir Ludhianvi, the famous lyricist. Dr. Atam Hamrahi,Surjeet pattar were/are prominent writers.

Ludhiana is well connected to the Indian capital city of Delhi through an airport, by road (GT road) and frequent train service. An international airport is coming up in Ludhiana

Lulu Sar Lake : 48 kilometers away from Naran, on Naran-Babusar road is Lulu Sar Lake which is wreathed in blue and gold wild flowers, and is the main source of river Kunhar.This river then flows through the entire Kaghan Valley through jalkhand, Naran, Kaghan, Jared, Paras, Balakot . Near Gittidas is the 11,000 feet high Lulusar Lake out of which river Kunhar issues anew with redoubled strength to flow down the valley first as placid blue stream and then a roaring torrent until it joins the Jhelum.

Lumbini : Lumbini (Sanskrit for "the lovely") is a Buddhist pilgrimage site located in Rupandehi District,

Lumbini Zone of Nepal near the Indian border. It is commonly recognized as the birth place of Gautama Buddha, the founder of Buddhism, who lived between approximately 563 BCE and 483 BCE. Lumbini is located 25kms east of the municipality of Kapilavastu, the place where the Buddha grew up and lived up to the age of 29. Kapilvastu is the name of place as well as the neighbouring district.

In 1896, Nepalese archaeologists (effort by Khadga Samsher Rana) discovered a great stone pillar at the site, attributed to Emperor Ashoka. Records made by the Chinese pilgrim Fa Xian were also used in the process of identifying this religiously acclaimed site. For Buddhists, this is one of four pilgrimage sites based around the life of Gautama Buddha, the other three being Kushinagar, Bodh Gaya, and Sarnath. Lumbini, as of 1997, is an UNESCO World Heritage Site specifically nominated for the international World heritage program.

Lumbini Park : This beautiful entertainment park in Hyderabad, which is situated on the shore of Hussainsagar lake. The landscaping here is a visual treat. A musically synchronized water fountain and a floral clock are major attractions.

Lunavada : Lunavada is a taluka and a small town in the Panchmahal District in the Northern part of Gujarat state of India. During British Raj, Lunavada was one of the princely states under the Gujarat division of Bombay Presidency, whose chieftain was a Rajput "maharana" of high linage. The capital was Lunavada town, said to have been founded in 1434 CE. The 1901 census records that the population had a decrease of 28% in the decade, due to famine.

Lungi : The lungi is a garment worn around the waist in India, Bangladesh, Sri Lanka, and Myanmar. While its origin is found in South Indian culture, it is worn by diverse communities across Southern Asia. It is normally woven in cotton with variety of designs and colors, though the most popular styles are either solid-colored or plaid. Depending on local tradition, lungis can be worn by men and/or women, are tied or fastened in various ways, and can be used in different cultural activities, ranging from normal daily life to elaborate wedding ceremonies. The lungi is thought to be quite comfortable, as its length can be adjusted rather easily. It is particularly popular in regions where the heat and humidity create an unpleasant climate for trousers.

Lyari River : Lyari River is located in Karachi, Sindh, Pakistan. It passes through the city of Karachi from north east to the center and drains into the Arabian Sea. Lyari is one of the two rivers passing through Karachi and the other is Malir River.

M

Maajhi : Maajhi is referred to as the standard dialect of Punjabi language. It is also used to refer to the people who speak this dialect and live mostly in central districts of Pakistani Punjab and in India around Amritsar region.

Maasti Venkatesh Ayengar : He (June 6, 1891—June 6, 1986) was a famous Kannada writer, and a Jnanpith (1983) awardee. Maasti Kannadada Aasti meaning Maasti is Kannada's Treasure is how he is treasured by Kannadigas. He is most renowned for his beautifully written short stories. His other works include historical novels such as Chikkaveera Rajendra and Channabasava Nayaka. He wrote under the pen name Srinivasa. Born in Kolar District of Karnataka, He secured an Master of Arts in 1914 with a brilliant academic career, and entered the Indian Civil Service. After working in various capacities including District Commissioner he retired in 1943.

Machiara National Park : Machiara National Park in Pakistan is one of three globally significant national parks selected for a Global Environment Facility sponsored project. The overall goal is to set-up management models demonstrating effective natural resource conservation and make a significant contribution to the development of Pakistan's capacity.

Machilipatnam : Machilipatnam, also known as Masulipatnam or Bandar or Masula (for short among Finnish mission workers), is a city on the southeastern or Coromandel Coast of India. Situated on one of the mouths of the river Krishna at the Bay of Bengal, Machilipatnam is the administrative center of Krishna District in the state of Andhra Pradesh. It was a 17th century port for French, British and Dutch trade. It is a small fishing town; has a carpet-weaving industry; other products include rice, oilseed, and scientific instruments. The town is a railway terminus and an educational center. Masulipatam is a station of the Church Missionary Society. Machilipatnam is known for its Kalamkari textiles and paintings created using vegetable dyes. As a kalam (pen) is used in the technique of painting, it was called "Kalamkari Painting". During the 17th century, western traders were attracted by this art.

Madan Kamdev : About 35 km from Guwahati, Madan Kamdev is famous for its impressive archaeological ruins and stone sculptures. It is more of a mystery in the sense that very little is known about the origin of this magnificent archaeological ruins. Other Places of Interests

Madanapalle : Madanapalle is a city in the Chittoor district of Andhra Pradesh state, India. It is a fast-growing town at the center of an agricultural region noted for its fruits and vegetables, especially tomatoes. Madanapalle is also a railhead and gateway to Horsley Hills, a small hill station and summer resort. Madanapalle is the birth place of the famous Indian philosopher J. Krishnamurthi who founded the Krishnamurthi foundation of America and the Krishnamurthi foundation of India. Madanapalle is also known for its high quality silks, which are spun into exquisite sarees and other types of clothing. It was also the site of a major flood in the year 1996 caused by the monsoon rains. 20 people died and there was wide spread damage.

Madaripur : Madaripur is a district im the Dhaka division of Bangladesh. With an area of 1144 sq km, the district is bounded by Faridpur and Munshiganj districts on the north, Barisal district on the south, Shariatpur district on the east, Gopalganj district on the west. Main rivers are Padma, Arial Khan and Kumar. Temperature: average maximum 35.8 C, minimum 12.6 C. Total rainfall 2105 mm. Madaripur subdivision was established in 1854 under the district of Bakerganj. In 1873 it was separated from Bakerganj and annexed to Faridpur district. Madaripur subdivision was turned into a district in 1984. It consists of 4 upazilas, 57 union parishads, 550 mouzas, 3 municipalities, 27 wards, 85 mahallas and 1035 villages. The upazilas are Madaripur Sadar, Shibchar, Rajoir and Kalkini. The most important historical event is the Faraizi Movement Fled by Haji Shariatullah (1781-1840). During the War of Liberation many direct encounters were held between the freedom fighters and the Pakistan army. The freedom fighters of Madaripur captured 40 Pakistani soldiers including a Major and a Captain.

Madei Wildlife Sanctuary : Madei Wildlife Sanctuary is located in the Sattari takula (district) of Goa, in India. The size of this area is about 208 sq km. This sanctuary covers much of the north-eastern portions of Goa and is connected to the Netravali Wildlife Sanctuary. Together the two wildlife areas have a total area of 420 sq km.

Madhav National Park : Madhav National Park is situated in Shivpuri District of Gwalior region in northwest Madhya Pradesh, India. Shivpuri town is located at 25°40' North, 77°44' East on Agra to Bombay National Highway-3. Shivpuri is steeped in the royal legacy of its past, when it was the summer capital of the Scindia rulers of Gwalior. Earlier its dense forests were the hunting grounds of the Mughal emperors. Emperor Akbar captured herds of elephants for his stables while returning from Mandu in year 1564. This National Park has a varied terrain of forested hills and flat grasslands around the lake. It is very rich in Biodiversity.

Madhavrao Scindia : Madhavrao Scindia (1945-2001) (alternatively His Highness the Maharaja of Gwalior) was a prominent Indian politician and minister from the Scindia family, who formerly ruled Gwalior.

Born on March 26, 1945, Madhavrao Scindia was the son of the last ruling Maharaja of Gwalior, Jiyajirao Scindia. A nine-term member of the Lok Sabha, Madhavrao Scindia never lost an election since 1971, when he won for the first time from Gwalior at the age of 26. He contested as an independent with the support of the Jan Sangh, a party that his family had for long patronised. In 1977, he switched to the Congress Party despite resistance from his larger family, and won the Gwalior seat a second time. In order to avoid a direct contest with his mother, he later shifted to the neighbouring constituency of Guna. But in 1984, he was nominated the Congress candidate in Gwalior as a last-minute manoeuvre to defeat the Bharatiya Janata Party's Atal Behari Vajpayee, and won by a massive margin. Since then Scindia contested from either Gwalior or Guna and won on each occasion. Scindia's political role and influence within the Congress party grew rapidly and he was seen as a potential prime ministerial candidate. His tragic demise in a plane crash demolished many hopes.

Madhubani Painting : Madhubani painting is a style of Indian painting, practiced in the Mithila region of Bihar state, India. The origins of Madhubani painting are shrouded in antiquity, and a tradition states that this style of painting originated at the time of the Ramayana, when King Janak commissioned artists to do paintings at the time of marriage of his daughter, Sita, to Hindu god Lord Ram. Madhubani painting has been done traditionally by the women of villages around the present town of

Madhubani (the literal meaning of which is forests of honey) and other areas of Mithila. The painting was traditionally done on freshly plastered mud wall of huts, but now it is also done on cloth, paper and canvas.

As the Madhubani painting has remained confined in a compact geographical area and the skills have been passed on through centuries, the content and the style have largely remained the same. Madhubani painting also uses three dimensional imageries, and the colors used are derived from plants. Traditionally, painting was one of the skills that was passed down from generation to generation in the families of the Mithila Region, mainly by women. The painting was usually done on walls during festivals, religious events, and other milestones of the life-cycle such as birth, Upanayanam (Sacred thread ceremony), and marriage.

Madhvacharya : Madhvacharya (1238-1317) was the chief proponent of Tattvavada (True Philosophy), popularly known as Dvaita or dualistic school of Hindu philosophy. It is one of the three most influential Vedanta philosophies. Madhva was one of the important philosophers during the Bhakti movement. He was a pioneer in many ways, going against standard conventions and norms. Madhvacharya is believed by his followers to be the third incarnation of Vayu, aka MukhyaPrana, after Hanuman and Bhima.

Madhya Bharat : Madhya Bharat is former state in west-central India. Madhya Bharat was created in 1950 from 25 former princely states, which were formerly part of the British Raj's Central India Agency. It was bordered by the states of Bombay (presently Gujarat and Maharashtra) to the southwest, Rajasthan to the northeast, Uttar Pradesh to the north, Uttar Pradesh and Vindhya Pradesh to the east, and Bhopal and Madhya Pradesh to the southeast. The state was mostly Hindu and Hindi-speaking. It had an area of 120,176 km^2 (46,400 mi^2). Gwalior was the winter capital and Indore was the summer capital. On November 1, 1956, Madhya Bharat, together with the states of Vindhya Pradesh and Bhopal, was merged into Madhya Pradesh. The Madhya Bharat plateau lies in central India, lying under most of northwestern Madhya Pradesh state and Central Rajasthan. It is bounded by the Indo-Gangetic plain to the north, the Bundelkhand upland to the east, the Malwa plateau to the south, and the East Rajasthan Uplands on the west.

Madhya Pradesh : Madhya Pradesh is a state in central India. Its capital is Bhopal. Madhya Pradesh was originally the largest state in India until November 1, 2000 when the state of Chhattisgarh was carved out. It borders the states Uttar Pradesh, Chhattisgarh, Maharashtra, Gujarat and Rajasthan.

Madhyamam : Madhyamam is a Malayalam daily newspaper established in 1987 by the initiatives of Jamaat-e-Islami. The name Madhyamam comes from a Malayalam word madhyamam which is the translation of media. Madhyamam has its core readership in the Malabar Muslim community. Madhyamam now has seven editions across the state of Kerala with am impressible readership. Apart from the daily edition, Madhyamam also publishes Madhyamam Weekly. An expatriate edition called Gulf Madhyamam is published from Bahrain, Doha, and Dammam. Madhyamam is owned by Ideal Publications Trust.

Madikeri : Madikeri is the district headquarters of Kodagu with about 28,729 population and 1200 meters altitude. Muddurajakeri named after the first ruler Mudduraja from this place since 1681 later became Madikeri. It is a picturesque hill town with Palace inside Fort, Omkareshvar temple, Raja's tomb, Raja's seat, Abbi falls, Cardamom Research Station at Appangala (7 km), Horticultural farm which develops varieties of citrus, fruits at Chettalli (18 km), World record holder in cardamom crop near Chettalli etc.

Madras Presidency : Madras Presidency, also known as Madras Province and known officially as Presidency of Fort St. George, was a province of British India. At its greatest extent, Madras Presidency included much of southern India, including the present-day Indian State of Tamil Nadu,the Malabar region of North Kerala, the Coastal Andhra and Rayalaseema regions of Andhra Pradesh, and the Bellary, Dakshina Kannada, and Udupi districts of Karnataka. The capital was at Madras, now known as Chennai.

Madras Rubber Factory (MRF) : Madras Rubber Factory, or (MRF) is a major manufacturing company located in Chennai, India. Established in 1946 by K. M. Mammen Mappillai, the company has grown to become a INR 30 billion enterprise. MRF is mainly involved in making vehicle tyres. It is India's largest tyre manufacturing company, and also exports to more than 75 countries worldwide. It is also involved in a range of other activities via subsidiaries. Funskool India, a joint venture between Hasbro and MRF is a major toy manufacturing company in the country. MRF Pretreads offers world class precured tyre retreading service, and MRF Muscleflex is involved in making conveyor belts.

Madras Treeshrew : The Madras Treeshrew (Anathana ellioti) is a monotypic species of treeshrew found in the hill forests of central and southern India, south of the Himalayas. The genus name is derived from the Tamil name of Moongil Anathaan which means bamboo squirrel and the species name is after Sir Walter Elliot of the Indian Civil Services in Madras.

Indian or Madras Treeshrews are found on the Indian subcontinent south of the Ganges River. Three subspecies have been described — A. e. ellioti of the Eastern Ghats, Biligirirangan and the Shevaroy Hills of Southern India, A. e. pallida from Central India primarily in Madhya Pradesh and Raipur, and A. e. wroughtoni from the Satpura Range and the Dangs near Bombay. However, it is more likely that these are just three populations and not distinct subspecies.

Madumalai National Park : Situated in the Nilgiri district the park extends over an area of 230sq.km. The Bandipur National Park of Karnataka is contiguous with this park separated by river Moyar. Kerala forests adjoin this park. The nearest town is Gudalur 16km from it. Octacmund, the nearest rail head is 64 km from he park. Nearest airport is Coimbatore,160 km from the park It is well connected by road with Mysore which is 97 km away from the park.

The park consist of tropical moist deciduous hill forests. It has thick forests of teak and eucalyptus and dense groves of bamboo. The fauna found in the park are tiger, panther, sloth bear, wild dog, elephant, gaur, mouse deer, pigs. The avifauna include great black wood pecker, barber, Malabar gray horn bill, owl, parakeet, hawk eagle and green pigeon.

Madurai : Madurai is situated on the banks of Vaigai River in Tamil Nadu, a southern Indian state. It is the second largest city of Tamil Nadu and has a population in excess of 1.1 million. It is well known for the Meenakshi temple situated at the heart of the town which attracts tourists as well as pilgrims. Madurai has a rich cultural heritage passed on from the great Tamil era more than 2500 years old, and has been an important commercial centre even as early as 550 AD. Madurai was the capital city of the Pandya kings of South India. Madurai is the headquarters of Madurai district

Madurai Meenakshi Temple : The Meenakshi temple is a Hindu temple in the Tamil Nadu city of Madurai. Initially there was only the Shiva temple. It was expanded by Vaishvanâtha of the Vijayanagara Empire in 1560 and took 120 years to complete, with most of the construction being done between 1623 and 1660 at the behest of Kulasekara Pandya. The massive structure measures 254 by 237 meters. The temple precinct is surrounded by nine gopurams (monumental gateways covered with sculpture) which rise up to 200 feet high. Its tallest spire rises 60 meters, and was for many years the tallest structure in its category in Asia.

The temple is dedicated to Shiva, known locally as Sundareshvara, and his consort Meenakshi, or Fisheyed One. The dual shrines dedicated to god and goddess add to the complexity of the plan. The Shiva shrine lies at the centre of the complex, suggesting that the ritual dominance of the goddess developed later. The shrines are small and crowned by modest shikaras (towers) with gold-plated finials. They are surrounded by their own walled and roofed enclosures with a connecting gate in their common side-wall. Within the outermost enclosure are various other features such as the Golden Lotus tank in which rainwater is collected for ritual ablution, the Marriage Hall that is used at the festival of the marriage of Shiva and Meenakshi, and the 16th century Hall of a Thousand Pillars. Outside the main entrance, the New Hall was constructed, an immense pillared pavilion, built in the 17th century by a Nayak ruler who commissioned life-size images of Nayak royalty to be carved against its granite columns. A massive unfinished gopuram precedes the New Hall. These gopurams are characteristic of Vijayanagara temple cities. Their tall and highly decorated concave profile increase in size from the inner to the outer enclosures. The gopuram to the south, for example, rises up to 60 m and is covered with over 1500 brightly painted figures of gods and demons. These sculptures are repainted every twelve years during the temple's reconsecration so that the colours remain as vibrant as they are today. The Meenakshi-Temple remains the symbol and heart of the city of Madurai and one of the holiest sites in India, attracting pilgrims and tourists.

Magadha : Magadha was an ancient Indo-Aryan kingdom of India, mentioned in both the Ramayana and the Mahabharata. It was also one of the four main kingdoms of India at the time of Buddha, having risen to power during the reigns of Bimbisara (c. 544-491 BCE) and his son Ajatashatru (c. 491-460 BCE). The core of the kingdom was that portion of Bihar lying south of the Ganges, with its capital at Rajagriha (modern Rajgir). Magadha expanded to include most of Bihar and parts of Bengal with the conquest of Anga, and then expanded up the Ganges valley annexing Kosala and Kashi. Magadha formed one of the sixteen so-called Mahajanapadas (Sanskrit, 'great country'). The Magadha empire included republican communities such as Rajakumara. Villages had their own assemblies under their local chiefs called Gramakas. Their administrations were divided into executive, judicial, and military functions. Bimbisara was friendly to both Jainism and Buddhism and suspended tolls at the river ferries for all ascetics after the Buddha was once stopped at the Ganges River for lack of money.

King Bimbisara of the Shishunaga dynasty led an active and expansive policy, conquering Anga in what is now West Bengal. Siddhartha Gautama himself was born a prince of Kapilavatthu in Kosala around 563 BCE. As the scene of many incidents in his life, Magadha was a holy land. After the death of Bimbisara at the hands of his son, Ajatashatru, the widowed princess of Kosala also died of grief, causing King Prasenajit to revoke the gift of Kashi and triggering a war between Kosala and Magadha.

Ajatashatru was trapped by an ambush and captured with his army; but in a peace treaty he, his army, and Kashi were restored to Magadha, and he married Prasenajit's daughter.

Accounts differ slightly as to the cause of Ajatashatru's war with the Licchavi republic. It appears that Ajatashatru sent a minister, who for three years worked to undermine the unity of the Licchavis at Vaishali. To launch his attack across the Ganga River (Ganges), Ajatashatru had to build a fort at a new capital called Pataliputra, which the Buddha prophesied would become a great center of commerce. Torn by disagreements the Licchavis were easily defeated once the fort was constructed. Jain texts tell how Ajatashatru used two new weapons – a catapult and a covered chariot with swinging mace that has been compared to modern tanks.

In 326 BCE, the army of Alexander the Great approached the boundaries of Magadha. Magadha was also the seat of the Mauryan Empire, founded by Chandragupta, which extended over nearly all India under Asoka; and, later, of the powerful Gupta Empire. The capital of the Mauryan Empire, Pataliputta (modern Patna), was begun as a Magadhan fortress and became the capital sometime after Ajatashatru's reign. Chandragupta destroyed the Nanda dynasty around 321 BCE, and became the first king of the great Mauryan Empire.

Magadhi Language : The Magadhi language (also known as Magahi) is a language spoken in India. Magadhi is closely related to Bhojpuri and Maithili and these languages are sometimes referred to as a single language, Bihari. These languages, together with several other related languages, are known as the Bihari languages, which form a sub-group of the Eastern Zone group of Indo-Aryan languages.

Magadhi has approximately 13 million speakers. It is spoken primarily spoken in the Magadh area of Bihar state. This area includes Patna, Gaya, Nalanda, Rajgir, and other surrounding districts. It is also spoken in some areas of Hazaribagh, Giridih, Palamau, Munger, and Bhagalpur, with some speakers in the Malda District of West Bengal. It is generally written using Devanagari script.

It sounds very similar to Hindi and can be easily understood by someone who is not familiar with it but knows either Hindi or any of the other numerous Bihari languages. It has a very rich and old tradition of folk songs and stories. An earlier form of Magadhi is believed to be the language spoken by The Buddha, and Magadhi may have been the language of ancient kingdom of Magadha, after which the Magadh area is named. Theravada tradition has long held that the Pali language was synonymous with the ancient Magadhi language; however, modern linguistic analysis has revealed that this is likely not the case.

Magadhi is also the name of one of the three Dramatic Prakrits, and was a language spoken in what is now Bihar in medieval times. Its successors include Bengali, Oriya and the complex of languages together called Bihari. Many of the texts of the Jain religion are written in old Magadhi.

Magpic-robin : The bird becomes quiet during the non-breeding season, but during the breeding season the male indulges in awkward puffing out of chest, pointing bill stiffly skyward, and strutting and posturing in front of rivals. The male vigorously defends his territory during the breeding season. It sings with its wings partly drooping and tail depressed. Its song is a spirited, clear, rather thin and varied whistling, and is divided in short phrases repeated over and over again, occasionally interlarded with mimicry of calls of other birds. The bird feeds on a variety of insects, snails, earthworms, centipedes, small lizards, and some vegetable matter. It breeds during February-July.

Maha Bodhi Society : Founded by Anagarika Dhammapala, the Maha Bodhi Society is a South Asian Buddhist society. The organization's initial efforts were to restore various Buddhist shrines that had been neglected under Hindu administration, and to open to the public various Buddhist sites and temples that had been destroyed in various periods of Muslim invasion. Their efforts involved Mahabodhi Temple at Bodhgaya and the site of the Buddha's parinibbana (physical death) at Kushinagar. The latter site has once again become a major attraction for Burmese Buddhists, as it was for many centuries previously.

Maha Bodhi Society branches have been established in several countries, most significantly in India and Sri Lanka. A United States branch was founded by Dr. Paul Carus. The Maha Bodhi Society has a robust tradition of publications, spanning from Pali translations into modern Indian vernacular languages (such as Hindi) to scholarly texts and new editions of Pali works typeset in Devanagari to appeal to a Hindi-educated Indian audience. They have also published books and pamphlets in local/regional languages and dialects, sometimes in partnership with other presses.

As of 2003, the Maha Bodhi Society of India's general secretary is Dombagoda Rewatha Thero. On September 27, 2004, B. K. Modi was elected president; he was previously vice-president. Modi was, until recently, an office-holder in the Vishwa Hindu Parishad.

Maha Siva Ratri : 'Maha Siva Ratri' means the great night of Siva. It is celebrated in the month of March. On this day, people fast. Some abstain from any kind of food, while others content themselves with one meal. Strict vigil is kept in the night. The people cluster round the Siva temple, and after bath they smear their bodies with holy ashes, and keep on reciting prayers to Siva. Enthusiasts, more devout than the rest perform rolling circumambulations round the temple, while the ordinary worshippers go round it on foot a number of times. Puja to the image of Siva is kept up all the night. Early next morning, people bathe once more, worship Siva and return to their ordinary avocations.

Maha Vir Chakra : The Maha Vir Chakra (MVC) is the second highest military decoration in India and is awarded for acts of conspicuous gallantry in the presence of the enemy, whether on land, at sea or in the air. It may be awarded posthumously.

The medal is made of standard silver and is circular in shape. Embossed on the obverse is a five pointed heraldic star with circular center-piece bearing the gilded state emblem of India in the center. The words "Mahavir Chakra" are embossed in Devanagari and English on the reverse with two lotus flowers in the middle. The decoration is worn on the left breast with a half-white and half-orange riband about 3.2 cm in width, the organ being near the left shoulder.

More than 155 acts of bravery and selfless courage have been recognized since the inception of the medal. The most number of MVCs awarded in a single conflict was in the Indo-Pakistani War of 1971, when eleven were given to the Indian Air Force.

Mahabalipuram : Mahabalipuram (also known as Mamallapuram) is a 7th century port city of the South Indian dynasty of the Pallavas around 60 km south from the city of Chennai in Tamil Nadu. It is believed to have been named after either the demon king Mahabali, or the Pallava king Mamalla. It has various historic monuments built largely between the 7th and the 9th century, and has been classified as a UNESCO World Heritage Site. The monuments are mostly rock-cut and monolithic, and constitute the early stages of Dravidian architecture wherein Buddhist elements of design are prominently visible. They are constituted by cave temples, monolithic rathas (chariots), sculpted reliefs and structural temples. The pillars are of the Dravidian order. The sculptures are excellent examples of Pallava art.

Most of the sculptures are not very intricate in details but rather tend to be rough sculptures. One point of view is that this area served as a school for young sculptors. The different sculptures, some half finished, may have been examples of different styles of architecture, probably demonstrated by instructors and practiced on by young students. This can be seen in the Pancha Rathas where each Ratha is sculpted in a different style

Mahabharata : The Mahabharata, sometimes just called Bharata, is one of the two major ancient Sanskrit epics of India, the other being the Ramayana. Traditionally ascribed to Vyasa, it is the longest literary epic poem in the world. Besides being hailed as one of the greatest literary accomplishments of humanity, it is also of immense religious and philosophical importance in India. In particular, the Bhagavad Gita, which is one of its chapters (Bhishmaparva), is a central sacred text of Hinduism.

The title may be translated as "History of the Great India" or, more accurately, "the Great Bharata Dynasty" (bharata means the progeny of Bharata, the king believed to have founded the Indian kingdom of Bharatavarsha; "Bharat" has equal status as the official name of India in all Indian governments today and is still commonly used today). The work is part of the Hindu itihaasas, literally "that which happened", along with the Puranas and Ramayana. The full version contains more than 100,000 verses (total over 200,000), making it around four times longer than the Bible, and seven times longer than the Iliad and the Odyssey combined. It is around 2.5 million words long.

Karma and dharma play an integral role in the Mahabharata. The epic is composed by Vyasa, who is one of the major dynastic characters within the epic. The first section of the Mahabharata states that it was Lord Ganesh (the Hindu god bearing the head of an elephant) who, at the behest of Vyasa, wrote the epic down on manuscript. Lord Ganesh is said to have agreed, but only on condition that Vyasa never pause in his recitation. Vyasa then put a counter-condition that Ganesh understand whatever he recited, before writing it down. In this way Vyasa could get some respite from continuously speaking by saying a verse which was difficult to understand. This situation also serves as a popular variation on the stories of how Ganesh's right tusk was broken (a traditional part of Ganesh imagery). This version attributes it to the fact that, in the rush of writing, the great elephant-headed divinity's pen failed, and he snapped off his tusk as a replacement in order that the transcription not be interrupted.

The Mahabharata is thought to have been derived from what was originally a much shorter work, called Jaya (Sanskrit for Victory). The dating of the events of this story is unclear. Some people find the events to be reliably placed in Vedic India. Scholars have studied the astronomical events described in the Mahabharata (such as eclipses) and have claimed to have dated it to around 1478 BCE or alternatively 3106 BCE. Linguistically, the language of the Mahabharata is classified as "Epic" Sanskrit, the oldest stratum post-dating late Vedic Sanskrit, dating to perhaps the 4th century BCE. Other estimates place it between 200 BCE and 200 CE. However, it is significant to realize that the debate about dating the 'events' of the

Mahabharata is secondary to the importance of the text in Classical Sanskrit literature and culture.

Mahabodhi Temple : The Mahabodhi Temple is a Buddhist temple in Bodh Gaya, the location where Siddhartha Gautama, the Buddha, attained enlightenment. Bodh Gaya is located about 96 km (60 miles) from Patna, Bihar state, India. Next to the temple is the holy Bodhi tree.

Traditional accounts say that, around 530 BC, Gautam Buddha, wandering as a monk, reached the sylvan banks of Falgu River, near the city of Gaya, India. There he sat in meditation under a peepul tree (Ficus religiosa or Sacred Fig), which later became known as the Bodhi tree. According to Buddhist scriptures, after three days and three nights, Siddharta attained enlightenment and the answers that he had sought. Mahabodhi Temple was built to mark that location.

In approximately 250 BC, about 250 years after the Buddha got Enlightenment, Buddhist Emperor Ashoka visited Bodh Gaya with the intention of establishing a monastery and shrine. As part of the temple he built, the diamond throne (called the Vajrasana), attempting to mark the exact spot of the Buddha's enlightenment, was established. Ashoka is considered the founder of the Mahabodhi Temple.

Mahabubnagar District : Mahabubnagar is the largest district in Telangana Region and the second largest in Andhra Pradesh State. This district consists of 1553 Revenue Villages, 1347 Gram Panchayats, 64 Mandals and 5 Revenue Divisions. Mahabubnagar District has 13 Assembly Constituencies and 2 Parliamentary Constituencies.

It is located in the semiarid region of India with recurring meteorological drought and worsened by overexploitation of meager groundwater resources. This is a backward District with diverse socio-economic problems like lowest literacy rate, migrations, extreme poverty, etc.

Mahadevi Varma : Mahadevi Varma (1907—11th September 1987) was one of the most famous modern Hindi poets. She is widely regarded as the 'modern Meera. Her descriptions of pain and sadness are extremely moving. She won the Jnanpith award in 1982.

Mahajanapadas : Mahajanapadas literally means "Great kingdoms" (from Sanskrit Maha = great, Janapada = foothold of tribe = country). Ancient Buddhist texts like Anguttara Nikaya make frequent reference to sixteen great kingdoms and republics (Solas Mahajanapadas) which had evolved and flourished in the northern/north-western parts of the Indian sub-continent prior to rise of Buddhism in India.

Mahakali River : The Mahakali is a river between Nepal and India. It is the current boundary limit between these countries. It is known as Kali in Nepal and Sarayu in India. It was named after Mahakali, the Hindu goddess of rage and courage. The main tributaries are the Limpiyadhura and the Chamelia.

Mahakoshal : Mahakoshal (also Mahakaushal) is a region of central India. Mahakoshal lies in the upper or eastern reaches of the Narmada River valley in the Indian state of Madhya Pradesh. Jabalpur is the largest city in the region. Nimar region lies to the west, in the lower reaches of the Narmada valley. The Vindhya Range forms the northern boundary of the region; north of the Vindhya Range lie the regions of Malwa to the northwest, Bundelkhand to the north, and Bagelkhand to the northeast. Chhatisgarh state lies to the east, and the Vidarbha region of Maharashtra state lies to the south across the Satpura Range.

Maham : In Tamil Nadu, Maham comes in the month of Maasi and the images of gods and goddesses are taken out to the sea for a dip. In areas away from the coast, the rivers or the tanks are the centres for this float festival. The Maham is an annual event. But once in twelve years, its importance exceeds bounds of imagination. When the planet Guru or Jupiter enters Simha sign, the Kumba Mela festival of south India is held at the famous Mahamaham tank at Kumbakonam. Vast crowds gather in Kumbakonam and ordinary folk have a dip in the tank, along with the saints and philosophers. All the rivers of India are said to meet at Mahamaham Tank on this day and so, a purificatory bath in this tank on this particular day is considered equal to the combined effect of dips in all the holy rivers of India.

Mahamaham : Mahamaham is a Hindu Kumb Mela festival celebrated every 12 years in a small temple-town called Kumbakonam in Tamil Nadu, India. Hindus consider taking a holy dip at the Mahamaham tank on the day of Mahamaham as sacred. Mahamaham was celebrated on March 6, 2004, with people from various places taking the holy dip in the Mahamaham tank. The next Mahamaham will be celebrated in 2016.

Mahanadi River : The Mahanadi River is a river of eastern India. The Mahanadi rises on the Amarkantak plateau in central India and flows east to the Bay of Bengal. The Mahanadi river system drains most of the state of Chhattisgarh, much of Orissa, and portions of Jharkhand and Maharashtra. It has a length of about 860 km. Near the city of Sambalpur, a large dam—the Hirakud Dam—is built on the river. It has a high Gandhi Minar (tower) for inspection of the dam.

The Mahanadi rises in Raipur District of Chhattisgarh. The fertile plains of the Mahanadi valley are home to intensive rice cultivation, and hinterland to the city of Raipur, one of the places located on its bank, is known as "the rice bowl". The Mahanadi and Brahmani rivers together form a large delta where they meet the Bay of Bengal. The city of Cuttack lies at the head of this delta. This delta houses one of the largest mangrove forests in peninsular India, and is a major rice producing area of the eastern coast of India.

Mahanagar Telephone Nigam Limited : The Mahanagar Telephone Nigam Limited is the government owned telephone service provider in the cities of Mumbai, Thane, New Delhi and New Bombay in India. The company was a monopoly till 2000 when telecom sector was thrown open to other service providers. MTNL provides fixed line telephones, cellular connection of both GSM — Dolphin and WLL (CDMA) — Garuda and internet services through dialup and DSL — TriBand. Phone numbers belonging to MTNL start with the prefix 2. MTNL also provides other services such as virtual private networking and leased lines through its sister concerns BSNL and VSNL (now Tata Indicom).

Mahananda River : Mahananda river is a major tributary of the Ganges in Bangladesh. Originating from the Himalayas, southwest of Nepal, the river crosses Karsiang and Shiliguri in West Bengal (India). Flowing southeast through the Purniah and Maldaha districts of West Bengal, it enters Bangladesh through Bholahat upazila of Nawabganj (Chapai Nawabganj) district. The Mahananda then falls into the Ganges at Godagari keeping Chapai Nawabganj town on the left. In Bangladesh, the length of the Mahananda is about 36 km. According to the survey of WW Hunter (1876), once the Mahananda was a wide and deep river allowing big cargo boats of 500 maund capacity (1 maund equals to 37.65 kg) to ply. It has neither any tributary nor any distributary. The

Mahananda is an important Trans-boundary river. India constructed a dam on the river 3 km north of the border near Shiliguri in spite of objections from Bangladesh

Mahananda Wildlife Sanctuary : Mahananda Wildlife Sanctuary is located on the foothills of Himalayas, between the Teesta and Mahananda rivers. Animal species found here are elephant, Indian bison, tiger, barking deer, Rhesus monkey, leopard, fishing cat, jungle cat, sambar (Cervus unicolor), and cheetal. The rare mountain goat (Serow) can be sighted here.

Mahant Ghasi Memorial Museum : Mahant Ghasi Memorial Museum is a museum in Chattisgarh is known for its collection of antiquarian finds like inscriptions, images, sculptures, coins etc. & also things of natural history & anthropology.

Mahar Regiment : The Mahar Regiment is an Infantry Regiment of the Indian Army. Although it was originally intended to be a regiment consisting of troops from the Mahars and other Backward Caste communities in Maharashtra, the Mahar Regiment is one of the only regiments in the Indian Army that is composed of troops from all communities and regions of India.

Maharaja Palace, Vadodara : The term Maharaja Palace actually refers to a series of palaces in Vadodara constructed since the Gaekwad family started ruling the Vadodara State. The first one was a building known as the Sarkar Wada. This building, not really a palace, was given up for the Nazarbaug Palace built in old classical style. This once a magnificent building is now in a dilapidated state.

After this the Lakshmi Vilas Palace, an extravagant building of the Indo-Saracenic school, was built by Maharaja Sayajirao in 1890 is till date the residence of the royal family. Its ornate Darbar Hall has an Italian mosaic floor and walls with mosaic decorations. The palace houses a remarkable collection of old armoury and sculptures in bronze, marble & terracotta. The Palace "compound" as it is known here is of over 700 acres and houses a number of buildings, particularly the Moti Baug Palace and the Maharaja Fateh Singh Museum building. Adjacent to the Motibaug Palace and the Museum is the Motibaug Cricket Ground. This ground was the home of the Baroda Cricket Association.

The Museum building was constructed as a school for the Maharaja's children. Today a large number of works of art belonging to the Royal family have been displayed in the museum. The most remarkable of these is the fabulous collection of the paintings of Raja Ravi Varma, who was specially commissioned by the then Maharaja of Baroda. The collection includes portraits of the Royal family in addition to the paintings based on Hindu mythology for which Raja Ravi Varma was famous. The Maharaja had constructed a miniature railway line from the school to the main Lakshmi Vilas Palace which circled the mango orchard within the palace compound. The palace also boasted of a small zoo. The only remenant of this zoo is the pond where a number of crocodiles remain. The Navlakhi (literally meaning "of nine hundred thousand") Well, a fine 'baoli' or step well, is 50 metres north of the palace.

A beautiful Golf Course has been set up by Gaekwad Baroda Golf Club, set up by the Royal Family for the citizens of Vadodara. The Motibaug Palace is now the club house for the club. Packs of langoors & peacocks can be spotted around the palace compound. The present management of the club have used the old british spelling Lukshmi Vilas Palace instead of the better known Lakshmi Vilas Palace.

Two other palaces in Baroda were the Makarpura Palace, built on the southern outskirts of Baroda which now houses a defence installation and Pratap Vilas Palace, which houses the prestigious Railway Staff College of India.

Maharaja Ranjit Singh : Maharaja Ranjit Singh (1780-1839) was a Sikh ruler of the Punjab. His tomb is located in Lahore, Pakistan. Maharaja Ranjit Singh was a Sikh born in 1780. At the time much of Punjab was ruled by the Sikhs, who had divided the territory between factions. Ranjit Singh's father Maha Singh was the commander of the Sukerchakia misl (faction) and controlled a territory in west Punjab based around his headquarters at Gujranwala. Ranjit Singh succeeded his father at just the tender age of 12.

After several campaigns he united the Sikh factions into one state and he took the title of Maharaja on April 12, 1801, with Lahore having served as his capital from 1799. In 1802 he took the holy city of Amritsar. He then spent the following years fighting the Afghans, driving them out of western Punjab. He also captured Pasthun territory including Peshawar. This was the first time ever that Pastuns were ruled by non-muslims. This event has a very important historical perspective. For more than a thousand years invaders had come down from the Khyber pass and ruled eastern lands. Ranjit Singh reversed this trend. When the Sikh empire finally fell to the English, they were able to retain this province. He captured the province of Multan which encompassed the southern parts of Punjab, Peshawar, Jammu and Kashmir and the hill states north of Anandpur, largest of which was Kangra.

He also modernised his army, hiring European mercenaries to create the first modern Indian Army, the effect was to create a powerful and heavily armed state and at this point Punjab was the only state not controlled by the British. He brought law and order, yet was relucant to use the death penalty. He stopped Indian secular style practises by treating Hindus and Muslims equally. He banned the secular "jizya" tax on Hindus and Sikhs. In his multi-ethnic empire he was famous for its tolerance with Muslims and Hindus holding high states of office. The Empire was effectively non-secular as it did not discriminate against Hindus and Sikhs, relatively modern and had great respect for all religions of the Empire. This was in sharp contrast with the ethnic & religious cleansing of past Moghul rulers. Ranjit Singh had created a state based upon sikh and hindu noble traditions, where everyone worked together, regardless of background. Where citizens where made to look at the things that they shared in common, e.g. being Punjabi, rather than any religious differences. The British at this time, on the subcontinent, where expanding and consolidating their grip on power. Whereas, in Punjab they had met a comprehensive road block for complete supremacy, on the subcontinent.

Ranjit is remembered for uniting the Punjab as a strong state and his possesion of the Koh-i-noor diamond. His most lasting legacy was the beautification of the Harmandir Sahib, holiest site of the Sikhs, with marble and gold from which the popular name of the "Golden Temple" is derived. He was also known as Sher-e-Punjab, the Lion of Punjab and is considered one of the 3 Lions of India, the most famous and revered heros in North Indian history (Emperor Rajendra Chola and Asoka were the 2 most powerful Indian kings of history yet are not named part of the 3 Lions) - the other 2 Lions are Rana Pratap Singh of Mewar and Shivaji the Maratha. The title of Sher-e-Punjab is still widely used as a term of respect for a powerful man.

Maharana Pratap : Maharana Pratap (1540-1597) was the ruler of Mewar, a state in north-western India. He belonged to the Shishodiya clan of Suryavanshi rajputs. His descendents bear the patronymic "Ranawat". The epitome of fiery Rajput pride and self-respect, Pratap has for centuries exemplified the qualities that Rajputs aspire to.

Maharashtra : It is India's third largest state in terms of area and second largest in terms of population after Uttar Pradesh. It is bordered by the states of Gujarat, Madhya Pradesh, Chhattisgarh, Andhra Pradesh, Karnataka, Goa and the Union territory of Dadra and Nagar Haveli. The Arabian Sea makes up the state's western coast. Mumbai (Bombay), India's largest city, is the capital of Maharashtra.

Maharashtra was known as "Rashtra" in the Rig Veda, "Rashtrik" in Ashoka's inscriptions, and "Maha rashtra" afterwards, as attested by Huein-Tsang and other travellers. The name appears to have been derived from "Maharashtri" in an old form of Prakrit, an ancient Indian language. However, there are other theories put forward by different schools of thought. One possible derivation is believed to be the corruption of the term "Maha Kantara", which means "Great Forest". Both these theories did not carry much weight, as can be seen from the name of Maharashtra.

Maharishi Mahesh Yogi : Maharishi Mahesh Yogi (born Mahesh Srivastava in 1917) is the founder of the Transcendental Meditation (TM) Movement. He brought Transcendental Meditation to the western world. Maharishi is believed to have been born near Jabalpur, India and graduated from Allahabad University with a degree in physics. He was secretary to Swami Brahmananda Saraswati, the Shankaracharya of Jyotirmath, for thirteen years.

In 1955, after spending two years in silence in UttarKashi, in the Himalayan foothills, he began teaching a basic meditation technique which he later dubbed "Transcendental Meditation". He set up an "Asharam" (Hermitage)- called "Shankaracharaya Nagar" in Rishikesh, Northern India on the bank of the river Ganges. In 1957 he founded The Spiritual Regeneration Movement, the first of several organizations collectively known as the TM Movement, and began the first of many tours to teach the Transcendental Meditation technique around the world.

Maharshi Dhondo Keshav Karve : Maharshi Dhondo Keshav Karve fought throughout his life for the upliftment of women. He started a college for them and established the first Indian University for women, named SNDT Women's University in Mumbai.

In 1958, he was awarded the Bharat Ratna, the highest civilian award of India. He was from the Ratnagiri district in Maharashtra, India.

Mahasamund : Mahasamund district is spread out in an area of 3902.39 km^2 in the Central-East of Chhattisgarh State, India. The district lies between 20°47' to 21°31'30° latitude and 82°00' to 83°15'45° longitude, surrounded by districts of Raigarh and Raipur of Chhattisgarh State and Nawapara and Bargarh of Orissa. From granite rocks of the Archean period to stratified rocks of Cuddupah group of Upper Cambrian age are and alluvial soil and sand of recent age are found in abundance in the district. Also found in this region are neo-granite, dolerite, and quartz in intrusive forms. Granite rocks can be found in the Bagbahra, Basna and Pithore region. Limestone rocks of Chhattisgarh group contemporary to Cuddapah group of Upper Pre-Cambrian age and comprising of limestone layers, shale, sandstone, or quartzite can be predominantly found. Hence there is a great scope of intense mining activity.

Mahasamund : Mahasamund district is spread out in an area of 3902.39 km^2 in the Central-East of Chhattisgarh

State, India. The district lies between 20°47' to 21°31'30° latitude and 82°00' to 83°15'45° longitude, surrounded by districts of Raigarh and Raipur of Chhattisgarh State and Nawapara and Bargarh of Orissa. From granite rocks of the Archean period to stratified rocks of Cuddupah group of Upper Cambrian age are and alluvial soil and sand of recent age are found in abundance in the district. Also found in this region are neo-granite, dolerite, and quartz in intrusive forms. Granite rocks can be found in the Bagbahra, Basna and Pithore region. Limestone rocks of Chhattisgarh group contemporary to Cuddapah group of Upper Pre-Cambrian age and comprising of limestone layers, shale, sandstone, or quartzite can be predominantly found. Hence there is a great scope of intense mining activity.

Mahasweta Devi : Mahasweta Devi (born 1926 in Dacca now known as Bangladesh) is an Indian writer. Born into a middle-class Bengali family, Mahasweta Devi studied at Vhisva-Bharati and Calcutta. She later earned a M.A. in English at Shantiniketan, a renowned experi-mental University. In 1964, she began teaching at Bijaygarh College in Jadavpur; an Indian college for working class women, while simultaneously working as a journalist and creative writer. She is noted in recent decades for her works related to the study of the rural tribal communities of West Bengal, women and dalits. She is also an activist who is dedicated to the struggle of tribal people in Bihar, Madhya Pradesh and Chhattisgarh. In her elaborate Bengali fiction, she often depicts the brutal opression of tribal peoples and the untouchables by potent, authoritary high-caste landlords, lenders, and venal government officials.

Mahatma Gandhi : Mohandas Karamchand Gandhi (October 2, 1869 – January 30, 1948) was a spiritual and one of the most prominent political leaders of India who led the movement for Indian independence from the

British Empire. Throughout his life, he rejected any form of violence as a means of achieving his goals. His philosophy of nonviolence, for which he coined the term satyagraha (struggle for the truth), has influenced nonviolent resistance movements to this day, across the world.

Ever since he became the leader of the freedom struggle, Gandhi was reverently addressed as Mahatma, or Great Soul by many Indians. Although he was much averse to honorary forms of address, Gandhi is still today commonly referred to as Mahatma Gandhi. During the freedom struggle and now, Gandhi was referred to as Bapu by Indians. He is acknowledged officially in India as the "Father of the Nation." His birthday on October 2, Gandhi Jayanti, is a national holiday in India.

At the age of 13 Gandhi married Kasturba, a girl the same age. Their parents arranged the marriage. The Gandhis had four children. Gandhi studied law in London and returned to India in 1891 to practice. In 1893 he took on a one-year contract to do legal work in South Africa. At the time the British controlled South Africa. When he attempted to claim his rights as a British subject he was abused, and soon saw that all Indians suffered similar treatment. Gandhi stayed in South Africa for 21 years working to secure rights for Indian people. He developed a method of action based upon the principles of courage, nonviolence and truth called Satyagraha. He believed that the way people behave is more important than what they achieve. Satyagraha promoted nonviolence and civil disobedience as the most appropriate methods for obtaining political and social goals. In 1915 Gandhi returned to India. Within 15 years he became the leader of the Indian nationalist movement.

Using the principles of Satyagraha he led the campaign for Indian independence from Britain. Gandhi was arrested many times by the British for his activities in South Africa and India. He believed it was honorable to go to jail for a just cause. Altogether he spent seven years in prison for his political activities. More than once Gandhi used fasting to impress upon others the need to be nonviolent. India was granted independence in 1947, and partitioned into India and Pakistan. Rioting between Hindus and Muslims followed. Gandhi had been an advocate for a united India where Hindus and Muslims lived together in peace. On January 13, 1948, at the age of 78, he began a fast with the purpose of stopping the bloodshed. After 5 days the opposing leaders pledged to stop the fighting and Gandhi broke his fast. Twelve days later a Hindu fanatic, Nathuram Godse who opposed his program of tolerance for all creeds and religion assassinated him.

By means of nonviolent civil disobedience, Gandhi helped bring about India's independence from British rule, ultimately dismantling the British Empire. This form of pacifist resistance has inspired other colonial nations to work towards their own independence. Gandhi's principle of satyagraha, has inspired other freedom activists such as Dr. Martin Luther King, the Dalai Lama, Lech Walesa, Stephen Biko, Aung San Suu Kyi, and Nelson Mandela. However, not all these leaders kept to Gandhi's strict principle of nonviolence and nonresistance. Gandhi often stated that his principles were simple and drawn from traditional Hindu beliefs: truth (satya) and nonviolence (ahimsa). 'My experiments with truth' is the famous autobiography written by Gandhiji.

Mahavatar Babaji : Mahavatar Babaji is a legendary Hindu saint, yogi, and culture hero first described by Paramahansa Yogananda in his best-selling Autobiography of a Yogi.

Yogananda describes Mahavatar Babaji as the guru of Lahiri Mahasaya and an avatar. Yogananda wrote that

Mahavatar Babaji is responsible for the revival, in 1861, of a spiritual technique known as Kriya Yoga, which is claimed to accelerate the spiritual aspirant's evolution. Yogananda said that Babaji was Krishna in a former lifetime, and he often prayed out loud to "Babaji-Krishna." Lahiri Mahasaya wrote in his personal diary that 'Krishna is Babaji'.

Mahaveer Harina Vanasthali National Park : The park is located at Vanasthalipuram in Hyderabad, at a distance of 20 km from the city and originally the area was under the Nizam. The park was established in 1977.

Mahaveer Wildlife Sanctuary : A wildlife sanctuary in Goa, India. Located in the Eastern Ghats and the borders of Karnataka. 240 square kilometres. Known as a place for avid bird-watchers to gather, one can also find many unique historical and geological features found in this area. They inculde Devil's Canyon, several important temples dating to the Kadamba Dynasty, and Dudhsagar Falls. The park land is also home to a community of nomadic buffalo herders known as the Dhangar.

Mahavir Harina Vanasthali National Park : The park is located in Vanasthalipuram, on the outskirts of Hyderabad city at a distance of about 15-km on the Hyderabad- Vijayawada road. Once the Nizam's (former Hyderabadi rulers) hunting grounds, it is now home to the beautiful black bucks with their spiral horns along with several species of birds.

The park named after the renowned Jain saint 'Lord Mahavira' was established in 1975, in commemoration of his 2500th birth anniversary. The deer park maintained by the Forest Department, has an undulating terrain, of 189 hectares dominated by acacia trees and grasslands. The park looks picturesque in the monsoon with the golden and white flowers of these trees on the lush green carpet of grass. Besides Acacias, neem, Bauhinias, Buteas (Flame of the forest) and a variety of thorny scrub species are found in this dry scrub forest.

Mahavira or Mahavir : Mahavira or Mahavir (the "Great Hero" — Also, Vardhamana (increasing) or Niggantha Nathaputta — 599 BC-527 BC, though possibly 549 BC-477 BC) was the 24th, and last, Jainist Tirthankara. Mahavira established what are today considered to be the central tenets of Jainism and was a contemporary of Siddhartha Gautama, the Buddha. He was born on the thirteenth day under the rising moon of Chaitra, in the ancient Kingdom of Vaishali, now a district of Bihar state, India. According to the Gregorian calendar, Mahavira was born in April. His birthday is celebrated as Mahavir Jayanti. He died at Pawapuri. He was known as "Vardhaman" (increasing) because it is said that his family's wealth grew after his conception. A growth of everything good was also noticed in the kingdom, like the bloom of beautiful flowers.

After his birth he was taken by Indra to bath the child in the celestial milk and perform the ritual befitting a future 'Tirthankar'. He was then returned back to his mother, who had dreamt of 14 auspicious symbols, before giving birth to her son. It was a sign to tell them the advent of a great soul. Being the son of King Siddartha and Queen Trisala, he lived the life of a prince; married Yashodhara, a princess and had a daughter also. At the age of thirty, he left his family, gave up his worldly possessions, and spent twelve years as an ascetic. At one point, it is said that Mahavir had more than 400,000 followers. He shed his body in 527 BC at the age of 72. Jains signify Dipavali, the last day of the Hindu and Jain calendars, as the anniversery of his death and, accordingly, the day he attained Moksha.

After he renounced his princehood, he spent the next twelve and half years in deep silence and meditation and took on the discipline of conquering his desires, feelings, and attachments. He carefully avoided harming or annoying other living beings including animals, birds, and plants. He also went without food for long periods. His enduring calm and peaceful character against all unbearable hardships presence the influence of his title, Mahavir (a Sanskrit word, meaning very brave and courageous), given to him by his peers. During this period, Jains believe his that he attained keval-jnana, or perfect enlightenment, in which spiritual powers fully become developed and perfect perception, knowledge, power, and bliss are realized.

Mahavira spent the next thirty years travelling around India preaching to the people the eternal truth he realized. The ultimate objective of his teaching is how one can attain total freedom from the cycle of birth, life, pain, misery, and death, and achieve the permanent blissful state of one's self, or Moksha, Sanskrit for "liberation". Mahavira preached that from eternity, every living being (soul) is in bondage of karmic atoms that are accumulated by good or bad deeds. Under the influence of karma, the soul is habituated to seek pleasures in materialistic belongings and possessions, which are the deep rooted causes of self-centered violent thoughts, deeds, anger, hatred, greed, and such other vices. These result in further accumulation of karmas.

As taught by Mahavira, Jains believe that these vows can not be fully implemented without the acceptance of a philosophy of non-absolutism (Anekantvada) and the theory of relativity (Syadvada, also translated "qualified prediction"). Monks and nuns are held to follow these vows strictly and totally, while the common people may follow the vows as far as their life styles will permit. In the matters of spiritual advancement, as envisioned by Mahavira, both men and women are on an equal footing and were taught by Mahavira that they may equally renounce the world in search of ultimate happiness.

Mahavira attracted people from all walks of life, rich and poor, kings and commoners, men and women, princes and priests, touchable and untouchable. He organized his followers into a four-fold order, namely monk (Sadhu), nun (Sadhvi), layman (Shravak), and laywoman (Shravika). This order is known as Chaturvidh Jain Sangh. Lord Mahavira's sermons were orally compiled by his immediate disciples in the Agam Sutras. These Agam Sutras were orally passed on to future generations. In the course of time, many of the Agam Sutras have been lost, destroyed, or modified. About one thousand years later the Agam Sutras were recorded on Tadpatris (leafy paper that was used in those days to preserve records for future references). Swetambar Jains have accepted these sutras as authentic version of His teachings while Digambar Jains use them as a reference.

Jainism existed before Mahavira, and his teachings were based on those of his predecessors. Thus, Mahavira was more of a reformer and propagator of an existing religious order than the founder of a new faith. He followed the well established creed of his predecessor Tirthankar Parshvanath. However, Mahavira did reorganize the philosophical tenets of Jainism to correspond to his times. A few centuries after Mahavira's death, the Jain religious order (Sangha) grew more and more complex. There were schisms on some minor points, although they did not affect the original doctrines as preached by Mahavira. Later generations saw the introduction of ritualistic complexities that some have criticized as almost placing Mahavira and other Tirthankars on the thrones of Hindu deities.

Mahayana : Mahayana is one of the major branches of Buddhism. Mahayana originated in the Indian subcontinent, and some of the areas in which it is practiced today are India, China, Tibet, Japan, Korea, Vietnam, and Taiwan. From Mahayana developed the esoteric Vajrayana which claims to encompass all previous schools.

Mahendra Singh (MS) Dhoni : Mahendra Singh (MS) Dhoni (born July 7, 1981 in Ranchi, Jharkhand) is an Indian cricketer. He is an aggressive right-handed batsman and wicketkeeper. He was picked to play for the Indian cricket team in December 2004 and has been a regular member of the Indian one-day international team since then. Dhoni is an alumnus of DAV Jawahar Vidya Mandir, Ranchi.

Dhoni (affectionately known as Mahi), made his debut for Jharkhand in the 1999-2000 season as an eighteen year old. He started off his career with modest performances at the local level. He was noticed by the national team selectors in 2004 after his performances in first class tournaments such as the Deodhar Trophy and the Duleep Trophy.

Dhoni's best performance for India thus far was an unbeaten score of 183 off 145 balls against Sri Lanka at Jaipur on 31 October 2005, equalling the second best score by an Indian in ODIs. It was also the highest innings recorded by a wicket-keeper, and the highest number of sixes in an innings for a wicketkeeper (with ten—all-rounders Sanath Jayasuriya and Shahid Afridi have hit 11). He also broke Saeed Anwar's record of most runs scored off boundaries by scoring a total of 120 runs off 4s and 6s eclipsing the previous record of 118. This has broken the record for the highest individual score for a team batting second. This has also established the new Indian record of number of sixes in a match, overtaking previous record holders, Sachin Tendulkar and Sourav Ganguly (both hit seven 6's in a match). Dhoni's current batting average in ODIs is just over 50 (as of February 2006), the highest by any Indian player with more than 20 innings.

With a career ODI batting strike rate of more than 100% he remains the only batsman with the unique double of a 50+ average scored at more than a run a ball.

Mahesh Bhupathi : Top league Doubles Tennis star Mahesh Srinivas Bhupathi, is one of India's outstanding sporting heroes. He is known for his booming serves and hard-hitting volleys. He was born on 7th June, 1974 in Madras, Tamilnadu. Bhupathi was educated in Dubai, Muscat and in USA. His father Mr. C.G. Krishna Bhupathi coached him right from his formative years, exclusively on hard courts in the Middle East and his son has proved that hard work pays.

Mahesh has traveled extensively from the age of 14 and has played in major tournaments all over the world. He had an outstanding two-year career at the University of Mississippi from 1994-95, earning singles and doubles All-America honors in '95. He was the finalist in doubles in the Under-18 at Wimbledon. He turned pro in 1995. He teamed with Ali Hamadeh in 1995 to win the NCAA doubles title and finished as the No. 1 player in doubles and No. 3 in singles. He was India's national champion in 1994 and 1995 and a member of the Indian Davis Cup team since 1995 and represents India in Davis Cup Singles and Doubles. He won a Silver and 3 Gold medals at the SAF Games, represented India at the Atlanta Olympics - 1996, took India to the Quarter Finals of the Elite World Group in Davis Cup along with Leander Paes. In 1997, he became the first Indian to win a Grand Slam when he took the mixed doubles French Open along with Japan's Rika Hiraki.

Bhupathi's partnership with Leander Paes formed a doubles 'dream' team which took Indian tennis to heights of glory. Their first major victory was at the 1997 ATP Gold Flake Open Tennis tournament at Chennai. They made it a hat-trick of triumphs by winning the Gold Flake open titles during 1998 and 1999. The duo captured six ATP doubles titles in seven finals and qualified for ATP World doubles Championship losing to Leach-Stark in final. In 1999, they showed their class by winning the French Open and Wimbledon and entering the finals of the two other Grand Slam Tournaments; the Australian and US Opens and became the first team since 1952 to reach the final of all four Grand Slam events in the same year. They also won the doubles title at Rolland Garros in 1999. But, as soon after they started dominating the World Tennis scene, the world top ranked pair separated due to mutual misunderstanding. Fortunately they came back together again after a gap of eight months, in time for the Sydney Olympics and started regaining their lost prestige at the end of 2000, winning the Men's Double title in Japan Open 2000 followed by Worlds Doubles Championship in Bangalore and in 2001 Verizon Atlanta Challenge, US Clay court Championship in Houston and at Roland Garros defeating the Czech pair of Petr Pala and Pavel Vizner, ranked no. 2 in the world.

Mahesh has won five doubles titles in 2002, with four different partners. Won titles in Chennai and Mallorca with Paes, captured TMS title in Hamburg with Gambill and in Long Island with M. Bryan, and the US Open with current partner Max Mirnyi of Belarus who teamed with him most of the year. In 2003, he won the TMS title in Monte Carlo and in Estoril. He received the ' Arjuna Award' in 1996 and India's highest honour 'Padma Shri' along with Paes on March 26, 2001. His father, the encouraging factor behind him runs 'The Tennis Village' at Bangalore, giving training to aspirants. Bhupathi residing in Bangalore got married on November 24th 2002 to a Chennai model girl Shwetha Jaishankar. This talented player keeps winning titles and making India proud.

Maheshwar : Maheshwar is a town in Khargone district of Madhya Pradesh state, in central India. The town lies on the north bank of the Narmada River, It is built on the site of the ancient city of Mahesvari, and was the capital of king Arjuna Kartavirya, who was mentioned in the Sanskrit epics Mahabharata and Ramayana.An ancient name of Maheshwar is Mahishmati. In the late eighteenth century Maheshwar served as the capital of Rajmata Ahilya Devi Holkar, ruler of the state of Indore. She embellished the city with many buildings and public works, and it is home to her palace, as well as numerous temples, a fort, and riverfront ghats, broad stone steps which step down to the river. The fort is home to a state archeological museum.

Maheshwar is noted as a center for weaving colorful cotton saris, with distinctive designs involving stripes, checks and floral borders.Near to Maheshwar is Sahastradhara(a water fall of thousand streams). Maheshawar was in news recently due to a big dam that will be constructed at some distance from here under Narmada valley development project. Noted movie of Shahrukh Khan "Ashoka" was also shot here.

Mahindra & Mahindra Ltd : Mahindra & Mahindra Ltd (The Mahindra Group) is a US$ 2.5 billion organization with businesses spanning various industries from automobile, auto components, and tractor manufacturing to information technology, trading and financial services, and infrastructure development. Mahindra is one of the most forward thinking and respected corporations in India and is among the top conglomerates driving globalization in India and establishing a multinational presence.

Mahiuddin Jahangir : Mahiuddin Jahangir (1948-1971) was an officer in the army Engineers Corps and a martyr in the war of liberation. He was born at village Rahimganj in Babuganj upazila of Barisal district in 1948. He passed Matriculation examination in 1964, I Sc in 1966, and joined Pakistan Military Academy as a cadet in 1967. He obtained commissioned rank in 1968. Mahiuddin Jahangir was posted in the 173 Engineer Battalion in West Pakistan during the War of Liberation. With an avowed object of joining the War Mahiuddin along with three of his fellow officers managed to escape from his station on 3 July, and passing through the inaccessible hilly tracts reached the camp of the freedom fighters at Mehdipur in Maldah district of west bengal.

Jahangir had displayed extraordinary skill and valour in some of the successful operations against the Pakistan occupation army, and was consequently placed in charge of the contingent of the freedom fighters deputed to capture Nawabganj in Rajshahi. Captain Mahiuddin along with Lieutenant Qayyum, Lieutenant Awwal and nearly fifty freedom fighters took position (10 December) at Bargharia on the west of Nawabganj town. At the dawn of 14 December, they crossed the Mahananda through Rehaichar on some country boats and surprised some trenches of the enemy. In a fiercely contested battle an enemy bullet struck Mahiuddin on his forehead and he succumbed to death (14 December). Undaunted the freedom fighters renewed their attacks and compelled the Pak-army to take to their heels. Mahiuddin was laid to rest at the premises of the chhota sona maosque. In recognition of his valour and sacrifice in the War of Liberation Mahiuddin Jahangir was honoured with the highest state insignia of Bir Srestha.

Mahmud of Ghazni : Mahmud of Ghazni (October 2, 971–April 30, 1030), also known as Yamin ad-Dawlah Mahmud (in full: Yamin ad-Dawlah Abd al-Qasim Mahmud Ibn Sebük Tigin) was the ruler of Ghazni from 997 until his death. Mahmud turned the former provincial city of Ghazni (in present-day Afghanistan) into the wealthy capital of an extensive empire which included today's Afghanistan, most of modern Iran, and parts of Pakistan and northern India.

Mahmud's grandfather was Alptigin, a Turkic general from Balkh in Turkestan who crossed the Hindu Kush mountains to seize Ghazni, located strategically on the road between Kabul and Kandahar. Alptigin was succeeded in 977 by his son Sabuktigin, who enlarged upon his Alptigin's conquests, extending his domain north to Balkh, west to Kandahar and Khorasan, and east to the Indus River. Sabuktigin was recognized by the Caliph in Baghdad as governor of his dominions. Sultan Alptigin died in 997, and was succeeded by his younger son Sultan Ismail of Ghazni. Mahmud rebelled against his younger brother, Sultan Ismail of Ghazni, and took over the Ghazni as the new Sultan.

Issuing forth year after year from his capital of Ghazni, Sultan Mahmud carried sixteen or seventeen campaigns into northern India and Gujarat, as well as others to the north and west. His first campaigns were against the Hindu Shahi kingdom, which occupied the Punjab from the Indus east to the Ganges. He had participated in his father's campaigns against the Shahi king Jayapala in the late 980s that captured the Khyber Pass region as far east as the Indus. Sultan Mahmud campaigned against the Shahis in 1001, and in 1004 raided deep into the Punjab, defeated a Shahi army and captured Bhatia and Multan. In 1008, he conquered most of the Punjab and captured the Shahi treasury at Kangra in the Punjab Hill States, which reduced the Shahi kingdom to a sliver of the eastern Punjab.

Mahmud's campaigns seem to be motivated by both religious zeal and an interest in wealth and gold. Mahmud followed the injunction to convert non-Muslims, whom he had vowed to follow every year of his life. Hindu temples were depositories of vast quantities of wealth, in cash, golden idols, diamonds, and jewellery—and these made them targets for a non-Hindu searching for wealth in northern India. The later invasions of Mahmud were directed to temple towns, including Nagarkot (1009), Thanesar (1012), Mathura and Kanauj (1018), Kalinjar 1021, and finally Somnath (1026). Mahmud's armies routinely stripped the temples of their wealth and then destroyed them; after Mahmud's raids on the cities of Varanasi, Ujjain, Maheshwar, Jwalamukhi, and Dwarka.

By the end of his reign, his empire extended from Kurdistan in the west to Samarkand in the northeast, and from the Caspian Sea to the Yamuna. Although his raids carried his forces across northern and western India, only the Punjab and Sindh, modern Pakistan, came under his permanent rule; Kashmir, the Doab, Rajasthan and Gujarat remained under the control of the local Hindu Rajput dynasties. The wealth brought back to Ghazni was enormous, and contemporary historians (e.g. Abolfazl Beyhaghi, Ferdowsi) give glowing descriptions of the magnificence of the capital, as well as of the conqueror's munificent support of literature. On April 30, 1030, Sultan Mahmud died in Ghazni, at the age of 59 years. Sultan Mahmud had contracted malaria during his last invasion. The medical complication from malaria has caused lethal tuberculosis.

The Ghaznavid Empire was ruled by his successors for 157 years, but after Mahmud it never reached anything like the same splendour and power. The expanding Seljuk Turkish empire absorbed most of the Ghaznavid west. The Persian Ghorids captured Ghazni c. 1150, and Muhammad Ghori captured the last Ghaznavid stronghold at Lahore in 1187. The Ghaznavids went on to live as the Nasher-Khans in their home of Ghazni until the 20th century.

Mahoba : Mahoba is a town in Mahoba District of the Indian state of Uttar Pradesh, in the Bundelkhand region. Mahoba is known for its closeness to Khajuraho and other historic places like Kulpahar, Charkhari, Kalinjar, Orchha, and Jhansi. The town is connected with railways and state highways. Mahoba was the capital of the Chandela Rajputs, who ruled Bundelkhand from the 10th to the 16th centuries. The Chandela king Vijaypal (1035-1045) built the Vijay-sagar reservoir, one of several artificial lakes in Mahoba created by the Chandela rulers. During the reign of king Paramardi, the Chauhan king Prithviraj III of Delhi and Ajmer captured Mahoba c. 1182, despite the resistance of his generals Allha & Udal. The Chandelas recaptured Mahoba a few years later, but the city was captured by the Muslim general Qutb-ud-din Aybak, later Sultan of Delhi, in 1203.

The Chandela ruler Keerat Pal Singh recaptured Mahoba in the 14th century. Emperor Sher Shah Suri campaigned against the Chandelas, and captured Mahoba before dying while besieging Kalinjar in 1545. The Mughal emperor Akbar captured Mahoba a few decades later.

The Bundela leader Chhatrasal captured Mahoba in 1680, during the reign of the Mughal Emperor Aurangzeb. Upon his death in 1732, Chhatra Sal bequeathed Mahoba and the surrounding area to the Maratha Peshwa Baji Rao I in return for Baji Rao's assistance against the Mughals. The Marathas ruled Mahoba until 1803, when it was ceded to British India by the Treaty of Bassein. Mahoba was made a subdivision of Hamirpur District.

Maihar : Maihar is a town in Madhya Pradesh state of central India. It is located in Satna District. The town was formerly the capital of the princely state of Maihar. The state was founded in 1778 by Rajputs of the Kachwaha clan, who were granted land by the ruler of the nearby state of Orchha. The state became a princely state of British India in the early 19th century, and was administered as part of Bundelkhand Agency in the Central India Agency. In 1871 the eastern states of Bundelkhand Agency, including Maihar, were separated to form the new agency of Bagelkhand in Central India. In 1933 Maihar, along with ten other states in western Bagelkhand, were transferred back to the Bundelkhand Agency. The state had an area of 407 square miles, and a population of 63,702 in 1901. The state, which was watered by the Tons River, consists mainly of alluvial soil covering sandstone, and is fertile except in the hilly district of the south. A large area was under forest, the produce of which provided a small export trade. The title of the ruler was maharaja. The state suffered severely from famine in 1896-1897. Maihar became a station on the East Indian Railway (now the West Central Railway) line between Satna and Jabalpur, 97 miles north of Jabalpur. Extensive ruins of shrines and other buildings surround the town.

Maithili : Maithili is of the family of Indo-Aryan languages, which are part of the Indo-Iranian branch of the Indo-European languages. It is spoken in the Indian state of Bihar and in the eastern Terai region of Nepal. It is considered by many to be a dialect of Hindi, and thus not a separate language. Nevertheless, a movement to give the language official status in the Indian Constitution so that it could be used in education, government, and other official contexts, resulted in Maithili being given official status in 2003.

The term Maithili comes from Mithila, which was an independent state in ancient times. Maithili is a separate language, having a large Maithili-speaking community (4.5 crore, or 45 million, people) with a rich literature. The most famous literary figure in Maithili is the poet Vidyapati. He is credited for raising the importance of 'people's langauage', i.e. Maithili, in the official work of the state by influencing the king of Darbhanga with the quality of his poetry. The state's official language used to be Sanskrit, which distanced common people from the state and its functions.

Linguists consider Maithili to be an Eastern Indic language, and thus a different language from Hindi, which is Central Indic. Most linguists do not consider it to be equated as a dialect of Hindi as this language developed separately from the advent of Hindi.

Maithili can be written in the Maithili script, which has some resemblance with Bengali script, or in the Devanagari script, which is also used for Hindi, Sanskrit, Nepali, and many other Indic languages. Maithili use to be written in Tirahuti script but in the later part of 20th century started using Devanagari script. Tirahuti script is the base script from which Maithali, Bengali and Oriya script have evolved.

Maithilisharan Gupt : Maithilisharan Gupt (1886-1965) was one of the most famous modern Hindi poets. He was designated as the National Poet by the first government of the independent India. He also wrote some dramas. Gupt entered the world of Hindi literature by writing poems in various magazines, including Saraswati. In 1910, his first major work, Rang mein Bhang was published. With Bharat Bharati, his nationalist poems became popular among Indians, who were struggling for independence. Most of his poems revolve around plots from Ramayana, Mahabharata, Buddhist stories and the lives of famous religious leaders. His famous work Saket revolves around Urmila, a lesser-known character from Ramayana, while another of his works Yashodhara revolves around Yashodhara, the wife of Gautama Buddha.

Maitraka Dynasty : The Maitraka dynasty ruled Gujarat in western India from the c. 475 to 767. The founder of the dynasty, general Bhatarka, was a military governor of Saurashtra peninsula under Gupta empire, who had established himself as the independent ruler of Gujarat approximately in the last quarter of 5th century.

The Maitraka is stated to be not a tribal name but a cognomen only. The name is said to derive from Mitra or Mithra, the Sun or Sun deity, also a synonym of Mihira, (old Persian Mihr). The Maitrakas, the worshippers of Mitra/Mithra i.e. Sun-worshippers, identified with the Mihiras (Zoroastrians) are regarded by one school of scholars as of foreign origin.

There is evidence that the Maitraka rulers had switched to Saivism, but when Chinese traveller Hieun-Tsang visited Vallabhi during second quarter of 7th century, he found its ruler to be a Buddhist follower. When I-Tsing, another Chinese traveller, visited Vallabhi in the last quarter of 7th century, he found Vallabhi as a great center of learning including Buddhism. Gunamati and Sthiramati were two famous Buddhist scholars of Vallabhi at the middle of 7th century. Vallabhi was famous for its catholicity and the students from all over the country, including the Brahmana boys, visited it to have higher education in secular and religious subjects. We are told that the graduates of Valabhi were given higher executive posts.

The Maitrakas ruled from their capital at Vallabhi. They came under the rule of Harsha in the mid-seventh century, but retained local autonomy, and regained their independence after Harsha's death. Maitraka rule ended with the sacking of Vallabhi by the barbarians in 524, according to James Tod and in second or third quarter of the 8th century by various other scholars. There is no agreement among the scholars as to who these barbarians were.

Majeed Amjad : Majeed Amjad was one of the founding fathers of the modern Urdu poetry. According to Intizar Hussain, " Some poets are deeply immersed in their own creative world. They seldom have the time to think or write about other creative individuals. Majeed

Amjad was one such verse-wielder. So, when he chose to write the preface to the collection of a young poet of his time, everyone took notice. He seemed to like the young poet. It also helped the reader to know how Majeed Amjad felt about the poetry of his days, especially about the genre of ghazal.

Majlis-e-Shoora : Majlis-e-Shoora (Council of Advisors in Urdu, although everyone calls it "Parliament")is the bicameral federal legislature that consists of the Senate (upper house) and the National Assembly (lower house). According to Article 50 of the Constitution of Pakistan, the Council consists also of the President of Pakistan. The Constitution gives the President of Pakistan the authority to dissolve (and thereby trigger new elections for) the National Assembly but not the Senate, which is not subject to dissolution. The National Assembly of Pakistan has 342 members; 72 of these members are women. Pakistani law requires that at least 20% of the members be women. The Senate has a 100 members; currently 18 of these members are women, one greater than the required number.

Major Muhammad Akram Shaheed : Born 4 April 1938 in Dingha, Gujrat District. Commissioned in the Frontier Force Regiment on 13 October 1963. He and a company of 4 FF Regiment which he commanded in the forward area in Hilli district, in East Pakistan in 1971, came under incessant air, artillery and armour attacks. But for an entire fortnight, despite enemy superiority in both numbers and fire power, he and his men repulsed every attack, inflicting heavy casualties on the enemy.

Major Akram died during this epic battle in 1971 at the age of 33.

Major Tufail Muhammad Shaheed : Born 1914 in Hoshiarpur. Commissioned into the 16th Punjab Regiment, 1943.

Early in August, 1958, Major Tufail, a Company Commander in the East Pakistan Rifles, and his patrol encircled an Indian post in the Lakshmipur area. And, though mortally wounded in the hand-to-hand encounter that followed, Major Tufail continued to lead his troops till the Indians were driven out, leaving four dead and three prisoners. He died the same day on 7 August 1958 at the age of 44.

Makar Sankranti : Makar Sankranti is a mid-winter festival of India. The day celebrates the northward journey of the Sun. Sankranti means the day the Sun enters a new zodiac sign according to Hindu astrology. There is a Sankranti for every month of the year. Makar means Capricorn. Makar Sankranti is the day the Sun enters Capricorn. The reason why Makar Sankranti is celebrated more than any other is that it marks the day the Sun starts moving north and the auspicious half of the year characterised by increasing daylight begins. The celebration is similar to winter solstice celebrations in other ancient cultures. Instead of the celebrating on the day of the Winter Solstice—Makar Sankranti is celebrated on January 14, the day the Sun enters the next zodiac sign according to Hindu astrology. Makar Sankranti is celebrated in regional festivals all over India

Makhad : Makhad is a hilly historical town in the Attock District in Northern Punjab of Pakistan. It is one of the last towns separating the Punjab province from the rugged North West Frontier Province (NWFP). The separation is marked by a fast flowing River Indus.

The Paracha tribe, which is one of the largest in Pakistan and today scattered all over the country and even India, is said to have become a large clan in Makhad in the 10th Century BC. The tribe which today mostly speak Pothohari dialect of Punjabi, migrated from North Yemen in the time of Prophet Muhammad (in 7th Century AD) and travelled to Iran where they were called "Ferashas" or people who were direct descendants of one Ali Yamani, a cloth trader who used to prepare the ground for Prophet Muhammad to prey upon. "Ferash" in Persian means ground.

Makki di Roti : Makki di roti is rolled flat bread cooked on an iron griddle. In Punjab it is often eaten with spinach and Lassi, a yoghurt-and-water drink. Makki di roti is a favorite of Punjabis at home and abroad. Makki is corn, so makke ki roti would be the roti made out of corn flour. Its extremely soft and has a golden yellow colour. Top it with butter and its so good you can forget about eating it with any sabji (vegetable). Made with sarson (mustard seeds) and palak (spinach) aka. Saag, this is one amazing curry to have. Extremely rich and usually takes a really long time to cook, for that exquisite flavour to come out.

Makrai : Makrai is a formerly princely state of India, administratively under the Bhopal Agency subdivision of the Central India Agency. The state covered an area of 401 square kilometers and had a population of 16,784 in 1892. Its rulers were styled "Raja". The principality was founded by Maratha Rajah Devi Shah in the 1850s. After Indian independence in 1947, the rulers of Makrai acceded to the Union of India, and the principality was incorporated into the new state of Madhya Bharat, which subsequently became Madhya Pradesh state on November 1, 1956.

Makran : Makran is the southern region of Balochistan, in Iran and Pakistan along the coast of the Arabian Sea and the Gulf of Oman. The Persian phrase Mahi khoran, (Fish eaters and Ichthyophagoi i.e. Fish eaters in Greek) which has become the modern word Makran. The narrow coastal plain rises very rapidly into several mountain ranges. The area possesses a very dry climate with very low rainfall. Makran is very sparsely inhabited, with much of the population being concentrated in a string of small ports including Chah Bahar, Gwatar, Jiwani, Gwadar (not to be confused with Gwatar), Pasni, Ormara and many smaller fishing villages. The total length of the coastline is about 1,000 km (of which 750 km is in Pakistan).

Makran Coastal Highway: The Makran Coastal Highway is located in Balochistan, Pakistan. It follows the Arabian Sea coast from Karachi to Gwadar. Previously there was a muddy track linking Karachi with the town of Gwadar. Journeys between the two could take several days as the safest route was to travel via Quetta. The journey time has now been reduced to six or seven hours with the construction of the new Coastal Highway. The highway was built as part of an overall plan to improve transport facilities in southern Balochistan; other parts of the plan include the new seaport and international airport at Gwadar and the construction of a road linking Gwadar to Khuzdar. In the coastal areas of Balochistan, the main livelihood is fishing. The catch could not be sold in Karachi because the fish would rot by the time they reached Karachi. However, the new highway has improved people's livelihoods by giving them the opportunity to sell fish in major markets in Karachi.

Malabar : Malabar is a region of southern India, lying between the Western Ghats and the Arabian Sea, and comprising the northern half of the state of Kerala. Geographically the name is sometimes extended to the entire southwestern coast of the peninsula, called the Malabar Coast. Malabar is also used by ecologists to refer to the tropical moist forests of southwestern India.

The Malabar Coast, in historical contexts, refers to India's southwest coast, lying on the narrow coastal plain of Karnataka and Kerala states between the Western Ghats range and the Arabian Sea. The coast runs from south of Goa to Cape Comorin on India's southern tip. The Malabar Coast is also sometimes used as an all encompassing term for the entire Indian coast from the western coast of Konkan to the tip of the subcontinent at Cape Comorin. It is over 525 miles or 845 km long. It spans from the South—Western coast of Maharashtra and goes along the coastal region of Goa, through the entire western coast of Karnataka and Kerala and reaches till Kanyakumari. It is flanked by the Arabian Sea on the west and the Western Ghats on the east. The Southern part of this narrow coast is the South Western Ghats moist deciduous forests.

The Malabar Coast features a number of historic port cities, notably Kozhikode (Calicut), Cochin, and Quilon, that have served as centers of the Indian Ocean trade for centuries. Because of their orientation to the sea and to maritime commerce, the Malabar coast cities feel very cosmopolitan, and hosted some of the first groups of christians (now known as Syrian Malabar Nasranis), Jews (today called as Cochin Jews), and Muslims (at present known as Mappilas) in India.

Malabar Civet : The Malabar Civet (Viverra civettina) is a civet belonging to the family Viverridae. Once common along the lowland coastal tracts of Western Ghats of Kerala and Karnataka of South India, the species became rare even by the turn of this century. Listed as Criticially Endangered by the IUCN, the species has never been photographed. The major threat facing isolated populations that have managed to survive in marginal habitats is changing cash crop practices and accidental hunting with dogs. Called Jawad in Malayalam, the local language of Kerala, the species is reportedly difficult to maintain in captivity for extracting civet, a secretion from anal glands of all civets that is used in oriental medicine and flavouring 'beedis' (local cigarettes).

A distinguishing feature of this small dog-sized civet is the presence of a crest of black erectile hair on the back, running from its shoulder to the tip of the tail. It feeds possibly on small mammals, reptiles, amphibians, fishes and birds. Like most species of civets, Malabar civet is terrestrial and nocturnal.

Malabar Coast : The Malabar Coast also known as the Malabarian Coast, is a long and narrow south-western shore line of the mainland Indian subcontinent. The Malabar Coast, in historical contexts, refers to India's southwest coast, lying on the narrow coastal plain of Karnataka and Kerala states between the Western Ghats range and the Arabian Sea. The coast runs from south of Goa to Cape Comorin on India's southern tip.

The Malabar Coast is also sometimes used as an all encompassing term for the entire Indian coast from the western coast of Konkan to the tip of the subcontinent at Cape Comorin. It is over 525 miles or 845 km long. It spans from the South—Western coast of Maharashtra and goes along the coastal region of Goa, through the entire western coast of Karnataka and Kerala and reaches till Kanyakumari. It is flanked by the Arabian Sea on the west and the Western Ghats on the east. The Southern part of this narrow coast is the South Western Ghats moist deciduous forests.

The Malabar Coast features a number of historic port cities, notably Kozhikode (Calicut), Cochin, and Quilon, that have served as centers of the Indian Ocean trade for centuries. Because of their orientation to the sea and to maritime commerce, the Malabar coast cities feel very cosmopolitan, and hosted some of the first groups of Christians, Jews, and Muslims in India. Geographically, the Malabar Coast, especially on its westward-facing mountain slopes, comprises the wettest region of southern India, as the Western Ghats intercept the moisture-laden monsoon rains.

Malabar Coast Moist Forests : The Malabar Coast moist forests is a tropical moist broadleaf forest ecoregion of southwestern India. It lies along India's Konkan and Malabar coasts, in a narrow strip between the Arabian Sea and the Western Ghats range, which runs parallel to the coast. It has an area of 35,500 square kilometers, and extends from northern Maharashtra through Goa, Karnataka and Kerala to Kanniyakumari in southernmost Tamil Nadu.

The ecoregion extends from sea level to the 250 meter contour of the Western Ghats. It is bounded on the east by the North Western Ghats moist deciduous forests in Maharashtra and Karnataka, and the South Western Ghats moist deciduous forests in Kerala. Very little of the natural vegetation of the ecoregion remains; it has largely been cleared for agriculture, grazing, and teak plantations.

Malabar Hill : Malabar Hill is a small hillock in southern Mumbai (formerly Bombay), India, and is the location of the Walkeshwar Temple, founded by the Silhara kings. The temple was destroyed by the Portuguese, but rebuilt again in 1715 by Rama Kamath. At a height of 50 metres (80 feet), this is the highest point in downtown Mumbai.

Malabar Rainforests : The term Malabar rainforests refers to one or more distinct ecoregions recognized by biogeographers. The Malabar Coast moist forests formerly occupied the coastal zone to the 250 meter elevation (but 95% of these forests no longer exist).

Malabari Paratha : Malabari paratha is a type of Indian bread, made by Malayalees (sometimes referred as Malabaries), who are the natives of Kerala, one of the southern states in India. These are layered breads, made with refined wheat flour and water and usually enriched with whole eggs. The dough is divided into equally shaped dumplings, and after giving it a rest for proofing, the dumplings are streched out with both the hands. Then it is grilled on a flat grill (usually called a tawa or a griddle). Usually served with spicy beef fry or chicken curry.

Malakand : Malakand is located in NWFP, Pakistan. Malakand agency lies at a strategically important position as it acts as a gateway to Swat, Dir, Chitral and Bajaur. It is in the lower Swat region amidst high mountains thick with evergreen olive and pine trees. It stands at the exit of a pass known as Malakand Pass or Darrah Malakand; now much less difficult to cross than before as one travels from Peshawar to Swat. In history the name has appeared as Malakhand or Mullah Khandao.

Malakand Pass : The Malakand Pass begins at Dargai. The road across the pass is in good condition, but is always crowded with a continuous stream of trucks. From a viewpoint about one kilometre before the top of the pass, one can see the Swat Canal in the valley below. It was built by the British to channel water from the Swat River through a tunnel under the Malakand Pass to the plains around Mardan. On the left, Malakand Fort guards the road at the top of the pass. On the other side of the pass, the road descends through the market town of Bat Khela, with a Hindu Shahi fort perched above it, and continues past the headworks of the Swat Canal to the Swat River. The first bridge across the river is at Chakdara, which carries the road to Dir and Chitral.

Malampuzha : Malampuzha is a tourist spot in Palakkad district of Kerala, South India. The main attractions is the dam built in 1955. Other attractions here are the Malampuzha Gardens, Rope Way, Snake Park, Rock

Garden and the aquarium. Another attraction in Malampuzha is a very big sculpture named Yakshi. This cement sculpture inside the Malampuzha Gardens is made by famous sculpturist Kanayi Kunhiraman.

Malappuram District : Malappuram District is a district of Kerala state in southern India. The district headquarters are at Malappuram. The district has a rich cultural and political heritage. Malappuram is known for national movements such as Khilafat Movement and Malabar Rebellion, in which the common man struggled against feudalism and colonialism alike. Though there were occasional religious overtones associated with such movements, many historians acknowledge them as part of Indian Independence Struggle. Before India's Independence in 1947, Malappuram was part of Malabar District in the Madras Presidency of British India. The area covered by the present district was administered as part of Kozhikode, Ernad, Valluvanad and Ponnani taluks.

Malavikagnimitram : Malavikagnimitram is a Sanskrit play by Kalidasa. It is his first play. The principal characters of Malavikagnimitram are Malavika and Agnimitra. The play tells the story of the love of Agnimitra, the Shunga king of Vidisha, for the beautiful hand-maiden of his chief queen. He falls in love with the picture of an exiled servant girl named Malavika. When the queen discovers her husband's passion for this girl, she becomes infuriated and has Malavika imprisoned, but as fate would have it, in the end she is discovered to be of royal birth and is accepted as one of his queens. The play contains an account of the Rajasuya sacrifice performed by Pushyamitra, and an elaborate exposition of a theory on music and acting.

Malayala Manorama : Malayala Manorama is a popular Malayalam newspaper in Kerala, India. The newspaper was once the world's largest circulated regional newspaper. The Manorama group, which manages the newspaper, also runs the Manorama Yearbook, the world's largest circulated yearbook. Malayala Manorama, which first appeared on 14th March 1890, as a weekly, currently has a readership of over 90 million, with a circulation base of over 1.4 million copies.

Malayalam : Malayalam is the language of the state of Kerala, in southern India. It is one of the 22 official languages of India, spoken by around 30 million people. A native speaker of Malayalam is called a "Malayali" (or sometimes a "Keraliyan" or "Keralite"). Malayalam is also spoken in the Lakshadweep Islands of India. It belongs to the family of Dravidian languages. Both the language and its writing system are closely related to Tamil. Malayalam has a script of its own.

Malayattoor : Malayattoor is one of the most prominent Christian pilgrim centers in Kerala. St. Thomas the Apostle established the church here, which has been designated by the Vatican as an International Shrine. The hilltop church is located 10km away from the town of Kalady. Historically, St. Thomas is believed to have landed in Kerala at Kodungallur (Cranganore) in AD52. While travelling through Malayattor, faced with hostile natives, he fled to the hilltop where he is said to have remained in prayer. According to beliefs, during prayer, he touched a rock, upon which blood poured from it.

Malda : Malda is a district of the Indian state of West Bengal. It lies 347 kilometres north of Kolkata, the state capital. It is famous for the production of mango and silk. The folk culture of gambhira is a feature of the district, being a unique way of representation of daily life's joy and sorrow of the common people, as well as the unique representation of national and international matters.

One time capital of Bengal, the district maintains the tradition of the past in culture and education.It lies just east of the confluence of the Mahananda and Kalindri rivers and is part of the English Bazar urban agglomeration. The town rose to prominence as the river port of the Hindu capital of Pandua. During the 18th century it was the seat of prosperous cotton and silk industries. It remains an important distributing centre for rice, jute, and wheat. Historical monuments include the mosque Jami' Masjid (1566) and the landmark Nimasari tower across the river. Constituted a municipality in 1867, it has several colleges affiliated with the University of North Bengal. Rice, jute, legumes, and oilseeds are the chief crops in the surrounding area. Mulberry plantations and mango orchards occupy large areas; mango trade and silk manufacture are the main economic activities.

Maldharis : Maldharis is an ethnic group lives inside the Gir Forest National Park –home to Asiatic lions -, Gujarat, India. They live in communities called nesses. Basically they are shepherds with a colorful lifestyle.

Malerkotla : Malerkotla is a town in the present-day Indian state of Punjab, which was the seat of the eponymous princely state during the British Raj. The state acceded unto the union of India in 1947 and was merged with other nearby princely states to create the Patiala and East Punjab States' Union (PEPSU). When that political entity was reorganised, the territories of the erstwhile state of Malerkotla became part of Punjab. Malerkotla, a Muslim pathan state, is most respected house in Punjab. Maler Kotla state was founded in 1600. It is a historic fact that during the 1947 riots when the whole of Punjab was in flames it was the State of Malerkotla which did not witness a single incident of violence. It was in island of peace. When the younger Sahibzadas of Guru Gobind Singh, the 10th and the last Sikh Guru, were ordered to be bricked alive by the governor of Sarhind, Wazir Khan, his close relative Sher Mohammed Khan, Nawab of

Malerkotla who was present in the court, lodged vehement protest against this inhuman act and said it is against the glorious tenets of Quran and Islam. Wazir Khan acquiesced and the Sahibzadas were tortured and bricked alive. At this the noble Nawab of Malerkotla walked out of the court in protest. Guru Gobind Singh on learning this kind and humanitarian approach profusely thanked the Nawab of Malerkotla and blessed him with his Hukamnama, Kirpan etc. In recognition of this act, the State of Malerkotla did not witness a single incident of violence during partition.

Malik Ayaz : Malik Ayaz was a Turkmen slave who rose to the rank of officer and general in the army of Sultan Mahmud of Ghazni (also known as Mahmud Ghaznavi). His rise to power was a reward for the devotion and love he bore his master. The romance of the Sultan and his slave boy Ayaz is part of Islamic legend. The Sultan is seen as an example of the man who, because of the power of his love, becomes "a slave to his slave." Ayaz became the paragon of the ideal beloved, and a model of purity in Sufi literature. The two have gained pride of place among the favorite pairs of lovers in Persian literature.

In 1021 the Sultan raised Ayaz to kingship, awarding him the throne of Lahore, which the Sultan had taken after a long siege and a firce battle in which the city was torched and depopulated. As the first Muslim governor of Lahore, he rebuilt and repopulated the city. He also added many important features, such as a masonry fort which he built in 1037-1040 on the ruins of the previous one, demolished in the fighting, and city gates (as recorded by Munshi Sujan Rae Bhandari, author of the Khulasatut Tawarikh in 1695-96 C.E.). The present Lahore Fort is built in the same location. Under his rulership the city became a cultural and academic center, renowned for poetry. The tomb of Malik Ayaz can still be seen in the Rang Mahal commercial area of town

Malinitha : Malinithan situated at Likabali, headquarters of sub-division of West Siang district in Arunachal Pradesh is a place of great sanctity, associated with the legend of Lord Krishna. There are ruins of a big temple belonging to the 14th -15th century here. Excavations have unearthed the beautifully designed basement of the temple, valuable sculptures of Indra and Airavata, Surya, Nandi Bull and other divine images, animal motifs and floral designs, carved columns and panels. The legend behind the place is that Krishna and Rukmini rested here on their way from Bhismakanagar to Dwarka and they were offered very fine flowers by Parvati. Krishna pleased with the offering praised Parvati and addressed her as Malini-Mistress of Garland. It is believed that, the place came to be known as Malinithan since then.

The legendary Akashi Ganga waterfalls is situated 5km from Malinithan in East Siang District. There is a beautiful view of the river Brahmaputra and its tributaries far below from here. Pilgrims come to Akashi Ganga to take a bath as the water is believed to wash away ones sins. The legend is associated with Parvathi narrated in the 8th century Kalika Purana. Parvati is believed to have been cut into pieces and her head fell somewhere near Akashiganga. The nearest Airport is Lilabari (Tezpur) and the nearest railway station is Silapathar. Can be reached by road from Silapathar.

Malir River : Malir River is located in Karachi, Sindh, Pakistan. Malir River passes through the city of Karachi from north east to the center and drains into the Arabian Sea. Malir river is one of the two rivers passing through Karachi and the other is Lyari River.

Mallika Sarabhai : Daughter of the dancing legend Mrinalini Sarabhai and the legendary scientist Vikram Sarabhai, Mallika Sarabhai is a renowned exponent of Bharata Natyam and Kuchipudi and an internationally known choreographer, who has to her credit compositions like *Draupadi, Shakti - The Powar of Woman, Sita's Daughters, Itan Kahani, Aspiration, Ganga, Surya, Mean Streets on Earth and "V for".*

She played the role of Draupadi in Peter Brooke's film *Mahabharata,* which was made in English and French. She has been an anchor on television for several programmes like *Turning Point, Eye Witness* and *Show Reeland Kaleidoscope.* She made an earlier unsuccessful attempt at acting in Hindi and Gujarati films. Later she directed many educational films on several general subjects. She is currently the co-director of the Darpana Academy of Performing Arts at Ahmedabad.

Malubiting : Malubiting (also known as Malubiting West) is the second highest mountain in the Rakaposhi-Haramosh mountains, a subrange of theKarakoram range of Pakistan. Malubiting lies in the heart of the Rakaposhi-Haramosh Mountains, which rise above the north bank of the Indus River between its tributaries the Hunza River and the Shigar River. Malubiting lies about 40km east-southeast of Rakaposhi, and about 50km east of Gilgit, the most important town in the region. Malubiting rises steeply over the Phuparash River to the southwest, while on the east the large Chogo Lungma Glacier starts on its slopes.

Malwa : Malwa is a region in western India occupying a plateau of volcanic origin in the western part of Madhya Pradesh state and the south-eastern part of Rajasthan. This region has been a separate political unit from the time of the Aryan tribe of Malavas until 1947, when the British Malwa Agency was merged into Madhya Bharat. Although political borders have fluctuated throughout history, the region has developed its own distinct culture and language. The plateau that forms a large part of the region is named the Malwa Plateau, after the region. The average elevation of the Malwa plateau is 500 metres, and the landscape generally slopes towards the north. Most of the region is drained by the Chambal River and its tributaries; the western part is drained by the upper reaches of the Mahi River. Ujjain was the political, economic, and cultural capital of the region in ancient times, and Indore is presently the largest city and commercial centre. Overall, agriculture is the main occupation of the people of Malwa. The region has been one of the important producers of opium in the world. Cotton and soybeans are other important cash crops, and textiles are a major industry.

Mamankam Festival : 'Zamorin' Samoothiri Rajas, the the rulers of the erstwhile Hindu state of Kozhikode had an interesting tradition which dictated that every Samoothiri who ruled over twelve years would have to publicly cut his throat. In the 17th century, this tradition was modified and led to an annual event where the Samoothiri declared that after an annual 12-day festival Mamankam festival, it was lawful for anyone wishing, to try to assassinate him. The Samoothiri would be seated in a national assembly, surrounded by guards. This revised tradition led to the development of suicide squads, called chaver, by neighbouring states (particularly Valluvakkonathiri) with the objective of killing the Samoothiri.

The land of ancient Mamankom, Thirunavaya is 7 km south of Tirur. Situated on the banks of Bharathapuzha, it is a place of historical importance. In olden days, Mamankam was a grand assembly of the rulers. held once in 12 years, in which one among them was selected as the emperor of Kerala. it was an enormous trade fair also. The

Mamankam festival was celebrated for 28 days with great pomp and pageantry where traders from outside came in ships and barges to Thirunavaya through Ponnani port. Thus the economical importance of Mamankam was high and hence the right to conduct and control it was important. The Mamankam is conducted in the banks of Bharathapuzha the second-longest river in Kerala, close to a holy town called Thirunava.

Mammootty : Mammootty (born at Chempu near Vaikom, Kottayam district, Kerala, 1953), whose real name is Muhammed Kutty, is a Malayalam film actor. He has acted in more than three hundred movies, most of them in Malayalam.

He is the only actor other than Kamal haasan to get National Award three times. So many other national and state appreciations are under his belt. Won Padmashree. He has a very large fan following in South India.

Manali : Manali is an important hill station in the mountains of Himachal Pradesh, India, near the northern end of the Kullu Valley. It is administratively part of the Kullu District. The population is approx. 30,000. The small town was the beginning of an ancient trade route to Ladakh and, from there, over the Karakoram Pass on to Yarkand and Khotan in the Tarim Basin. Manali offers the best of northwestern Himalayan beauty, second only to Kashmir valley. The twin towns of Kullu and Manali, approximately 40 km apart lie on the Beas River valley. The Beas River is snow fed by scores of tributaries originating in the glacial peaks surrounding the valley. The highest peaks average 6000 to 6500 m above sea level.

Manali is well connected by road to Delhi through NH-21 which goes on the Leh and is the world's highest motorable road. Leading up to Manali from New Delhi are the towns of Panipat and Ambala in Haryana, Chandigarh and Ropar in Punjab, and Bilaspur, Sundernagar, and Mandi in Himachal. The road to Manali features a gradual change in flora, fauna, lifestyle, and language. Despite being at high altitudes, the twin towns are still at the bottom of the valley. Past Manali, the change in climate and lifestyle is abrupt, moving further and higher into the mountains at the periphery of the windward side led by high mountain passes on to the dry plateau type leeward side. The road from Manali to Leh features a strong Buddhist influence, with frequent Buddhist gompas and stupas along the arid stretch.

Manali is a popular Himalayan tourist destination, and is visited by many trekkers who follow the hashish trail. Manali's charas is considered to be the best in India. It also offers hot springs, spectacular religious shrines and temples, Tibetan Buddhist temples, and trekking in the surrounding mountains.

Manas National Park : Manas National Park, a Project Tiger reserve, lies among the foothills of the Himalayas, in the far eastern state of Assam, India. It is about 175 km away from Guwahati, the capital of Assam. The sanctuary constitutes the river Manas which also gave its name to the area. The park, which spreads over 2,837 km^2, is a vast, relatively unspoilt expanse of low-lying sal forests and grasslands. The core area of the reserve lies in Kokrajhar and Barpeta districts, whereas its outlying areas spread over the neighbouring forest reserve divisions of North Kamrup, Western Assam Wildlife Division, Kachugaon and Haltugaon. To the north lies the Royal Manas National Park, in Bhutan.

Initially known as North Kamrup, Manas was designated a wildlife sanctuary way back in 1928. In April 1973 the santuary was established as the core of the Manas Tiger Reserve, and in 1985, was declared a 'World Heritage in Danger' site by UNESCO. Manas became a national park on September 7, 1990. The only tiger reserve in Assam and also famous for the rare golden langur and the red panda, Manas is one of the best-kept national parks in India. Its home to India's second-largest tiger population. Manas' other denizens include elephants, rhinoceros, swamp deer, gaur, and more elusive species, such as the clouded leopard, golden cat, pangolin, fishing cat, pygmy hog and leopard. Manas has more than 450 species of birds, of which the great pied hornbill and the Bengal florican are among the leading stars.

Manchar : Lake Manchar is the largest freshwater lake in Pakistan and one of Asia's largest. It is located west of the Indus River in Sindh. The area of the lake fluctuates with the seasons from as little as 350 km^2 to as much as 520 km^2. The lake collects water from numerous small streams in the Kirthar mountains and empties into the river Indus.

Manddo : Manddo is a song or rather a poignant story of love told in the form of a lovely song. The word Manddo, derives from the Sanskrit 'Mandalam' meaning circular movement. It is believed that originally the Konkani Manddo dance involved movement in circle. At present such circular patterns are noticed when the dancers get into a feverish pitch in the concluding stages of the dance. In the normal course the dance moves along parallel lines, with graceful movements to and fro, advancing and reading, the men displaying in a flourish towards the women their colourful handkerchiefs and the women admiring their toy fans, with an eye on the men. The Manddo music appears to have been strongly influenced by Latin or rather Italian music. The dance-song Manddo may be called a synthesis of the Italian minuet and the temple Devadasi dance-song.

Mandi : Mandi is the central district of Himachal Pradesh, India. There is also a town called Mandi, which has a distinguished history and interesting architecture. It is also an important transportation hub for the district. Sundernagar is one of the emerging towns of this district. Mandi has a highly educated middle class and people speak a dialect of Hindi called "Mandyali".

Mandi-Bahaudddin District : The district of Mandi-Bahaudddin is situated in Punjab and is bounded on the northwest by the Jhelum River, on the South-East by the Chenab River which separates it from Gujranwala District and Gujrat District and on the southwest by Sargodha District. Mandi-Bahauddin is spread over an area of 2673 km2 comprising of three Tehsils : Mandi Bahauddin, Phalia, Malakwal.

Mandla : Mandla is a town in Madhya Pradesh in India, situated on the banks of Narmada River. It is connected by road to nearby cities like Jabalpur and Nagpur. A part of the famous Kanha National Park is situated in Mandla district. Kanha has the largest number of tigers in India. The park has won national awards for good management and infrastructure. The park is open year round except for July and August. The area is largely tribal and backward. The district consistently ranks among the 20 most backward districts in India. It is a tribal district and Gond tribe inhabits the interior of the district. It has a fort also but in absence of proper care the fort has gone to ruins.Mandla also has railway line(narrow gauge). The river Narmada is worshipped here and many beautiful ghats have been constructed on the banks of the river.

Mandla Plant Fossils National Park : Mandla Plant Fossils National Park is situated in Mandla district of Madhya Pradesh in India. This national park has got plants in fossil form, which existed in India anything between 40 million and 150 million years ago. In seven villages of Mandla District, Ghuguwa, Umaria, Deorakhurd, Barbaspur, Chanti-hills, Chargaon and Deori Kohani spread over 274,100 square metres; we have the Mandla Plant Fossils National Park. Such fossils are to be found in three other villages of the district also, but they lie outside the national park.

Mandleshwar : Mandleshwar is a town of historical and religious importance situated in Khargone district of Madhya Pradesh, India, on the banks of Narmada River at a distance of 5 km from Maheshwar. The town was founded by Mandana Mishra, and has a stone fort constructed by Muslim rulers. It also has a fine flight of 123 steps leading down to the river and expanding below into a wide ghat. Tukoji Rao Holkar II built a palace here. It was also the headquarters of the Nimar Agency and cantonment under the British from 1819 to 1864. The town is an important retail marketing and trade centre.

Mandovi River : The Mandovi River, is described to be the lifeline of the state of Goa, India. The river, with its cerulean waters is also known as the Gomati in a few places, has its origin at Bhimgad in the Western Ghats. Mandovi, along with the Zuari River, form the two primary rivers in the state. In the state of Goa, the river has a length of 77 kilometres.

The Cumbarjuem Canal, which links both rivers, has made the interiors of the Mandovi accessible to ships which ferry iron ore, Goa's prime mineral, mined in the eastern hills. Three large freshwater isles — Divar, Chorao and Vashee are present in the Mandovi near the town of Old Goa. The island of Chorao, is home to the Salim Ali Bird Sanctuary, named after the renowned ornithologist Salim Ali. A regular ferry transports the inhabitants between the isles to the mainland.

Mandsaur : Mandsaur or Mandsaor is a city in the Malwa region and district of Madhya Pradesh state of central India. It is the administrative headquarters of

Mandsaur District. Mandsaur and its neighborhood are full of archaeological interest. An inscription discovered near the town indicated the erection of a temple of the sun in 437, and at Sondani are two great monolith pillars recording a victory of Yasodharman, king of Malwa, in 528. The fort dates from the 14th and 15th centuries. Hindu and Jain remains are numerous, though the town is predominantly Muslim.

Before India's independence in 1947, Madsaur was part of the princely state of Gwalior. It gave its name to the treaty with the Holkar Maharaja of Indore, which concluded the Third Anglo-Maratha War and the Pindari War in 1818. At the turn of the 20th century it was a centre of the Malwa opium trade.

Mandsaur District : Mandsaur District is a District of Madhya Pradesh state in central India. The town of Mandsaur is the administrative headquarters of the district. The district has an area of 9,791 sq. km., and a population of 1,555,481 (1991 census). The district is part of the Malwa region, and is bounded by Neemuch District to the north, Rajasthan state to the east and west, and Ratlam District to the south. It is part of Ujjain Division.

Mandu : Mandu, or Mandogarh, is a ruined city in the Dhar district in the Malwa region of western Madhya Pradesh state, Central India. Mandu was the capital of the fifteenth-century Muslim kingdom of Malwa. This fortress town on a rocky outcrop 100 km from Indore is celebrated for its fine architecture. Mandu is celebration in stone of life and joy, of the poet-prince Baz Bahadur for his beautiful consort, Rani Roopmati.The balladeers of Malwa still sing of the romance of these royal lovers, and high on the crest of a hill, Rani Roopmati's pavilion still gazes down at Baz Bahadur's palace, a magnificent expression of Afgan architecture.

The Mandu city is situated at an elevation of 2079 ft. and extends for 8 miles along the crest of the Vindhya Range, overlooking the plateau of Malwa to the north, and the valley of the Narmada River to the south. Mandu with its natural defences was originally the fort-capital of Parmara rulers of Malwa. Towards the end of the 13th century, it came under the sway of the Sultans of Malwa, the first of whom renamed it as Shadiabad- the city of Joy.It was founded by Dilawar Khan, who was governor of Malwa province under the Delhi Sultanate, and in 1401 declared himself Sultan of Malwa.

The city reached its greatest splendour under Hoshang Shah (1405-1435). Sultan Mahmud Khalji (reigned 1436-69) expanded the state to include portions of Gujarat, Rajasthan, and the Deccan. The circuit of the battlemented wall is nearly 23 miles, enclosing a large number of palaces, mosques and other buildings. The oldest mosque dates from 1405; the finest is the Jama Masjid or great mosque, a notable example of Pathan architecture, founded by Hoshang Shah. The marble domed tomb of this ruler is also magnificent.

Maneka Gandhi : Maneka Gandhi was born on 26 August 1956 in Delhi and educated at the prestigious Lawrence School, Sanawar. She is the widow of Sanjay Gandhi, the son of Indira Gandhi. A former model and editor of Surya India magazine, Ms. Gandhi entered politics in 1982 after her husband's death.

After Sanjay's death in an aircrash relations broke down between Maneka and the Nehru-Gandhi family. In a public spat covered by the media Maneka stormed out of the Prime Minister's residence with her son Varun. The next decade she joined various parties opposed to the Congress and tried to stake her own claim to what she perceived as Sanjay's legacy.

She formed the Sanjay Vichar Manch in 1983 and joined the Janata Dal in 1988. She was the general secretary of JD 1988-1989. She served as Minister of the Environment from 1989 to 1991 in the cabinet of V.P. Singh. Maneka is an environmentalist who mainstreamed the issue of animal rights in India. She was appointed chairwoman of the Committee for the Purpose of Control and Supervision of Experiments on Animals (CPCSEA). Under her direction, unannounced inspections of laboratories where animals are used for scientific research were conducted, and abominable conditions and cruelty were documented and exposed. The CPCSEA imposed restrictions that brought some of the abuse to a stop. Political upheaval caused by vested interests eventually forced her to resign from the position.

In 1996 and 1998, she was reelected to the Lok Sabha as an independent member from Pilibhit in Uttar Pradesh and served on a number of BJP led governments as Minister of State for Social Justice and Empowerment. In December 2001 she converted Sanjay Vichar Manch into a political party, Shakti Dal. In the 2004 elections she formally contested on the BJP ticket. Maneka and Varun Gandhi's presence on the BJP remains a source of embarrassment to the Congress Party led by the other branch of the Nehru-Gandhi's. In the 2004 election campaign Varun's criticism of his aunt Sonia Gandhi made headlines.

Mangal Pandey : Mangal Pandey (d. 8 April 1857) also known as Shaheed Mangal Pandey (Shaheed means martyr in Arabic and Hindustani), was a sepoy (soldier) in the forces of the British East India Company. He is primarily known for attacking his British superior in an incident that sparked what is known to the British as the Sepoy Mutiny of 1857 and to Indians as the First War of Indian Independence.

Pandey was born in village Nagwa in district Ballia, Uttar Pradesh. He joined the British East India Company forces, and was part of 5th Company of the 34th Bengal Native Infantry (BNI) regiment.

Mangalkavya : Mangalkavya (literally, poems of well-being) a genre of Bangla epic poems written approximately between the 13th-18th centuries, depicting the greatness of popular, indigenous deities as well as the social scenario. The poems are known as mangalkavya because it was believed that listening to these poems about the deities brought both spiritual and material benefits. The poems used to be rendered as musical plays but with more emphasis on the story than on the music.

Mangalkavya describe the greatness of a particular deity, usually one indigenous to Bengal or an indigenous deity fused with an Aryan god. They also depict the conflict between the indigenous deities and the alien deities which ended with the victory of the indigenous gods. The word mangal also means vijay or victory, and indicates that the poems were written to celebrate the victory of the local gods over the Aryan gods. Some of these poems have the word vijay as part of their names, such as Manasavijay by Bipradas Pipilai.

Mangalore : Mangalore, originally called Mangalooru, is the chief port city of the state of Karnataka, India. It is the capital of Dakshina Kannada (South Kanara) district. Situated on the west coast of the country on the Arabian Sea, the Western Ghats lie to Mangalore's east. Mangalore is known for its beaches, temples and industries. The city is virtually a Tower of Babel, with the sounds of several languages mingling on the streets. The main languages of Mangalore are Tulu, Kannada, Konkani, and Byari (somewhat of a mixture of Tulu and Malayalam).

Mangan : Mangan is the capital of the district of North Sikkim in the Indian state of Sikkim. The town is connected to the capital Gangtok by a metalled road. North Sikkim is the largest district of Sikkim in terms of area. The town lies in the geographic south of the district. After the opening up of the district, Mangan has witnessed a spurt in its economy in mostly tourism. The town opens up the Tibetan Plateau. Mangan also serves the towns of Lachung, Chungthang and Lachen in the far north. Owing to its elevation, the town enjoys a temperate climate.

Chhaang or chang (Nectar of Gods) is a popular alcoholic beverage in the eastern Himalayas. Chhaang is a relative of the more universally known beer. Millet or rice is used to brew the drink. Semi-fermented seeds of millet are served, stuffed in a mug of bamboo called the Domru. Then boiling water is poured and sipped through a narrow bore bamboo pipe called the Pipsing. The brew tastes like ale. Alcohol content is quite low, but it produces an intense feeling of heat and well-being, ideal for enduring the temperatures which go well below freezing in winter.

Mangla Dam : Mangla Dam is the twelfth largest dam in the world. It was constructed in 1967 across the River Jhelum, about 60 miles southeast of the federal capital, Islamabad. The main structures of the dam include 4 embankment dams, 2 spillways, 5 power-cum-irrigation tunnels and a power station. The main dam is 10,300 feet long and 454 feet high (above core trench) with a reservoir of 97.7 square miles. Since its first impounding in 1967, sedimentation has occurred to the extent of 1.13 MAF, and the present gross storage capacity has declined to 4.75 MAF from the actual design of 5.88 MAF. The live capacity has declined to 4.58 MAF from 5.34 MAF. This implies a reduction of 19.22% in the capacity of the dam.

Mango Dance : The Hill Reddis or Konda Reddis also called the Reddis of the Bison hills dwell in Khamman, East Godavari and West Godavari districts. These parts are famous for mangoes. Before plucking the mangoes, the

Konda Reddis have a ceremonial festival with a community Dance. They neither decorate nor paint their body like the Gusadis. As an act of worship to Mutyalamma and Konda devata, they dance rhythmically to the accompaniment of drums. This dance commences during the night, with a gentle beat of drums.

Three to four women hand in hand with the castanet like sound of dry nuts join the dance. The men and women both join the dance but they form separate groups. Leaning towards the left they circumambulate around the place. The women, while tapping the ground with the foot, take four steps forward. This is done in a particular manner. Stepping forward with the right foot four times, leaning towards one side, they come back with one step in the same manner. The circle of men and women moving rhythmically to the centre and retreating with waving arms and the clatter of nuts provide a fascinating pattern for the dance. Keeping the feet apart and jumping with the right and left foot alternately with the other foot forward is another feature of this dance. The dance steps of the men are different from those of the women. The men while stepping forward, put the right foot first and bring the left foot up to the heel of right foot. This facilitates stepping forward again with the right foot. The drummers and other instrumentalists stand in the centre in the beginning, later they join in the dances and step accordingly forward and backward along with the whole group. The two types of drums used as accompaniment provide regular rhythm to this foot work.

Mango Festival : The Mango festival is held in June. Mango-growers from all over India are invited to enter their prize fruits in the various competitions. Visitors to the fair can see and taste all the traditional varieties of the fruit as well as the latest hybrids from the agricultural universities. It is also an occasion for agro-industries, and food industries processing mango into jams, pickles and canned fruit to display their wares.

Mangopir : Mangopir or Manghopir is one of the neighborhoods of Gadap Town in Karachi, Sindh, Pakistan. There are several ethnic groups in Gadap Town including Urdu speakers, Punjabis, Sindhis, Kashmiris, Seraikis, Pakhtuns, Balochs, Memons, Bohras, Ismailis. Over 99% of the population is Muslim. The population of Gadap Town is estimated to be nearly one million. Manghopir is a remote, less developed area of Karachi, named after Pir Mangho. The area has the oldest Sufi shrines in the city, hot sulphur springs that are believed to have curative powers, and many crocodiles—believed locally to be the sacred disciples of Pir Mangho. Balochs often call this place as 'Mangi' or Garm-aap / Sard-aap (due to the presence of the hot & cold springs).

Mangueshi Temple : This temple is located at Priol, in Goa, India and is dedicated to Lord Mangueshi who was an incarnation of Shiva. The general beliefs is that this temple built in the 17th century was made far away so to escape the destructive conquest of the Portuguese who had destroyed a similar temple at Cortalim. The main hall is known for wooden carvings of eighteen avataars of Vishnu.

Mani Ratnam : Mani Ratnam (born June 2, 1956, Madras, India) is a leading movie maker (screen writer and director) of the Indian film industry. He was educated at Jamnalalal Bajaj Insitute of Management, a noted management school in India. He got into film direction with the help of his late brother, film producer G. Venkateswaran. He consistently chooses realistic, contemporary themes and complex plots for his movies in an industry often accused of making commercial, fairy-tale-like, formulaic movies. With a career spanning over two decades, he has been praised for handling serious issues whilst retaining a high entertainment factor in his films. Familial and marital hardships, terrorism, love, class and religious conflict, war, politics, adoption, history and disability are just some of the socio-political issues to have been featured in his films.

Mani Ratnam's movies are generally made in the Tamil language, but are usually also dubbed into other languages like Telugu and Hindi, owing to their national appeal. He has also made films in other languages like Hindi, Malayalam, Telugu and Kannada. His works have come to be recognised nationally and internationally, and in 2002, he was awarded the Padma Shri.

Manik Bandopadhay : Manik Bandopadhay (1908-1956) is one of the most influential novelists in Bangla literature. His important works include Padma Nadir Majhi (The Boatman of River Padma) and Putul Nacher Itikotha (A History of Puppet Dance) and numerous short stories. His writing stands in stark contrast to that of other luminaries like Bibhutibhushan Bandopadhyay who portrayed life in rural Bengal in a gentle, lyrical light.

Manik's writing dealt with the pettiness and wretchedness of existence in a village context. His primary concern was the dark alleyways of the human mind, even among the supposedly simple village folk, and not the serene beauty of nature that was always in the background in his novels. In Putulnacher Itikotha he took on rather savagely the touchy topic of hypocrisy in villages: an elderly couple are canonised as saints after committing morpheine - induced suicide; the daughter of one of the village's elders gets married off to a wealthy businessman in Kolkata who treats her as a 'kept'woman, she develops a drinking habit and comes back to her old home just a shadow of her former self. However, the people around her keep pretending that nothing untoward has happened. Numerous other examples abound.

Manikganj : Manikganj is a district in central Bangladesh. It is a part of the Dhaka Division. It has an area of about 1379 sq. km, and is bounded by Tangail District on the north, Dhaka District on the east and Faridpur District on the south. It has 1 municipality, 7 Upazillas, and 65 union parishads. The Upazillas are Manikganj Sadar, Singair, Shivalaya, Saturia, Harirampur, Ghior and Daulatpur. Manikganj was formerly a subdivision of Dhaka District. It was turned into a district in 1984. On the April 26, 1989 Manikganj was the site of, what was at the time, the world's worst tornado interms of loss-of-life. 1,300 people were initially reported as having been killed with 12,000 injured. The towns of Saturia and Manikgank Sadar were levelled and about 80,000 people were made homeless.

Manimekalai : Manimekalai, written by Seethalai Saathanar, is one of the masterpieces of Tamil literature and belongs to The Five Great Epics of Tamil Literature. Saathanaar had a title known as "Seethalai" which means a "a head covered by wounds, festered with blood and pus". Being a great lover of tamil, every time Saathanar heard someone speak the language improperly (wrong in either the grammatical or syntactical sense) he used to hit his head hard with his "Ezhuthaani" (wooden pen). Hence, the title.

Manipur : Manipur is a state in northeastern India making its capital in the city of Imphal. Manipur is bounded by the Indian states of Nagaland in the north, Mizoram in the south and Assam in the west; it also borders the country of Myanmar to the east. The Meiteis from the valley region is one of the ethnic group in Manipur. Their language is Meitei (also known Meiteilon or Manipuri) which is also the lingua franca in the state. It was recognized as a national Indian language in 1992. Manipur is considered a sensitive border state. Foreigners entering Manipur (including foreign citizens born in Manipur) must possess a Restricted Area Permit which can be obtained from the Foreigners' Regional Registration Office in the "metros" (Delhi, Mumbai, Kolkata) or certain other state government offices. Permits are valid for only 10 days, and visitors must travel only on tours arranged by authorised travel agents, in groups of four. Furthermore, they may come to Imphal only by air and will not be permitted to travel outside the capital.

Manipuri : Manipuri or Meithei is the predominant language and lingua-franca in the state of Manipur, in northeastern India. It is the official language in government offices. Meithei has proven to be a large integrating factor among all ethnic groups in Manipur who use it to communicate among themselves. Meithei has been recognized as the Manipuri language by the Indian Union and has been included in the list of scheduled languages (included in the 8th schedule by the 71st amendment of the constitution in 1992). Meithei is taught as a subject up to the Post-graduate level in Universities of India, apart from being a medium of instruction upto the undergraduate level in Manipur.

Manipuri Dance : Manipuri Dance can be called a house of many mansions. There is a belief that Radha and Krishna were the original author and creator of Manipuri Dance. This Rasa -dance was repeated by Uma and Shiva in Lasya style in Manipur. After many centuries the same Rasa-dance was performed the third time by two mortal human beings, princess Toibi and Khamba. These two star-crossed lovers died in tragic circumstances. The dance than these two lovers performed is known as Lai Haraoba. There are many myths and legends which reveal the Manipuris passionate love for arts, particularly for dance, music and mime. These are woven into the very fabric of their life like a beautiful pattern.

Today Manipuri Dance has become a ruling passion and an aesthetic obsession for initiated artists and the spectators alike because of its colourful adornment, lightness of dancing foot, delicacy of abhinaya, lilting music and poetic charm.

Manmohan Singh : Manmohan Singh, best known as 'father of Indian Reforms', has emerged as the Congress party's frontrunner, the 14th Prime Minister of India and also the first Sikh to have reached the country's top legislative position. Hailed to be the cleanest man in Indian politics, he was Former Finance Minister and author of the post-1991 economic reforms. He was Born to Mr Gurmukh Singh and Mrs Gursharan Kaur on September 26, 1932 in a small village Gah (West Punjab), now in Pakistan. A brilliant student, Manmohan Singh secured top marks in almost all the major examinations he wrote. After his Masters in Economics from Amritsar's Hindu College under Punjab University he won scholarships to Cambridge and Oxford, earning a doctorate with a thesis on the critical role of exports and free trade in India's economy. Manmohan Singh won the prestigious Adam Smith prize in 1956 from Cambridge University.

The following year, he returned to India as a university lecturer and for the next nine years remained at Punjab University before being posted for international duty with UNCTAD (United Nations Conference on Trade and Development). He then joined the Delhi School of Economics as a professor. Two years later, his academic career was cut short and he joined the government to serve in various capacities.

Singh held several positions throughout the 1980s and early 1990s. He served as Economic advisor to the finance ministry in the late 70s, Deputy Chairman of Planning Commission and Chairman of University Grants

Commission in 1980s and early 1990's and as the Governor of the Reserve Bank of India from 1982 to 1985 etc.

An academician, he was discovered by former prime minister Shri. P.V Narasimha Rao. Rao offered him the finance ministry in 1991 under the Congress Government, and the chance to rescue a sickly economy threatened by an acute balance of payments crisis. During his stint as the finance minister (1991-1996), the suave, soft-spoken Sikh guided India out of financial trouble and put the country on course to becoming an economic power by opening up the economy to foreign investment and slashing trade barriers.

Singh was always an unlikely politician, who was routed in a parliamentary election in 1999. In fact, he has never won an election and sits in the upper house. Politically, Manmohan Singh is the classic example of the stateless politician. The 71 year old prime minister is married to Gursharan Kaur, they have three daughters.

Manna Dey : Prabodh Chandra Dey, better known by his nickname as Manna Dey (born 1920) is a popular playback singer in Hindi films and other vernacular Indian films, especially Bengali. He was the nephew of the legendary K. C. Dey. He did his graduation in arts from the Scottish Church College in Calcutta.

Manna Dey currently lives in Bangalore.

Mannargudi : Mannargudi is a town in the Tiruvarur district (formerly part of Thanjavur district) of Tamil Nadu state in southeastern India. Mannargudi is also known as Raja Mannargudi or Mannai. Mannargudi can be reached by road from Thanjavur and Kumbakonam which are situated around 40 km from the place. The nearest railway station is 12 km away at Needamangalam. The most famous landmark in Mannargudi is the one thousand year old Hindu Temple Sri Rajagopala Swami Temple. A festival called Panguni Tiruvizha is celebrated every year during the Tamil month of Panguni (March/April) in the Sri Rajagopala Swami Temple. People around the town gather in great numbers to celebrate this grand event. There are lots of temples around this town like the famous Alangudi (Guru Sthalam) temple.

Manoj Night Shyamalan : Manoj Night Shyamalan, alias Manoj Nelliyattu Shyamalan, director, screenwriter and actor was born on 6th August 1970 in Pondicherry. His parents Nelliyate C Shyamalan and Jayalakshmi were both doctors and the family moved to the United States when Shyamalan was still a young boy and he was raised in a suburban area of Penn Valley of Philadelphia. He had his early education at a Catholic Private School and Philadelphia's Episcopal Academy. Although he received scholarships to several medical schools, Shyamalan chose to attend the Tisch School of Arts at New York University to study film-making.

Shyamalan had a very early passion for filmmaking and as a child, he revelled in making up stories. At the age of 10, inspired primarily by Steven Spielberg's films, he began making film with his father's 8mm camera and by age 16, he had made over 45 short films. Shyamalan graduated from NYU and during his final year, he wrote, directed and starred in his first full-length feature film, 'Praying With Anger'. In 1995 he was asked to write the script for a combined live action-animated version of the E B White children's classic 'Stuart Little' and it was released onto the big screen in 1999. In 1997 he made his second film 'Wide Awake'.

Following the success of the this film he directed another supernatural thriller 'Unbreakable' in 2000. In 2002, Shyamalan directed another film 'Signs' an emotional story which deals with crop circles in a rural Pennsylvania town. In 2003 Shymalan comes the chilling tale of a close-knit community that lives with the frightening knowledge that creatures reside in the woods around, and the courage of one young man who challenges the unknown creatures in the film 'The village'.

Mansa Devi Mela : Mansa Devi Mela is held in Bilaspur village near of Mani Majra in Haryana. There are two temples dedicated to the goddess here. The fairs are held twice a year in March-April (Chat shudiashtami) and September-October (asoj shudi ashtami).

Mansa District : Mansa District is situated in Punjab, India. The main town is Mansa. The district has an area of 2174 km^2 and a population of 688,630 (2001 census), with a population density of 317 persons per km^2. The district is roughly triangular in shape, and is bounded on the northwest by Bathinda District, on the northeast by Sangrur District, and on the south by Haryana state. The district is divided into three tehsils, Budhlada, Mansa, and Sardulgarh. The Ghaggar River flows through Sardulgarh tehsil in the southwestern corner of the district.

Mansehra : Mansehra is a district in the North-West Frontier Province of Pakistan that contains the town of Mansehra, and the Kaghan Valley area, an adventure-tourism destination. The Karakoram Highway passes through the district.

Mansoor Ali Khan : Mansoor Ali Khan, the 9th Nawab of Pataudi (Jr.), nicknamed Tiger is a former Indian cricketer and former captain of the Indian cricket team. Mansoor was born on January 5, 1941, at Bhopal in the Indian state of Madhya Pradesh to Iftikhar Ali Khan, eighth nawab of Pataudi and his wife Sajida Sultan, second daughter of the last ruling nawab of Bhopal. He was educated at the Winchester College and at Oxford

University. By happenstance, his father died on Mansoor's 11th birthday in 1952, whereupon Mansoor succeeded as the ninth Nawab of Pataudi. While the princely state of Pataudi had been merged with India after the end of the British Raj in 1947, Mansoor did inherit the titular dignity of nawab of Pataudi.

Pataudi Jr., as Mansoor came to be known in the cricket world, was a right-hand batsman and a right-arm medium pace bowler. He played in 46 Test matches for India between 1961 and 1975. In March 1962, at the relatively young age of 21, Pataudi Jr. was elevated to the captaincy of the Indian cricket team. This was a few months AFTER a car accident permanently damaged vision in his right eye. He also captained Sussex in 1966. Pataudi Jr. was captain of the Indian cricket team in 40 matches, only 9 of which resulted in victory for his team. He was however captain when the Indian team recorded its first ever overseas Test victory, against New Zealand in 1967.

Mansura : Mansura was the capital of the Arab empire in Pakistan. When Mohammad Bin Qasim conquered Sindh, then a part of Hindustan and currently a part of Pakistan, in 711 A.D., he chose Brahmanabad as his capital city. According to Idrisi, the name of the city was changed to Al-Mansura in honor of Caliph Al-Mansur (754-775 AD) the second Khalifa of the Abbasid dynasty. Mansura enjoys an important position in Muslim history as this was the first city which was built according to the principles of town-planning. And the experience gained over here was used in Baghdad seventeen years later. According to historians, Mansura was a beautiful town which had vast orchards of mangoes and groves of date palms. The ruins of Mansura are spread over an area of four miles in circumference near the modern city of Shahdadpur. The most significant ruins found in Mansura is of the big courtyard of a Jamia Masjid.

Manthani : Manthani is a village in India approximately 70 kilometers from Karimnagar. It is situated on the banks of the river Godavari. It is a very ancient center of Vedic learning, and even today houses many scholars well versed in Vedas & Sastras. Among several temples situated here, the most important are those of Lord Saileshwara, Laxminarayana Swamy, Omkeshwara Swamy & Mahalaxmi. It is also a main centre for Jainism & Buddhism.

Manu River : Manu river is one of the Trans-boundary rivers of Bangladesh and also a tributary of the Kushiyara river. The Manu takes its rise under the Kahoisib peak of the Sakkanklang range located in the Hill Tripura (India) and for some distance passes through various narrow gorges with escarpments of naked rock rising often 30m and more, and cutting into deep and clear pools. As it descends into the more level plain, it becomes a broad sluggish stream with a meander course. Its course is northward until it reaches the Sylhet plains. The river enters Bangladesh through Kulaura upazila in Maulvi Bazar district, when it changes to northwest and north to meet the Kushiyara at Manumukh.

Manusmriti : The Manusmriti, translated "Laws of Manu" or "Institutions of Manu", is regarded as a foundational work of Hindu law and ancient Indian society, compiled and written quite late, c.200 CE in India. It is one of the eighteen Smritis of the Dharma Sastra (or "laws of righteous conduct"); Smriti means "what is remembered" and is applied in general to a Hindu text other than the Vedas, including traditional Indian epics, the Puranas, and science and grammar treatises. Unlike the Vedas which are considered to be eternal or of divine origin, the Smritis are considered to be of human origin and therefore susceptible to the flaws of humans. They contain laws, rules and codes of conduct to be applied by individuals, communities and nations. Some of these laws codify the Hindu caste system and discuss the "stages of life for a twice-born man". The book is ascribed to Manu, said to be the forefather of all human race. Manu's writings condemned the indian sub continent into the dark ages which still continue for more than 250 million people living under the hindu belief in the oppressive caste system.

Manusmriti was quoted, especially by the British Colonial rulers of India as "the law-book" of the Hindus. Some Hindus allege that the colonial rulers, like Robert Clive and Lord Macaulay, would have found it a useful tool. The caste system as prescribed by the Manusmriti developed a society and a civilization that was very easy to subjugate and rule. The British found a society already deeply divided and under an oppressive system easy to govern. Some people over the ages have quoted or interpreted the Manusmriti to justify Brahmin supremacy, the sanctity of the caste system and the lower status given to the so-called Dalits.

Manusmriti is attributed for having rendered the caste system secure by the elaboration of a system of conventional precepts. The society consisted of four (later hereditary) classes—Brahmanas (teachers and priests), Kshatriyas (administrators and armymen), Vaishyas, also called as Aryas (traders, farmers and herdsmen) and Shudras (servants). It clearly defined the relative position and the duties of the several castes, and determined the penalties to be indicted on any transgressions of the limits assigned to each of them.

Manzoor Alam Beg : Manzoor Alam Beg was a famous Fine Art Photographer and a founder member of BPS (Bangladesh Photographic Society). He was the leader of fine art photographic movements in Bangladesh. He had been recognized by FIAP for his excellence in photography. He was honored with a title "Alokchitracharjo" by Bangladeshi photographers community. He is considered as the Father of Fine Art Photography Movements in Bangladesh.

Mappilas : The Mappilas are a Muslim community in Kerala and neighbouring states and territories of India. They are the earliest known Indian Muslim community, having existed since the 8th century AD, when Arab merchants who had long been trading with the Chera kingdom converted to Islam, based on the preachings of monotheism by Prophet Muhammad in Arabia. They propagated their faith along the Malabar Coast.

In the 16th and 17th centuries they are known for their fight against Portuguese inquisition and conversion to Christianity of native people of malabar coast. 19th and early 20th centuries, Mappilas were known for active armed attacks against the British, including the 1921 Moplah rebellion.

Mapusa : Mapusa is a town in Goa, India. It is situated 13 km north of the capital Panaji. The town is the headquarters of Bardez taluka. It is located on the main highway NH-17, linking Mumbai to Trivandrum. Mapusa is one of the main centres of Goa's tourism industry, with its proximity to the beaches in north Goa. Mapusa comes alive on Friday, the traditional market day. People from surrounding villages and towns come to Mapusa to sell their wares. Its close proximity to many beaches in the north make it a very suitable place to make a base while exploring north Goa. Book well in advance to avoid disappointment during the tourist season (October to January).

Maratha Empire : The Maratha Empire, of India, was founded by Chhatrapati Shivaji in 1674 when he carved out an independent Maratha zone around Pune from the

Bijapur Sultanate. After a lifetime of exploits and guerrilla warfare with the Mughal emperor Aurangzeb, Shivaji died in 1680, leaving a Maratha kingdom of great extent but strategically and vulnerably located. The Mughal invasion started around 1682 and lasted till 1707: so for 25 years the Marathas fought one of the longest ongoing battles in human history. Shahu, a grandson of Shivaji became ruler until his death in 1749.At the time of death he appointed peshwa as head of the state with certain conditions to follow. The battle of Panipat in 1761 crippled the Maratha empire and corroded the power of Peshwa forever. Now the Maratha Confederacy was the real authority, with titular king and prime minister. The last Peshwa, Baji Rao II, was defeated by the British in the Third Anglo-Maratha War. But the memory of Shivaji kept their cause alive, and during the late 19th century a wave of socio-political breakthrough revolutions caused a transformation of the entire State and nation.

Marathas : The Marathas" is a collective term referring to a group of Hindu, Marathi-speaking castes of warriors and peasants, hailing mostly from the present-day state of Maharashtra, who created a substantial empire, covering a major part of India, in the 17th and 18th centuries.

The "Marathas" were known by that name since their native tongue was almost invariably Marathi (an Indo-Aryan language); however, not all those whose native tongue is Marathi are Marathas. The term "Maratha" refers only to those marathi-speaking people who also belong to certain specific Hindu castes: for two available listings, refer to Maratha Clan System.Thus, the terms "Marathi people" and "Maratha people" are not interchangable and should not be confused for each other.

Historians, researchers and scholars are divided over the origins of Marathas. Some of the Maratha clans are descendants of the local dynasties. Earlier, historians put the origin of Marathas as Indo-Aryans. However, recent genetic studies put the origin of Marathas as Aryans. There is a kunbi or kurmi kshatriyas group apart from 96 royal clans of marathas. Linguistically, they belong to exclusively Indo-Aryan linguistic group.

The Marathas have contributed a glorious chapter to the history of India. They first came into historical prominence under the leadership of Chhatrapati Shivaji in the 17th century. Shivaji Maharaj, born into the Bhonsle clan of marathas, secured an independent state by dint of lifelong struggle and thereby founded an empire, the remnants of which lasted until the independence of India in 1947. The state thus founded by Chhatrapati Shivaji attained its zenith under the tutelage of the Peshwas in the 18th century, extending from the Indus in present-day Pakistan to Orissa in the east and Thanjavur in the south excluding the kingdom of Mysore which remained independent. At its peak, the Maratha Empire established a protectorate over the mughal emperor and commanded the allegiance of the numerous rajput chieftains of Gujarat, Rajasthan, Central India and elsewhere. This vast empire declined gradually after the third battle of Panipat in 1761; by 1818, all of present-day India had fallen to the British East India Company.

Marathi : Marathi is one of the twenty-two official languages spoken in India, and has a long history purportedly dating back to the 8th century in inscriptions. The first Marathi inscription was discovered in the Karnataka state and is said to date back to 981 AD. There are approximately ninety million speakers of Marathi in the Maharashtra state. Marathi's grammar and syntax is primarily based on Sanskrit. Marathi is alternatively spelt "Maharathi" in English.

Marble Palace : Marble Palace is located on C R Avenue in north Calcutta at Muktaram Babu Street. This palace was constructed by Raja Rajendra Mullick Bahadur in 1835. Italian marble was lavishly used to complete its construction. This palace set behind a large lawn has the sculptures of Jesus Christ, the Virgin Mary, Hindu Gods, the Buddha and Christopher Columbus. A large pool near the small granite bungalow has ducks, peacocks and ostriches. The rooms have hundreds of statues and oriental urns. The walls of these rooms are covered with enormous paintings and mirrors. Gigantic chandeliers hang on its ceilings. The lamps on the stair cases are detailed creations.

Mardol : Mardol is a historic street in Shrewsbury, Shropshire. Shuts and passages leading from the street include the King's Head Passage, Phoenix Place, Mardol Gardens, Carnarvon Lane, Hill's Lane and Roushill Bank. At the top of Mardol now stands a new modern monument, Darwin's Gate. It has been criticised by many in the town as being out of place and meaningless.

Margalla Hills National Park : The Margalla Hills National Park is in Northern Punjab Pakistan at the foothills of the Himalayas and is a beautiful park. The hills lie in several towns including Islamabad. There is a Shaker-Parian park, and there are also several hiking trails, with the most famous being Trail 3. It is home to the leopard, gray goral, barking deer, wild boar, asiatic leopard, jackal, red fox, fruit bat, porcupine and even gazelle. It is also home to some bird and reptiles such as larks, pheasants, spotted doves, egyptian vultures, falcons, hawks and Russell's viper, indian cobra and saw scaled viper.

Margao : Margao, is also called Madgaon, Margaon and Margão. It is Goa's biggest city, the commercial capital of the state and the administrative headquarters of South Goa District. The name may be pronounced as 'Modgow' in Konkani, the local language. Margão is the Portuguese form, and the form Margaon is also common. It is derived from Mathagram which means a place with a matha.

The Madgaon Railway station is Goa's biggest and most important as it is a railway junction positioned at the intersection of the Konkan Railway and the South Western Railway. All trains passing through Goa stop here. Hence Margao is used more commonly as a transit stop rather than as a tourist destination, by many people who either head off down south to Palolem or to Benaulim and Colva which is about six kilometers away.

The city has many sights and destinations. These include the 'Closed' Market called Pimpalakatta, the municipal building also called 'Camara', Anna Fonte (natural springs), Old Market, Holy Spirit Church, grand colonial mansions in Borda, the view and chapel at Monte Hill, the Hindu crematorium or 'Smashant' on Pajifond's Rua de Saudade. Some of the city suburbs include Pajifond, Aquem, Gogol, Borda, Malbhat, Kharebandh, Old Market and Comba, the last two being the oldest parts of the city. Though the town is also known as the cultural capital of Goa, however, the culture center is still in construction in Fatorda, and when completed will be called the Ravindra Bhavan. It also has Goa's only sports stadium, and hosts the test track for Skybus, an elevated rail system.

Margazh : Margazh is an important festival observed by Vaishnavites. They are the followers of Ramaṇuja. It is observed during the whole month of Margasira. It is dedicated to Andal also called Godavere or Chudukuduta, one of the twelve Alwars or Vaishmavite saints. She loved Lord Ranganatha and become one with him. On this day everyone gets up early in the morning before 4.00 am, they bathe and go to a Vaishnava temple to attend puja. This continues for one month and the festival concludes with the celebration of the wedding of Godavari with Lord Ranganatha. This is done on grand scale and with great devotion.

Maridamma Festival : Maridamma temple is located in Peddapuram taluk in East Godavari district. Maridamma festival is celebrated for thirty-one days from the Amavasya in the month of Jyeshtha to the Amavasya in the month of Ashadha. Thousands congregate with dances like Kolatoms and display physical feats and skills with sticks. They also revel in music, dance drumming, Garaga dances, processions and other communal activities. A wide variety of house hold articles are sold in the fair held during the festival. Cycle races, cattle shows, parrot circuses and agricultural exhibitions are also held here. 'Kumbham' is carried in decorated vessels, kept in open carts. Sometimes men and women dressed to resemble those personages stand on the carts. These carts are taken in procession to the temple to the accompaniment of music and dance and offered to the God, then food is distributed as 'prasadam'.

Marina Beach : Marina Beach, at 13 km long, is one of the longest beaches in the world. It forms the shoreline of Chennai. Unlike the short, rocky formations that make up the Juhu Beach in Mumbai on the west coast of India, the Marina is primarily sandy. Another famous characteristic of the beach is the set of beautiful stone statues that adorn the roadside area of the beach. Most statues are of Indian/ local legends (like Mahatma Gandhi, Thiruvalluvar), while others have symbolic significance (like the Statue of Labour).

The Marina used to be famed for its pristine beauty, jolly ambiance, and rich ecosystems. However, since the middle of the 20th century, the beach and water has become polluted. A proliferation of plastic bags, human waste and other pollutants have rendered many parts of the beach unusable. In recent years, many voluntary organisations have taken up the task of cleaning up the Marina and protecting the ecosystem. Particular efforts include protection of Olive Ridley turtle nests along the Neelangarai section of the beach. Despite these problems however, a visit to the Marina is a sine qua non for any tourist coming to Chennai.

Marine Drive : Marine Drive is a 3 km long boulevard in South Mumbai in the city of Mumbai. It is an inverted 'C'-shaped six lane concrete road along the coast which is a natural bay. The road links Nariman Point to Babulnath and Malabar Hill. Marine Drive is situated over reclaimed land facing west-south-west. The bay is part of the Arabian Sea.

The official name for this road, though rarely used, is: Netaji Subhash Chandra Bose Road. The highlight of Marine drive is the beautiful promenade along the road where many of the citizens take in a breath of fresh air and view the daily sunsets. The promenade is lined with palm trees. At the northern end of Marine Drive is Chowpatty Beach. This is a popular beach is famed for its Bhel puri (local fast food). However the sea is too polluted to safely enter. Many restaurants also line this stretch of the road. Further down this road lies Walkeshwar, a wealthy neighbourhood of the city, also home to the governor of Maharashtra.

Marine National Park, Andaman and Nicobar Islands : This new National Park was set up in the Andaman and Nicobar Islands at a distance of 20km from Port Blair which is the nearest town and airport. The park covers an area of 281sq.km. The park is spread over 15 islands of Labrynth group of Islands of the west coast of south Andaman. Each Island has distinct vegetation which comprise littoral moist deciduous evergreen forests and mangroves in small pockets, creeks and estuarine bags. The island shores are nesting grounds for 5 species of tropical sea turtles. The coral reefs and associated coral fish attract many tourists, water-monitor, lizard, wild boar, sea snakes are other animal forms.

Marine National Park, Gujarat : India's first Marine Sanctuary and National park is found in the Gulf of Kutch, Jamnagar District in Gujarat. The Gulf of Kutch located on the west coast of India is an arm of the Arabian Sea, separating the Saurashtra Peninsula from the Great and Little Rann of Kutch. At its seaward (western) end it is 58 km wide, from which point it tapers gradually eastwards, extending for nearly 170 km with maximum depth of 60 mts and an average depth of about 20 mts. The Marine sanctuary and the park located on the southern shore of the Gulf of Kutch were established in 1980 and 1982 respectively under the provisions of the Wildlife (Protection) Act, 1972 for the protection of threatened marine flora and fauna in the area.

Marine National Park, Tamil Nadu : This Marine National Park is located in the districts of Tirunelveli and Ramanathapuram, covering an area of 6.25sq.km. Spread over 21 Islands. The nearest town and rail head is Tuticorin and the airport is at Madurai. The forests consists of littoral scrubs in patches. Some Islands have babul plots raised artificially. The fauna found are several species of birds, squirrel, hare, dugong,dolphin, sea turtles etc. All the islands are egg laying sites for not less than six species of turtles.

Markanda : This small parish is located on the left bank of Vainganga river in Maharashtra. The land gets its name from Sage Markandeya. A cluster of temples exist here housing 'Shiva Linga' which Markandeya is believed to have worshipped. The cluster has an approximate 24 temples and the architecture strongly resembles that of the Khajuraho temples.

Marma : The Marma are a tribe inhabiting the Chittagong Hill Tracts of Bangladesh. Ethnically related to the Chakma, they are largely followers of Theravada Buddhism.

Marriage of Bhadrakali and Virabhadra : Tegada in Nagur, independent sub-taluk of Khannan district, has Bhadrakali and Virabhadraswami temple as a place of worship. The marriage of Bhadrakali and Virabhadra is celebrated for two days on the 13th and 14th days of the dark fortnight in the month of Magha. On the morning of Trayodasi Lord Virabhadraswami is taken to the river Godavari, which is about three kilometers from this place to the accompaniment of music and Abhishekam is performed with the holy waters and the idol is brought back to the temple. Then 'sunku' is measured before the Lord. Sunku is explained as follows. Some rice is measured before the image of the Lord with a new earthen pitcher and poured into a new pot, then it is covered with an earthen plate and is wrapped in a new cloth. The seal of the Lord is affixed on the knot of the cloth and the pot is kept to the left of the pedestal of the image.

Before the procession of the Lord starts in the night, the pot is opened and the same person measures that rice again with the same pitcher, more rice is found, than what was measured into the pot in the morning. If it is found that the quantity of the rice in the pot has increased, the festival is celebrated considering it as a good omen. There is a procession throughout the night. During the procession some devotees pierce their tongues or cheeks with marasalu, coconuts, jaggery, fruits and pumpkins are offered.

Marthanda Varma : Marthanda Varma (1706—1758) was the son of the Rani of Attingal. He inherited the throne of Venad, a small principality on the southernmost tip of peninsular India, from his uncle, according to the matrilineal system of inheritance. A shrewd tactician and a brilliant general, he signed a treaty with the English East

India Company in 1723, in his capacity as the crown prince. He is known as "the maker of modern Travancore" for developing a small kingdom into a powerful state. He appointed his former prisoner, Admiral D'lennoy, as his commander-in-chief and gave him the status of a local noble. D'lennoy modernised the Travancore army and equipped the army with firearms and artillery. Marthanda Varma also took steps to improve trade, and built waterways and roads. He passed away in 1758, leaving his kingdom to his nephew Karthika Thirunal Rama Varma (Dharma Raja), during whose reign, the kingdom withstood the Mysorean invasion.

Martyr's Memorial : The martyr's memorial in Bihar is a sculpture near the Secretariat honouring the seven freedom fighters who sacrificed their lives in the Quit India Movement of August 1942. They were shot dead when they attempted to hoist the national flag.

Marumalarchi Dravida Munnetra Kazhagam (MDMK) : Marumalarchi Dravida Munnetra Kazhagam, a political party in the Indian state of Tamil Nadu. It is led by Vaiko. The party was a member of the National Democratic Alliance until the winter of 2003. But although the party was participating in the national NDA-government, Vaiko was arrested for 19 months under the Prevention of Terrorism Act. Since the 2004 Lok Sabha elections the party is a member of the broad Tamil alliance, the Democratic Progressive Alliance, together with Dravida Munnetra Kazhagam, Indian National Congress, Pattali Makkal Katchi, Communist Party of India, Communist Party of India (Marxist) and Indian Union Muslim League.

Maruti Udyog Ltd : Maruti Udyog Ltd is one of India's leading automobile manufacturers and the market leader in the car segment, both in terms of volume of vehicles sold and revenue earned. 18.28% of the company is owned by the Indian government, and 54.2% by Suzuki of Japan. The Indian government held an Initial Public Offering of 25% of the company in June of 2003. Maruti Udyog Limited (MUL) was established in February 1981, though the actual production commenced in 1983. Through 2004, Maruti has produced over 5 Million vehicles. Marutis are sold in India and various several other countries, depending upon export orders. Cars similar to Marutis (but not manufactured by Maruti Udyog) are sold by Suzuki in Pakistan and other South Asian countries.

Masala Dosa : Masala Dosa is a South Indian tiffin dish that has now become extremely popular all over India and abroad. The batter made is similar to regular Dosa batter with some additional ingredients. One variant of Masala dosa, the Mysore Masala Dosa, described here uses two types of chutneys.

Masherbrum : Masherbrum is the highest peak of the Masherbrum Mountains, a subrange of the Karakoram mountain range. It is a large and striking peak, which is somewhat overshadowed by the nearby 8000m peaks of the Karakoram, including K2. The meaning of the name is not entirely clear. It may come from mashadar (muzzle-loading gun) plus brum (mountain), from the resemblance of the double summit to an old muzzle-loader. It may also come from masha (queen or lady), giving "queen of peaks." Other meanings have also been suggested.

Mashru : Mashru, a mixed fabric, woven with a combination of cotton and silk, was essentially for the use of Muslim men as there was a prohibition on their wearing pure silk. The tradition of Mashru may have been influenced by weaving tradiions prevalent in Iraq and the Arab countries where the habits were strictly adhered to Mashru was woven all over India, though it survives today only in Gujarat.

Masjidpara Mosque : Masjidpara Mosque is situated in the locality of Hoarshi about three miles to the north of Pakundia upazila headquarters, Kishoreganj. Now a protected monument of the Department of Archaeology, Bangladesh, it is also called Hoarshi Mosque. A Persian inscription, fixed over the central doorway of the mosque, records that it was built in 1675-76 AD during the reign of Aurangzeb.

The mosque provides an interesting example of a synthesis of the Sultanate and Mughal building styles. The Sultanate features are exemplified by the terracotta ornamentation and the Bengali pendentives, while the Mughal constructional peculiarities are corroborated by the bulbous shape of the dome on drum, the horizontal parapets and cornices, the rectangular panels and smooth plastering in the walls.

Mass Upsurge, 1969 : Mass Upsurge, 1969 was started in Bagladesh with the student unrest of 1968 against the tyrannical rule of Ayub Khan, President of Pakistan. The movement soon engulfed the whole of the then East Pakistan peasants, artisans, workers joined the movement almost en masse. Due to continuous exaction of undue demands the labouring class of the industrial belts and low and medium income groups soon turned the movement into a struggle for economic emancipation. The racial repression and the deprivation of the Bengalis within the frame work of Pakistan and, to the contrary, starting from the Language Movement the feeling of separate identity together with struggle for autonomy had direct influence on the mass upsurge of 1969. Indeed, this mass upsurge was the greatest mass awakening ever since the creation of Pakistan.

Master Tara Singh : Master Tara Singh (24 June 1885, Rawalpindi, Punjab - 22 November 1967, Chandigarh) was a prominent Sikh political and religious leader in the first half of the 20th century. He was instrumental in organizing the Shiromani Gurdwara Prabhandak Committee, in organizing Sikhs politically, and guided the Sikhs during the Partition of India, and later led their demand for a Sikh-majority state in Punjab, India.

Master Tara Singh was born on 24 June 1885 in the village Harial in Rawalpindi District, now in Pakistan. His childhood name was Nanak Chand and his father's name was Bakshi Gopi Chand, who by caste was a Malhotra, and a Hindu. He had four brothers and a sister. His father was the village patwari by profession and was held in great esteem by the villagers, and his mother was Mullan Devi, a very pious lady. The entire family, especially their parents believed in Sikh Gurus and Gurbani.

Masti Gate : Masti Gate is one of the 13 gates of Lahore Fort in the city of Lahore, Pakistan. It is located on the east side of the fort. The "Masti" name comes from the word "masjidi", relating to a mosque. The area of the city named after it is known for its many wholesale shoesellers.

Mastung : Mastung is a district in the north west of Balochistan province of Pakistan. Prior to 1991 Mastung was part of Kalat District. Due to administrative reasons Mastung was separated from Kalat and made a new District in 1991. The district consists Three Tehsils, Tehsil Mastung, Tehsil Dasht and Tehsil Kirdgap. District Mastung consists 12 union councils, Khadkocha, Ghulam Parenz, Karez Noth, Mastung-1, Mastung-2, Sorgaz, Dasht, Isplinji,Kanak, Shaikh Wasil, Kirdgap and Soro, one more union council formed with the name of Alizai in 2006. Over 99% of the people of the area are Muslims

Mataji Nirmala Devi : Shri Mataji Nirmala Srivastava (or Shrivastava) or Shri Mataji Nirmala Devi (born March 21, 1923 in Chindawara, India) is the founder of Sahaja Yoga. Nirmala Srivastava was born to Christian parents, Prasad and Cornelia Salve, having descended from the royal Shalivahana dynasty. Her parents named her Nirmala, which means "immaculate." Srivastava occasionally visited the ashram of Mahatma Gandhi. Like her parents, she was involved in the Indian independence movement; as a young woman she was a youth leader, and participated in the Quit India Movement. Shortly before India achieved independence Nirmala married Chandrika Prasad Srivastava and had two daughters.

Srivastava has stated that the potential for all humanity to gain spiritual self awareness was realised on May 5, 1970, which she characterizes as a historical process of en-masse self-realization and inner transformation. Prior to this day it was possible to attain self-realisation as Buddha did, but this required much penence, introspection and meditation before the understanding of the 'self' was attained.

Matamuhuri River : Matamuhuri river is a river that originates at 21 14 N and 92 36 E, only 1 to the north and 1 to the east of the source of the Sangu river in the ranges of hills that divide Arakan from Chittagong. Matamuhuri is the Bangla version of the Magh name Mamuri. Like the Sangu, this river also flows northwest in the Hill Tracts and enters Cox's Bazar district from the east. Flowing west it falls into the Bay of Bengal at 21 45 N and 91 57 E forming a broad delta at its mouth extending from Bhola Khal to Khuta Khali. The delta is of the same character as the Sundarban, consisting of groups of islets intersected by a network of tidal creeks and covered by mangrove vegetation. The entire area has been brought under cultivation by erecting Embankments. The principal upazila adjoining this river is Chakaria. The length of the river is about 287 km.

Matha Amritanadamayi Math : Mata Amritanandamayi Math, is situated at Amritapuri in Vallickavu, a small fishing village near Quilon (Kollam),

South Kerala. The ashram which houses more than 2,500 disciples and householders as full-time residents is located at the site of the birth place and childhood home of Mata Amrithanandamayi or Amma or Ammichi as she is popularly known. Thousands of people around the world come to experience her unique 'darshan', in which she holds each devotee in her arms like a mother embracing a child.

Mata Amrithanadamayi's principal teaching is not her words, but the experience of being with her. She has a special earthy aura a sense of peace about her, a special healing touch, experienced by people who come to see her or receive her 'darshan'. Amma gives darshan on Wednesdays, Thursdays and Saturdays. She personally receives every person who comes to her with a radiant smile, talking to them, consoling and blessing them finally giving them a divine motherly hug. She is been known to embrace over 15,000 devotees in one night. On Sundays Amma gives a special 'Devi Bhava' darshan, a ritual in which she dresses in a spectacular costume and a crown, enters a trance and assumes the form of the Divine mother. This special darshan lasts the whole night past sunrise the next morning. Her devotees believe her to be an incarnation of the Hindu Goddess Kali. Some of them even worship her picture or small Ammachi dolls. Tuesdays and Fridays are set aside for ashram residents when Amma comes to the temple to give them 'Satsang'.

Mathrubhumi : Mathrubhumi is a Malayalam newspaper started in 1923. It evolved in the crucible of the national struggle for freedom. From a tri-weekly it grew into a daily in 1930. The founders of Mathrubhumi were in the forefront of the social movements also. Mathrubhumi is now a fullfledged professional newspaper with printing units in 12 cities in and out of Kerala. It has it's headquarters in Kozhikode in the northern part of

Kerala. Apart from the daily newspaper the group has eight other periodicals including an illustrated weekly, a film publication, a health magazine, sports magazine etc. K.P.Kesavamenon, the veteran freedom fighter and close disciple of Mahatma Gandhi was the founder editor. A newspaper born out of a relentless passion to explore the truth and lay bare issues of life changing significance before its readers. A newspaper that incisively cuts to the core of the Indian polity. Staunchly upholding its values. And of course, keeping pace with the digital age to meet its readers changing needs.

Mathura : Mathura is a city in India, located approximately 50 km north of Agra, and south of Delhi. It is the administrative center of Mathura District of Uttar Pradesh. During the ancient period, this was an economic hub, located at the junction of some relatively important caravan routes. Mathura is the reputed birthplace of Krishna, Krishnajanmabhoomi. The Keshav Dev temple was built in ancient times on the site of Krishna's supposed birthplace (an underground prison). In the 6th century BCE Mathura became the capital of the Shursen republic. The city was later ruled by the Maurya empire (4th to 2nd centuries BCE) and the Shunga dynasty (2nd century BCE). It was then ruled by the Indo-Greeks between 180 BCE and 100 BCE. It briefly reverted to Indian rule, and was then occupied by the Indo-Scythians during the 1st century BCE. Archaeological evidence seems to indicate that, by 100 BCE, there was a group of Jains living in Mathura.

Mathura served as one of the Kushan Empire's two capitals from the first to the third centuries. The Mathura Museum has the largest collection of redstone sculptures in Asia, depicting many famous Buddha figurines. In 634 Xuanzang had visited the Mathura town. He went east to Jalandhara in eastern Punjab, before climbing up to visit predominantly Theravada monasteries in the Kulu valley and turning southward again to Bairat and then Mathura, on the Yamuna river.

The city was sacked and many of its temples destroyed by Mahmud of Ghazni in 1018. The Keshav Dev temple was partially destroyed by the Mughal Emperor Aurangzeb, who built the city's Jami Masjid (Friday mosque) on the same site, re-using many of the temple's stones. The main Krishna shrine is presently the Dwarkadeesh temple, built in 1815 by Seth Gokuldas Parikh, Treasurer of Gwalior. The city is mentioned in the Sherlock Holmes story 'The Sign of Four.' Mathura is home to a large, technologically advanced oil refinery owned by the Indian Oil Corporation.

Mathura District : Mathura District is a district of Uttar Pradesh state of northern India. The historic town of Mathura is the district headquarters. The district is bounded on the northeast by Aligarh District, on the southeast by Hathras District, on the south by Agra District, and on the west and northwest by Haryana state. The district is part of Agra Division.

Matiur Rahman : Matiur Rahman was a (1941-1971) martyr in the War of Liberation of Bangladesh. He was born in Dhaka on 29 November 1941. He received his primary education at Dhaka Collegiate School. Next he got himself admitted into Pakistan Air Force Public School at Sargoda in West Pakistan. After completing his twelfth class course there he entered Pakistan Air Force Academy. He was commissioned in June 1963 and was posted at Risalpur, West Pakistan. He successfully completed the Jet Conversion Course in Karachi before he was appointed a Jet Pilot in Peshawar.

Rahman made a secret plan of hijacking an aircraft. His aim was to join the liberation forces with the hijacked plane. On the morning of 20 August Pilot Officer Minhaz

Rashid was scheduled to fly in a T-33 aircraft from Masrur Airbase in Karachi with Matiur Rahman as his trainer. The T-33 aircraft was code-named 'Bluebird'. During the training flight Matiur Rahman attempted to take control of the aircraft into his own hands, but failed. The plane crashed in Thatta, a place near the Indian border. Matiur's dead body was found near the crash sight, but no traces of Minhaz's dead body could be discovered. Matiur Rahman was buried at the graveyard of fourth class employees at Masrur Airbase. Matiur Rahman was awarded the highest state title of honour 'Bir Srestha' in recognition of his patriotism and sacrifice.

Matka Nritya: It is a variation of the Dandiya Raas in which the performers strike their fingers against empty pots to generate a distinctive beat.

Matki Dance : On wedding occasions, the countryside women of this part perform the 'Matki' dance with an earthen pot balanced on the head, the Matki is mostly danced solo in MP. Sometimes just for merriment a couple of women join the main dancer who usually dances with a veil on her face. The two other variations of the Matki are the Aada and Khada Nach.

Matsyanyayam : Matsyanyayam is reffered as the condition of Bengal in the century following the death of Shashanka and before the rise of the Palas (c 750-850 AD) has been described as matsyanyayam (matsyanyayam). In a near contemporary inscription, the Khalimpur copperplate of the 32nd year of the second Pala ruler Dharmapala, and the 12th century Ramacharitam kavya of Sandhyakaranandi the anarchical condition of Bengal preceding the rise of the Pala dynasty is found mentioned as matsyanyayam.

Matsyendranath : Matsyendranath (9th-10th century) was one of the eighty-four Mahasiddhas, and is the patron deity of Nepal. He was guru of Gorakshanath, with whom he founded the school of Hatha yoga, one of the branches of Yogic practices. Matsyendranath was the son of Minanath, a fisherman. He is considered by many to be the founder of the Nath Sampradaya of sadhus. While the Naths had actually been known much earlier, from the time of Dattatreya, Matsyendranath did initiate a revival by combining the three viewpoints of Siddha, Tantra, and Nath philosophy.

Mattancherry Palace : The Mattancherry Palace, also known as the Dutch Palace, is a large construction in Mattancherry, Kochi, Kerala, India. It features Kerala murals depicting Hindu temple art, portraits and exhibits of the Rajas of Kochi. It was built by the Portuguese and presented to the Raja of Kochi, Veera Kerala Varma, in 1555. It became known as the Dutch Palace in 1663, when the Dutch renovated the palace and built some extensions.

Maulana Abul Kalam Azad : Abul Kalam Ghulam Muhiyuddin (1888—1958), better known as Maulana Abul Kalam Azad was a great scholar, poet, freedom fighter and leader of the Indian National Congress in India's struggle for Independence. He was well versed in many languages viz. Arabic, English, Hindi, Persian and Urdu and a prolific debater as his name depicts Abul Kalãm which literally means father or lord of dialogue.

He was independent India's first Education Minister. The title Maulana is of a highly-qualified Islamic scholar and religious cleric. Azad was not a practicing cleric, however. He was posthumously awarded India's highest civilian honor Bharat Ratna in 1992.

Maulana Bhashani : Maulana Bhashani (full name Maulana Abdul Hamid Khan Bhashani) was a popular political leader in East Pakistan and Bangladesh. He was born in 1880 in Dhangara, Tangail in erstwhile Bengal(now Bangladesh). He gained immense popularity among peasants. He fought against Colonialism, both British and Pakistani. He died on 17 November 1976 in Dhaka, Bangladesh.

Maulana Mohammad Ali : Maulana Mohammad Ali (1878—1931), also addressed with the suffix Jauhar, which was his pen name, was an Indian Muslim nationalist and leader of the Khilafat movement. Mohammed Ali had attended the founding meeting of the All India Muslim League in Dhaka in 1906, and served as its president in 1918. He remained active in the League till 1928.

Now accorded the respectful title of Maulana, Ali formed in 1921, a broad coalition with Muslim nationalists like Maulana Shaukat Ali, Maulana Azad, Hakim Ajmal Khan, Mukhtar Ahmed Ansari and Indian nationalist leader Mahatma Gandhi, who enlisted the support of the Indian National Congress and many thousands of Hindus, who joined the Muslims in a demonstration of unity. Ali also wholeheartedly supported Gandhi's call for a national civil resistance movement, and inspired many hundreds of protests and strikes all over India. He was arrested by British authorities and imprisoned for two years.

Maulana Mohammad Ali was however, disillusioned by the failure of the Khilafat movement and Gandhi's suspension of civil disobedience in 1922, owing to the Chauri Chaura incident. Mohammad Ali opposed the Nehru Report's rejection of separate electorates for Muslims, and supported the Fourteen Points of Muhammad Ali Jinnah and the League. He became a critic of Gandhi, breaking with fellow Muslim leaders like Maulana Azad, Hakim Ajmal Khan and Mukhtar Ahmed Ansari, who continued to support Gandhi and the Indian National Congress. Ali attended the Round Table Conference to show that only the Muslim League spoke for India's Muslims. He died soon after the conference in London, on January 4, 1931 and was buried in Jerusalem according to his own wish.

Maulana Mufti Mehmood : Maulana Mufti Mehmood was born in January 1919 in Paniala, District Dera Ismail Khan, NWFP, Pakistan. He was an Islamic scholar and political activist. After the 1970 General Elections, he led his party the Jamiat Ulema-e-Islam (JUI—F) into a coalition with the National Awami Party. On March 1 1972, he was elected as the Chief Minister of the North-West Frontier Province. He alongwith his cabinet resigned in protest at the dismissal of the NAP—JUI (F) coalition government in Balochistan on 14 February 1973. He supported Afghan Jihad against the invasion of Afghanistan by USSR. He died on 14th October 1980. He was buried in Dera Ismail Khan his home town.

Maulana Shaukat Ali : Maulana Shaukat Ali was an Indian Muslim nationalist and leader of the Khilafat movement. He was the brother of Maulana Mohammad Ali He was born in 1873 in Rampur state in what is today Uttar Pradesh. He was educated at the Aligarh Muslim University. Shaukat Ali helped his brother Mohammed Ali publish the Urdu weekly Hamdard and the English weekly Comrade. In 1919, while jailed for publishing what the British charged as seditious materials and organizing protests, he was elected as the first president of the Khilafat conference. He was re-arrested and imprisoned from 1921 to 1923 for his support to Mahatma Gandhi and the Indian National Congress during the Non-Cooperation Movement (1919-1922). His fans accorded him and his brother the title of Maulana.

Along with his brother, Shaukat Ali grew disilliusioned with the Congress and Gandhi's leadership. He opposed the 1928 Nehru Report, demanding separate electorates for Muslims, and attended the first and second Round Table Conferences in London. His brother died in 1931, and Ali continued on and organized the World Muslim Conference in Jerusalem. In 1936, Ali joined the All India Muslim League and became a close political ally of and campaigner for Muhammad Ali Jinnah, the future founder of Pakistan. He served as member of the Central Assembly from 1934 to 1938. Shaukat Ali died in 1938.

Maulana Zafar Ali Khan : Maulana Zafar Ali Khan (1873–1956), was a writer, poet, and journalist who took an important part in Pakistan Movement. He was born at Kot Mehrath, Sialkot. He received his early education in Mission High School, Wazirabad, then he went to Aligarh Muslim University, and graduated from there.

After graduation he was appointed secretary to Nawab Mohsin-ul-Mulk who was then in Bombay. Then he worked for some time as a translator in Hyderabad, Deccan, rising to the post of Secretary, Home Department. He returned from Hyderabad and launched his daily Zamindar from Lahore which was founded by his father Maulvi Sirajuddin Ahmad.

Maulvi Bazar : Maulvi Bazar is a district in the Sylhet division of Bangladesh with an area of 2799.39 sq km, is bounded by Sylhet district on the north, Tripura state of India on the south, Assam and Tripura states of India on the east, and Habiganj district on the west. Main rivers are Manu, Dhalai, Juri, Gopala, etc; noted depressions: Hakaluki, Hail and Kawadighi Haors. Annual temperature: maximum 33.2 C, minimum 13.6 C; annual rainfall 3334 mm. The total forest area is 413.65 sq km; noted forest ranges are Patharia, Sanrer Gaz or Longla, Rajkandi and Vanugachh. Maulvi Bazar subdivision was established in 1960 and was turned into a district in 1984. It consists of 6 upazilas, 4 municipalities, 36 wards and 123 mahallas, 66 union parishads, 876 mouzas, 2030 villages. The upazilas are Barlekha, Kamalganj, Kulaura, Maulvi Bazar Sadar, Rajnagar and Sreemangal.

Mauryan Empire : The Mauryan Empire was the first and largest political and military empire in the history of the South Asia. Originating from the kingdom of Magadha in the Indo-Gangetic plains of modern Bihar and its capital city of Pataliputra (near modern Patna), the Empire was founded in 321 BCE by Chandragupta Maurya, who had overthrown the Nanda Dynasty and began expanding his power across central and western India. The Empire stretched to the north along the natural boundaries of the Himalayas and to the east, stretching around the modern boundaries of Assam and West Bengal. To the west, it reached beyond modern Pakistan and included significant portions of modern Kandahar in Afghanistan and Baluchistan, which also stretches into Iran. The Empire was expanded into India's central and southern regions by Emperor Bindusara, but excluded a small portion of unexplored trial and forested regions near Kalinga. Following the conquest of Kalinga in a major war, Ashoka ended the military expansion of his empire. The kingdoms of Pandya and Chola thus preserved their independence, accepting the supremacy of the Mauryan emperor. Its decline began fifty years after Ashoka's rule ended, and it dissolved in 185 BCE with the foundation of the Sunga Dynasty in Magadha.

Under the rule of the Maurya Dynasty, ancient India was liberated from conquest by the armies of Alexander the Great, and subsequent rule by Indo-Greek kingdoms under his generals. After uniting the plethora of regional kingdoms under his rule, Emperor Chandragupta Maurya successfully defeated the invasion led by Seleucus I, a Greek general from Alexander's army. Under Chandragupta and his successors, internal and external trade, agriculture and economic activities thrived and expanded across India, with the creation of a single and efficient system of finance, administration and security. After the Kalinga War, the Empire experienced half a century of peace and security under Ashoka. Under him, India was a prosperous and stable empire of great economic and military power whose political influence and trade extended across West and Central Asia and Europe. Mauryan India was also exposed to an era of social harmony, religious transformation and expansion of the sciences and knowledge. Chandragupta Maurya's embrace of Jainism increased social and religious renewal and reform across society, while Ashoka's embrace of Buddhism was the foundation of the reign of social and political peace and non-violence across India. Ashoka sponsored the spreading of Buddhist ideals into Sri Lanka, South East Asia, West Asia and Mediterranean Europe.

Chandragupta's minister, Kautilya Chanakya wrote the Arthashastra—the greatest collection of treatises exploring economics, politics, foreign affairs, administration, military arts, war, religion in the East, often compared to the medieval-era Italian expert Niccolo Machiavelli's The Prince. Archaeologically, the period of Mauryan rule in South Asia falls in the Northern Black Polished Ware (NBPW). The Arthashastra and the Edicts of Ashoka are the greatest sources of written records of the Mauryan times. The Mauryan empire is considered one of the greatest periods in Indian history. The Lion Capital of Asoka at Sarnath, is the emblem of India.

Mausoleum of Hazrat Baha-ud-Din Zakaria : Standing at the north-eastern fringe of the ancient fort of Multan, is the eternal abode of Al-Sheikh Al-Kabir Sheikh-ul-Islam Baha-ud-Din Abu Muhammad Zakaria Al-Qureshi Al-Asadi, one of the greatest saints of the Suhrawardiya Silsila and one of the most distinguished disciples of Sheikh Al-Shuyukh Shahab Al-Din Suhrawardy. He was the founder of Suhrawardiya Silsila in the Sub-Continent. He was born in 1170 AD. The prime attraction of the Fort area is the Mausoleum generally known as Bahawal Haq (the ornament of the Faith). The dome of the Mausoleum is visible from miles and dominate the skyline of Multan. Sheikh Baha-ud-Din Zakariya known as Bahawal Haq was born at Kot Kehror a town of District Laiah near Multan, around 1170 AD. For fifteen years he went from place to place to preach Islam and after his wanderings Bahawal Haq settled in Multan in 1222 AD. This great man passed away in 1267 AD. The Mausoleum is a square of 51 feet 9 inches, measured internally. Above this is an octagon, about half the height of the square, which is surmounted by a hemispherical dome. The Mausoleum was almost completely ruined during the siege of 1848, but was soon afterwards restored by the Muslims.

Mausoleum of Musa Pak Shaheed : The Mausoleum of Moosa Pak Shaheed is inside the Pak Gate. Sheikh Abul Hassab Musa Pak Shaheed was a descendant of Abdul Qadir Jillani and was born in Uch. The Shrine of Musa Pak Shaheed is also frequented by a large number of Pathans from all parts of Pakistan.

Mausoleum of Shah Gardez : Within the city there is another shrine of Muhammad Yusaf Gardezi commonly known as Shah Gardez just inside the Bohar Gate. It is a rectangular domeless building decorated with glazed tiles, a work of considerable beauty. He came to Multan in 1088 AD and settled here for good.

Mausoleum of Shah Rukn-i-Alam : The tomb of Shah Rukn-i-Alam grandson of Shaikh Bahauddin Zakaria, which was built between 1320 and 1324, is an unmatched pre-Moghul masterpiece. The Mausoleum of Rukn-i-Alam is the glory of Multan. From whichever side the city is approached, the most prominent thing that can be seen from miles all around is a huge dome. This dome is the Shrine of Sheikh Rukn-ud-Din Abul Fath commonly known by the title Rukn-i-Alam (pillar of the world). The tomb is located on the southwest side of the Fort premises. This elegant building is an octagon, 51 feet 9 inches in diameter internally, with walls 41 feet 4 inches high and 13 feet 3 inches thick, supported at the angles by sloping towers.

Over this is a smaller octagon 25 feet 8 inches, on the exterior side, and 26 feet 10 inches high, leaving a narrow passage all round the top of the lower storey for the Moazzan, or public caller to prayers. The whole is surmounted by hemispherical dome of 58 feet external diameter. The total height of the building, including a plinth of 3 feet, is 100 feet. As it stands on the high ground, the total height above the road level is 150 feet.

Besides its religious importance, the mausoleum is also of considerable archaeological value as its dome is reputed to be the second largest in the world after 'Gol Gumbad' of Bijapur (India), which is the largest. The mausoleum is built entirely of red brick, bounded with beams of Shisham wood, which have now turned black after so many centuries. The whole of the exterior is elaborately ornamented with glazed tile panels, stringcourses and battlements. Colors used are dark blue, azure, and white, contrasted with the deep red of the finely polished bricks. The tomb was said to have been built by Ghias-ud-Din Tughlak for himself, but was given up by his son Muhammad Tughlak in favor of Rukn-i-Alam, when he passed away from this world during 1330 AD.

Mausoleum of Shah Shams Sabzwari : The mausoleum of Shams-ud-Din, commonly known as Shah Shams Tabrez is located about half a mile to the east of the Fort Site, on the high bank of the old bed of the River Ravi near Aam-Khas Garden. He was a descendant of Imam Jaffer and was born in 1165 AD. He passed away in 1276 AD and the shrine was built by his grandson in 1330 AD. The Tomb is square, 30 feet in height surmounted by a hemispherical dome. It is decorated with ornamental glazed tiles.

Mayura Dance : It is practised by the Kondh tribe during marriages and in the April festivals. 'Pirodi' is the flute used during this dance.

Mayurbhanj : Mayurbhanj is a district of Orissa, India that is situated in the northern part of the state of Orissa. There are four subdivisions: Baripada, Karanjia, Udala, and Rairangpur. Mayurbhanj is famous for its Chhau Dance. In the back drop of Rofty Similipal Forest with gorgeous waterfalls, winding rivers, huge summits and lush green valleys, the district of Mayurbhanj unfolds a vast panorama of nature's beauty. Amid the surroundings evolved a beautiful yet virile dance form, known as famous Chhau Dance. The fame of Mayurbhanj Chhau has crossed geographical limitations and has claimed world wide fans for its beauty, vigour and marvel of the art.

Though Chhau is famous not only in India but World over the origin of word Chhau is yet in mystery. Chhau is believed to have found its origin from "Chhaya" the shadow. But the Chhau performers of Purulia use Mask while dancing and that mask is told as "Chhau". Perhaps Chhau Dance might have derived its name from that mask,the Chhau. Some chhau pundits opine the Chhau has got its name from "Chhaushree". Inarguably, the word chhau has been derived from the word 'CHHAUNI' the camp camped at the time of military operation. The folks say that chhau was performed to entertain the Oriya warriors inside the camp and has spread now knowing no boundaries.

Mazar-e-Quaid : Mazar-e-Quaid refers to the mausoleum of the founder of Pakistan, Muhammad Ali Jinnah. It has now become an icon of Karachi throughout the world. The mausoleum is situated at the heart of the city, completed in 1960s. It is made of beautiful white marble with curved Moorish arches and copper grills reset on an elevated 54 square meters platform. The cool inner sanctum reflects the green of a four-tiered crystal chandelier gifted by the peoples of China. Around the mausoleum there is a park fitted with strong beamed spot lights which at nights project light on the white mausoleum.

The mausoleum is a nice, calm and relaxing place. The glowing tomb can be seen for miles at night.

M Balamuralikrishna : Mangalampalli Balamurali Krishna ((b July 6, 1930) is a legendary Carnatic music composer, poet, vocalist, multi-instrumentalist, innovator and musical iconoclast. His magnificiently rich and instantly recognizable voice extends, with perfect control, over three octaves.

Nearly 400 Carnatic musical compositions are credited to him. New raga(Ganapathi Raga is an Example) some with only three or four notes, and a new tala (rhythm) system are among his iconoclastic innovations. Such innovations have provoked many criticisms, but his musical inventiveness remains unblunted. Top Hindustani (north Indian classical) musicians have collaborated with him in "jugalbandhis" (duets akin to jamming): including Pandit Bhimsen Joshi, Pandit Hariprasad Chaurasia and Smt. Kishori Amonkar, among others.

He appeared as featured soloist with an award-winning British choir, performing the "Gitanjali Suite" with words from Rabindranath Tagore's Nobel Prize-winning poetry and music by Dr. Joel, the noted UK-based Goan composer. His clear diction in several languages prompted an invitation to record Tagore's entire Rabindra Sangeet compositions in Bengali, preserving them for posterity. He has sung in French, and even ventured into jazz fusion, collaborating with the top Carnatic percussion teacher, Sri T.H. Subash Chandran, in a concert for Malaysian royalty.

Honours have pursued him. He was awarded the prestigious "Padma Vibhushan" title by the Indian government, five doctorates, the pro-chancellorship of

Telugu University and numerous top musical honours including Sangeetha Kalanidhi of the Madras Music Academy. The city of Vijayawada in Andhra Pradesh, India, has named a road after him. The record-buying public have supported him enthusiastically, prompting record labels to issue hundreds of his recordings. He has become increasingly interested in music therapy, and now performs only occasionally.

McMahon Line : The McMahon Line, which was originally created by the British during their colonial rule in British India, provides the basis for the eastern sector of the Line of Actual Control between the People's Republic of China (PRC) and Republic of India, running from the border of Bhutan in the west to Myanmar in the east. It is regarded by India as a permanent national border, but is not recognized by the PRC as anything more than a temporary line of control. The PRC claims most of the Indian state of Arunachal Pradesh, which lies to the south of this line, as part of its Tibet Autonomous Region and considers the McMahon Line to be an illegal line of occupation. Currently the armies of both countries are posted on each sides of the Line of Actual Control. The two sides also disagree over the position of the line itself. The Sumdorong Chu Valley, at the westernmost point of the line, is claimed by both sides to lie within their zone of control.

British administrator Sir Henry McMahon drew up the 550-mile McMahon Line as the border between British India and Tibet during the Simla Conference, as Britain sought to advance its line of control and establish buffer zones around its colony in South Asia. The conference took part between Britain, Tibet, and Chinese Empire, which was acknowledged by the British as having suzerainty over Tibet. The Tibetan and British representatives at the conference agreed to the line, which ceded Tawang and other Tibetan areas to British India; however the Chinese representative refused to accept the line because of domestic pressures. The Chinese position since then has been that since China was sovereign over Tibet, the line was invalid without Chinese agreement. As a result, China has not accepted the validity of the McMahon Line and regards India's control of Arunachal Pradesh as an illegal occupation.

For the first two decades after the Simla Conference, the Survey of India did not show the McMahon Line as the border between British India and Tibet either; only in 1937 did they publish a map showing it as the official boundary; in 1938 the Survey of India published a map showing Tawang as a part of Tibet. In 1944, Britain established administrations in the area, from Dirang Dzong in the west to Walong in the east. The situation developed further as India became independent and the People's Republic of China was established in the late 1940s: with the PRC poised to take over Tibet, India unilaterally declared the McMahon Line to be the boundary in November 1950, and forced the Tibetan administration out of the Tawang area in 1951, despite Tibetan and PRC protests.

The issue was quiet during the next decade or so of cordial Sino-Indian relations, but erupted again during the Sino-Indian War of 1962. Troops of the PRC crossed the McMahon Line on the August 26, 1959, and captured an Indian outpost at Longju, a few miles south of the line. They abandoned this in 1961 but in October 1962 crossed the line once again, this time in force, beginning the Sino-Indian War. After striking toward the Tanglha ridge and Tawang, which is near the Bhutan border, the PRC later extended their attack across the whole frontier. Deep inroads were made at a number of points. However, the PRC agreed to withdraw back to the McMahon Line and returned Indian prisoners of war in 1963. The Indian government attributes this to the preparedness of India to defend the plains of Assam, the superiority of the Indian Air Force, and logistical problems of the PRC; the PRC government maintains that political considerations were the only factor in their retreat.

Mecca Masjid : Mecca Masjid in Hyderabad, India is one of the oldest and the biggest mosques in India. Muhammed Quli Qutub Shah, the 6th Sultan of Hyderabad began building it in 1617 under the supervision of Mir Faizullah Baig and Rangiah Choudhary. The work continued during the reign of Abdullah Qutub Shah and Abul Hassan Tana Shah and was completed in 1694 by the Moghal Emperor Aurangzeb. It took about 8000 masons and 77 years to be completed.

This mosque stands 100 yards southwest of the Charminar and is believed to be comprised of bricks brought from Mecca, which were built into the central arch and hence the name.

The hall of the mosque is about 75 feet high, 220 feet wide and 180 feet long, each of the two octagonal columns on either side are made out of a single piece of granite, which took five years to quarry. The courtyard houses a large pond flanked by slab seats. Legend has it that a visitor who sits on one of these seats will definitely return to Hyderabad. The mosque is also said to contain sacred relics, one of which is the hair of Prophet Muhammad.

Medak : Medak is located in Medak District in Telangana region of Andhra Pradesh, India. It is 100 km to the north of Hyderabad. Medak, a historic town originally called Siddapur, reached its pinnacle during the kakatiya reign. Medak has a citadel dating back to the Kakatiyas. It was built during the reign of Kakatiya emperor Prataparudra. Strategically built on a hillock, it was called the Methukudurgam, from the Telugu word Methuku - meaning cooked rich grain. The main entrance proudly displays the double-headed bird "Gandabherundam" of the Kakatiyas. The Medak fort stands as an epitome of architectural excellence of the Kakatiya Empire.

Pocharam Forest & Wildlife Sanctuary, located 15 km from Medak and 115 km from Hyderabad, was the favourite hunting ground of the Nizam and was declared a wild life sanctuary in the early part of 20th century. Named after the Pocharam lake formed from bunding of the Allair in the years 1916 - 1922, it is spread over 9.12 km^2. Surrounded by lush green forest, it is rich in flora and fauna and attracts a lot of winged visitors, like the bar-headed goose, Brahminy bucks and open-billed stork. There is a center for Eco-Tourism where visitors can see five species of antelopes and deer.

Medha Patkar : Medha Patkar is an eminent social activist from India. As the leader of Narmada Bachao Andolan (Save Narmada Movement), she alongwith Baba Amte, tribal activists, environmentalists and human rights activists, spearheaded the movement against Sardar Sarovar Dam being built across Narmada river in Gujarat, India.

Prior to being a social activist, Medha did her M.A. is Social Work from Tata Institute of Social Sciences. She left her position on the faculty of Tata Institute of Social Sciences as well as her unfinished Ph.D. when she became immersed in the tribal and peasant communities in Maharashtra, Madhya Pradesh and Gujarat eventually organized as the Narmada Bachao Andolan. She gained fame through the andolan making her a known name throughout India. She is one of the recipients of Right Livelihood Award for the year 1991. Medha Patkar has received numerous other awards, including the Deena Nath Mangeshkar Award, Mahatma Phule Award, Goldman

Environment Prize, Green Ribbon Award for Best International Political Campaigner by BBC, and the Human Rights Defender's Award from Amnesty International.

Meera Jasmine : Meera Jasmine is a leading South Indian actress, who has acted in hit movies in Malayalam, Tamil, Telugu and Kannada, and won India's National Award for Best Actress.

Meera has consistently impressed in good roles in all South Indian languages, and made herself a reputed name in the South Indian film circuit.

Meerut : Meerut is an ancient city located to the north-east of New Delhi in the state of Uttar Pradesh, India. Meerut also has one of the major army cantonments in this part of the country. Meerut can also refer to the district in which Meerut is located. Meerut is famously associated with the Indian rebellion of 1857 against the British East India Company when chants of popular Urdu slogan "Dilli Chalo" (lets march to Delhi) were first raised here. Meerut cantonment is the place where the rebellion started when Hindu and Muslim soldiers were given rifle cartridges with a coating made of animal fat. The bullet wrapping was to be opened by mouth before use, which affected religious sensibilities of both Muslims and Hindus as the animal coating was alleged to be composed of pork and beef. Meerut was also the place of severe religious strife between Hindus and Muslims in 1987. The city was afflicted with more communal violence in the late 80s and early 90s. Things have somewhat calmed down since the early 90s and there have been no major communal skirmishes between Hindus and Muslims for over a decade now.

Meghaduuta : Meghaduuta is a lyrical poem written by Kalidasa, considered to be one of the greatest Sanskrit poets. A short poem of only 111 stanzas, it is one of

Kalidasa's most famous works. It recounts how a yaksha, after being exiled for a year to central India for some unknown transgression, convinces a passing cloud to take a message to his wife on Mount Kailasa in the Himalayan Mountains. The yaksha accomplishes this by describing the many beautiful sights the cloud will see on its northward course to the city of Alakaa, where his wife awaits his return. Meghaduuta has gained a lot of attention in recent years beacuase of a queer fact that it includes the exact description of terestrial forms as could be seen from a high flying aircraft, which supposedly did not exist during those days.

Meghalaya : Meghalaya is a small state in north-eastern India. It is a hilly strip in the eastern part of the country about 300 km long (East-West) and 100 km wide, with a total area of about 22,429 sq km. The population numbered 2,175,000 in 2000. The state is bounded on the north by Assam and by Bangladesh on the south. The capital is Shillong, which has a population of 260,000. Meghalaya was originally part of Assam. On 21 January 1972 the Garo, Khasi and Jaintia Hills districts of western Assam became the new state of Meghalaya.

Meghalaya is known as "The Abode of Clouds". The climate of Meghalaya is moderate but humid, the average annual rainfall going as high as 1200 cm in some areas, making it the wettest state of India. The town of Cherrapunji, south of capital Shillong holds the world record for most rain in a calendar month while the village of Mawsynram, near town of Cherrapunji holds the distinction of seeing the heaviest yearly rains. About one third of the state is forested. The ranges of the Garo Hills in the west, Khasi Hills, and Jaintia Hills in the east are not especially high, with Shillong Peak the highest point at 1,965 m. Many caves are known to exist with unique limestone structures forming curious stalactites and stalagmites.

Tribal peoples make up about 85 percent of Meghalaya's population. The Khasi, the largest group, followed by the Garos, were among those known to the British as "hill tribes". Other groups include the Jaintias and the Hajong (40,000). About fifteen percent of the population is defined as non-tribal; these include about 54,000 Bengalis and 49,000 Shaikhs. Meghalaya is one of three states in India to have a Christian majority; the other two (Nagaland and Mizoram) are also in the north-east of India. A sizeable minority (16%) of the population follow an ancient Animist philosophy.

Meghalaya Subtropical Forests : The Meghalaya subtropical forests is a montane subtropical moist broadleaf forest ecoregion of eastern India. The ecoregion covers an area of 41,700 square kilometers (16,100 square miles), encompassing the Khasi Hills, Garo Hills, and Jaintia Hills of India's Meghalaya state, and adjacent portions of Assam state. The ecoregion covers those portions of the Khasi, Garo, and Jaintia hills lying above 1000 meters elevation. The subtropical forests lie between the tropical lowland lowland Lower Gangetic Plains moist deciduous forests to the south and west, and the Brahmaputra Valley semi-evergreen forests to the north. The ecoregion is one of the wettest in the world, with some places, notably Mawsynram and Cherrapunji, receiving up to eleven meters of rain in a year. The ecoregion is considered one of the most species-rich in India, with a rich diversity of birds, mammals, and plants.

Meghna River : Meghna river is one of the major rivers in Bangladesh, specially famous for its great estuary that discharges the flows of the Ganges-Padma, the Brahmaputra-Jamuna and the Meghna itself. The downstream of Surma river from Ajmiriganj is often referred to as the Meghna. The matter would be simpler but for the fact that from Madna downstream for about

26 km (in a straight line) one of the two channels of the Surma-Meghna is known as the Dhaleshwari. The channel from Ajmiriganj down to the confluence with the Dhanu is referred to as the Surma. This confluence is five kilometres east of Kuliarchar and north of Bhairab Bazar. Downstream from this point, the river is referred to as the Meghna. The Meghna has two distinct parts. The Upper Meghna from Kuliarchar to Shatnol is a comparatively small river. The Lower Meghna below Shatnol is one of the largest rivers in the world because of its wide estuary mouth. The Lower Meghna is at times treated as a separate river.

Meghnad Saha : Meghnad Saha, one of the famous Physicist was born in Saroyatali village in Dacca (now in Bangladesh). He invented an instrument to measure the weight and pressure of solar rays.

Dr. Saha produced the famous equation which he called 'equation of the reaction—isobar for ionization' which later became known as Saha's "Thermo-Ionization Equation". Saha was the leading spirit in organizing the scientific societies like the 'National Academy of Science' (1930), 'Indian Institute of Science' (1935) and the 'Indian Association for the Cultivation of Science' (1944). The lasting memorial to him is the 'Saha Institute of Nuclear Physics' founded in 1943 in Calcutta. He was the chief architect of river planning in India. He prepared the original plan for Damodar Valley Project.

Mehdi Hasan : Mehdi Hasan is a well-known Pakistani ghazal singer. He was born in Luna, Rajasthan, India, and has lived and worked in Pakistan. The King of Ghazal started his career from Radio Pakistan in 1952 by singing the hit ghazal "Gulon me rang bharey bad-e-naubahar chale". And, thereafter, he never looked back but went on singing one hit after the other over a span of 50 years totaling over 30,000 geets and ghazals. His popularity among the masses shot him to the pinnacles of glory and made him Pakistan's supreme vocalist.

Mehdi Hassan has now made Karachi his permanent residence and whenever he visits Lahore he spends most of his time with his children and other family members. Mehdi Hassan's voice and unique performance skills in ghazal singing were unmatched in the world of South Asian music. The 60s and 70s can be named Mehdi Hassan's decades', as there was hardly any hero of the Pakistani musical scene on whom Mehdi Hassan's songs were not filmed. Mehdi Hassan hails from a family with a rich music tradition. Talat Aziz is one of his famous disciples. He is universally acclaimed as the finest ghazal singer of his time, perhaps of all time. His unsurpassable vocal range and his mastery over even the most difficult of raags makes him the undisputed emperor of ghazals. His popularity amongst the masses, appreciation by the masses, and continued success over five decades makes him on par with Noor Jehan and Nusrat Fateh Ali Khan in the league of the greatest Pakistani singers of all time. There is no better tribute to his greatness than the observation by the eternal nightingale, Lata Mangeshkar, that "God sings through Mehdi Hassan".

Meherangarh Fort : This fort is situated at the Fort Road in Rajasthan. Opens at 0830 to 1300 and 1430 to 1700. Entry fee -Rs.50, This fort was build in the year 1459 by Rao Jodha. This fort included several palaces.The Moti Mahal (Pearl palace), Phool Mahal (flower palace), Sheesh Mahal (glass palace) and the other apartments exquisitely decorated, with paintings on ceilings, walls and even on the floors. The museum at the palace have rooms filled with lavish royal palanquins, thrones, paintings. We get an excellent view of the city from the ramparts of the Fort.

Mehrgarh : Mehrgarh was an ancient settlement in South Asia and is one of the most important sites in archaeology for the study of the earliest neolithic settlements in that region. The remains are located in Balochistan, Pakistan, on the Kachi plain near the Bolan Pass, to the west of the Indus River valley and between the present-day cities of Quetta, Kalat and Sibi.

Mehrgarh is sometimes cited as the earliest known farming settlement in South Asia, based on archaeological excavations from 1974 (Jarrige et al). The earliest evidence of settlement dates from 7000 BCE. It is also cited for the earliest evidence of pottery in South Asia. Archaeologists divide the occupation at the site into several periods. The chalcolithic people of Mehrgarh also had contacts with northern Afghanistan, northeastern Iran and even with the southern part of central Asia.

Meiteis : The Meiteis are the majority ethnic race of valley of Manipur, and because of this are sometimes refered to as Manipuris. The Meitei people are made up of seven tribes, or clans, which trace their history back to around the 1st century. Meitei women have always enjoyed equal status with men, and today they work in nearly every social and economic sphere of society; in particular, they control the Meitei markets and the trade in vegetables and traditional clothing. The Meitei people are well-known for their sporting prowess, hockey and polo are traditional and the Meitei for of martial art, thang ta, has recently been recognised as one of the official forms of international martial arts.

The major population is concentrated in the Imphal valley of Manipur, Cachar valley of Assam, Tripura, Bangladesh and Myanmar. Majority of the Meiteis are followers of Vaishnavite Hinduism mixed with traditional beliefs. A section of the Meiteis follows ancient Meitei religion called Sanamahi laining. Meitei Pangal, a section of the larger Meitei ethnic group follows Islam. There are some individuals who follow religions like Christianity and the Bahá'í Faith.

Meithei Language : Meithei/Manipuri (also Meitei, Manipuri, Meiteilon) is the predominant language and lingua-franca in the state of Manipur, in northeastern India. It is the official language in government offices. Meithei has proven to be a large integrating factor among all ethnic groups in Manipur who use it to communicate among themselves. Meithei has been recognized as the Manipuri language by the Indian Union and has been included in the list of scheduled languages (included in the 8th schedule by the 71st amendment of the constitution in 1992). Meithei is taught as a subject up to the Post-graduate level (Ph.D.) in Universities of India, apart from being a medium of instruction upto the undergraduate level in Manipur.

Melli : Melli is a town on the West Bengal-Sikkim border on the River Teesta. The appellation Melli in Nepali means the place where the dead are cremated. Melli is one of the few towns present in India that lie in two different states. A bridge connects the two parts of the town. The part of the town in West Bengal is also called as Melli Bazaar. The town lies on National Highway 31A connecting Siliguri to Gangtok.

The town lies at an elevation of about 100 m. It is located 7 km upstream from Teesta Bazaar. On the Sikkimese side, the Yuksom Breweries, which produces most of the beer in the region, is based. The breweries and a biscuit factory are the major industries in the region. River rafting can also be undertaken from this point. Kalimpong, the largest town in the region lies 20 km away from Melli. Local made rum and whisky are available in the Sikkimese side at prices which are lower than most of India.

Memon : The Memon people are an Indo-Aryan ethnic group that originated in Sindh province of what is now Pakistan and later settled in Gujarat. They speak an Indo-Aryan language called Memoni, that is similar to Sindhi and Gujarati. Some estimates put the number of Memons worldwide over one million. The word Memon is derived from Arabic word Momin meaning faithful. Memons are Sunni Hanafi Muslims, and they originated when a group of Hindus from Sindh belonging to the Kshatriya Lohana caste converted to Islam by Sufi missionaries of the Qadiri order.

Memons are known for their involvement in business and philanthropy, with Memon immigrants having played a major part in the building of Pakistani industry, although an increasing number of Memons are turning to professional occupations. The success of many Memons has aroused some jealousy from other ethnic groups, who sometimes stereotype Memons as being stingy. Owing to their tradition of management and attention to detail, the Memons are one of the most prosperous communities in South Asia and else where. They have built vast business legacies and most Memons around the world belong to the upper-middle class. The Memon language is falling into disuse in many parts of the world.

Memorial Obelisk : There are no architectural remains of the British period except a memorial obelisk, which is located in the center of the Fort. It was built in the memory of Agnew and Anderson who were murdered in 1848. It is 50 feet high with five steps to a pedestal five feet high.

Menander I : Menander I (also known as Milinda in Sanskrit, Pali), was one of the Greek kings of the Indo-Greek Kingdom in northern India from 155 or 150 to 130 BC. His territories covered the eastern dominions of the divided Greek empire of Bactria (from the areas of the

Panjshir and Kapisa) and extended to the modern Pakistani province of Punjab with diffuse tributaries to the south and east, probably as far as Mathura. His capital is supposed to have been Sagala, a very prosperous city in northern Punjab (modern Sialkot). Sagala, modern Sialkot, was a city of located in northern Punjab, Pakistan. Sagala was used as a capital by the Greco-Bactrian (alternatively Indo-Greek or Graeco-Indian) king Menander during his reign between 160 and 135 B.C.

Though many Graeco-Bactrian, and even some Indo-Greek cities were designed along Greek architectural lines, Sagala was clearly an Indian city. In contrast to other imperialist governments elsewhere, literary accounts suggests the Greeks and Indians of cities like Sagala lived in relative harmony, with some Indians adopting the responsibilities of Greek citizenship—and more astonishingly, Greeks converting to Buddhism. The best descriptions of Sagala however, come from the Milinda Panha, a dialogue between king Menander and the Buddhist monk Nagasena. Historians like Sir Tarn believe this document was written around 100 years after Menander's rule, which is one of the best enduring testimonies of the productiveness and benevolance of his rule, which has made the more modern theory that he was regarded as a Chakravartin—King of the Wheel or literally Wheel-Turner in Sansrkit—generally accepted.

Meola Glacier : Meola Glacier or Athasi-Balati glacier is the Himalayan glacier situated in the eastern part of Uttaranchal in the Pithoragarh district of India.Meola Glacier is located at the base of five peaks of Panchchuli in the Lassar Yankti valley.With Sona glacier it forms the famous Panchchuli glacier as mixed glacial system.One can reach here as glacial trek through Tawaghat-Bailing-Son—Duktu-Tidang.Sona glacier and Meola glacier serves the route to climb Panchchuli peaks from east direction.Sona glacier is situated north to Meola glacier.The snout of the Meola glacier is at one hour's trek along Duktu Nala from Duktu village.Snout of Meola is situated at an altitude of 3,600 M. This place also serves as BC for Panchchuli expeditions. Meola glacier is divided in to Lower and upper parts.

Mer Dance : It is another variation of the Dandiya Raas in which the dance begins with a slow tempo but gains momentum gradually.

Mer Raas : The Mers of Saurashtra are known for their folk dance called the Mer Raas. White shepherds perform what is called the Gher Raas. The Gheria Raas is a dance performed by the agriculturists of south Gujarat. Hallisaka a group dance, in the Harivamsa Purana is very significant. This is a group dance, in a circular formation with the hands joined together forming a chain. The time (Tala) is kept by clapping and is accompanied by singing. A young man (Krishna) stands in the middle of the damsels. The feet movements, toes, heels and legs first start their journey to explore rhythmic expression measured steps, long, short, quick, and slow accompanied in single, double and triple timings.

Metumniu Festival : In Nagaland, the Yimchungrüs celebrate Metumniu festival from 4th to 8th August every year. This festival is connected with prayers for the souls of the departed ones. The festival is spread over five days and has separate names for the days, SHITO, ZHIHTO, ZUMTO, KHEHRESUK, SHERESUK. The festival also has strong agricultural base and the agricultural implements are sharpened and worshipped.

Mewar : Mewar is a region of south-central Rajasthan state in western India. It includes the present-day districts of Bhilwara, Chittorgarh, Rajsamand and Udaipur. The region was for centuries a Rajput kingdom that later became a princely state under the British. It was ruled by the Guhilot and Sisodia dynasties for over 1200 years.

The northern part of Mewar is a gently sloping plain, drained by the Banas River and its tributaries, which empty northwest into the Chambal River, a tributary of the Yamuna River. The southern part of the region is hilly, and marks the divide between the Banas and its tributaries and the headwaters of the Sabarmati and Mahi rivers and their tributaries, which drain south into the Gulf of Cambay through Gujarat state. The Aravalli Range forms the northwestern boundary of the region, composed mostly of sedimentary rocks, like marble and Kota stone, which has traditionally been an important construction material. The Marwar region lies across the Aravalli Range to the northwest, Gujarat and the Vagad region of Rajasthan lie to the south, the Malwa region of Madhya Pradesh state lies to the southeast, and the Hadoti region of Rajasthan lies to the east.

The region is part of the Kathiawar-Gir dry deciduous forests' ecoregion. Protected areas include the Jaisamand Wildlife Sanctuary, the Kumbhalgarh Wildlife Sanctuary, the Bassi Wildlife Sanctuary and the Sitamata Game Sanctuary. Mewar has a tropical climate. Rainfall averages 660 mm/ year, and is generally higher in the southwest and lower in the northeast of the region. Over 90% of the rain typically falls in the period June to September every year, during the southwest monsoon.

Mewat : Mewat is a region of Rajasthan and Haryana states in northwestern India. Mewat's boundaries are not precisely determined, but generally include Alwar, Bharatpur, and Dholpur districts of Rajasthan, and Gurgaon and Faridabad districts of Haryana. The region corresponds to the ancient kingdom of Matsya, founded in the 5th century BCE. Mewati is the chief language or dialect of the region.

MGR : Dr Marudur Gopalamenon Ramachandran (January 17, 1917–December 24, 1987), popularly known as Dr MGR and Puratchi Thalaivar (tamil: Revolutionary Leader), was a long time Tamil film actor and Chief Minister of the Indian state of Tamil Nadu from 1977 until his death.

MGR was born at Kandy, Sri Lanka, to Maradhur Gopala Menon and Satyabhama who were of the Nair caste from the state of Kerala in Southern India. After his father's death, MGR settled with his family at Kumbakonam in Tamil Nadu. Making his film debut in 1936, in the film Sati Leelavathi, MGR did not attain great popularity until his role in the 1947 film Rajakumari. He rose to stardom by playing characters that potrayed him as the saviour of the poor. His movies were the medium of communication for the Dravidian movement. For the next twenty-five years he remained one of the biggest celebrities in Tamil cinema.

He was a vocal Tamil and Dravidian nationalist and prominent member of the DMK (Dravidian Progressive Federation). In 1953, MGR joined the Dravida Munnetra Kazhagam. He became a member of the state Legislative Council in 1962. He was first elected to the Tamil Nadu Legislative Assembly in 1967. He added glamour to the Dravidian movement which was sweeping Tamil Nadu. He enjoyed unending support during his time as Chief Minister. He placed great emphasis on social development, especially education. He was posthumously awarded the "Bharat Ratna" by the President of India. After his death, his political party, the All India Anna Dravida Munnetra Kazhagam, split between his wife Janaki Ramachandran and his long time companion and political protege, J. Jayalalitha.

Mian Mohammad Nawaz Sharif : Mian Mohammad Nawaz Sharif was born on December 25, 1949 in Lahore,

Punjab, Pakistan. Nawaz Sharif was twice elected as Prime Minister of Pakistan, serving two non-consecutive terms. His first term was from November 1, 1990 to July 18, 1993, and his second term was from February 17, 1997 to October 12, 1999. His party is the Pakistan Muslim League N (Nawaz group). His rule came to an abrupt end following the overthrow of his government by the General Pervez Musharraf-led military coup in 1999 months after the Kargil War.

Sharif was born in Lahore, the son of Mian Mohammad Sharif, then the owner of a relatively modest cast-iron parts business who later became a prominent industrialist and later a joint owner of the Ittefaq Group of Industries. Nawaz Sharif became politically prominent after General Muhammad Zia-ul-Haq declared martial law over Pakistan in 1977. Sharif served as finance minister of the province of the Punjab under the dispensation of General Zia, and was later the provincial (Punjab) chief minister. Although the military government is credited with his political debut, Sharif became an important figure in Pakistani politics when elected government was restored in 1988 after General Zia's death, gaining a significant electoral constituency in his hometown Lahore that he has managed to retain.

Michael Madhusudan Dutt (Datta) : He is a famous 19th century Bengali poet and dramatist. He was born in the village Sagardari, Jessore District, Bengal (now in Bangladesh). He was an important pioneer in dramatic writing. He wrote Meghnadh-bodh Kabbo, a grand heroic-tragic epic in nine cantos which is quite unique in the body of Bengali literature. He also wrote poems about the sorrows and hurts of love spoken by women.

Michael Madhusudan Dutt : Michael Madhusudan Dutt (Datta), (1824-1873) is a famous 19th century Bengali poet and dramatist. He was born in the village Sagardari,

Jessore District, Bengal (now in Bangladesh). He was an important pioneer in dramatic writing. He wrote Meghnadh Bodh Kabya, a grand heroic-tragic epic in nine cantos which is quite unique in the body of Bengali literature. He also wrote poems about the sorrows and hurts of love spoken by women. From an early age he had a desire to be like an Englishman. To the displeasure of his family Michael converted to Christianity, taking the Christian name of Michael. However, at his later age, he repented for his desire for England and talked ardently of his homeland. His poems and sonnets from this period reflect his emotions. Madhusudan is widely considered to be one of the greatest poets in Bengali literature. He died in Kolkata, India on 29 June 1873.

Mid-day : Mid-day is an afternoon newspaper in Mumbai (Bombay). It was established in 1979 as a family owned newspaper. Mid-day is owned by Mid Day Multimedia Ltd., a publishing house listed on the Bombay Stock Exchange and National Stock Exchange. It publishes the the newspaper in three languages: English, Gujarati and Urdu. It also has a special sunday edition, the Sunday Mid-day. The newspaper publishes three editions: An early morning, a noon and a late evening edition. Its slogan is Delivering Mumbai.

Middle Button National Park : This park set up in 1979 is spread over an area of 64sq.km in the Andaman district. It is 60km away from the nearest town of long island. The capital town and the airport Port Blair is at a distance of 200km. It is an Island with most deciduous forests. The fauna of the park consists of spotted deer, monitor, lizard and marine species. The suitable period for visit is December to April.

Mihir Sen : Mihir Sen was the first Asian who have crossed the English Channel. He was born on 16th

November 1930 in Purulia (West Bengal). He was a lawyer by profession, a barrister of Kolkatta High court.

In 1966, he established 5 important records and became an extra ordinary salt water swimmer. In 1958, Mihir Sen swam across the English Channel, in 1966 he crossed the Palk strait, followed by Gibralter Dar-E-Daniyal, Wasphorus and Panama. He thus established the record of swimming the longest distance. He is a matchless swimmer, having swam more than 600km in sea/ocean water. In 1959 he was awarded "Padma Shree" and in 1967 "Padma Bhushan". He brought glory to his motherland by creating records and earning a place in Guinness Book of World Record.

Miji : The Miji, also known by the names of Sajolang and Damai, inhabit in the districts of West Kameng and East Kameng in Arunachal Pradesh. Their population of 5,000 are found near the lower parts of the sub-Himalayan hills bordering Assam. Combining ancestry of their Tibetan and Assamese counterparts, most Assamese possess a reddish-red and fair complexion. Isolated from the rest of the world, they sustain their livehood through Swidden agriculture.

Yet simple, the dress of the Miji reflects elegant styles. The women wear an ankle-length white garment with another additional external beautifully decorated red jacket. Large silver ring-shaped earrings and coloured necklaces, usually made of jade serves as the principal ornaments for the women. A fillet of silver chains may also be worn around the head by the richer women, and pine-resin is sometimes extracted to manufacture indigenious cosmetics. The Miji are followers of the Animistic Donyi-Polo faith, known as Phong kelum, with some Buddhist influence, notably in their rites. Of late, they have subtly adapted the Roman script for writing their language, because they did not have an indigenous script of their own. A few have adopted Christianity.

Mikir Hills : Mikir Hills regarded as the north-eastern corner of the Indian Shield separated by the Rangpur Saddle. In the northeast of the Shillong Plateau, the Mikir Hills constitute an Archaean inlier, projecting through the Alluvium and fringed with more or less horizontal Tertiary beds (66 to 2 million years ago), and in one small area overlain by a probable Mesozoic trap (245 to 66 million years ago). The Mikir Hills are comprised of coarse-grained porphyritic granites and fine-grained strongly banded gneisses. The general strike of the foliation of the gneisses is E-W; the dip is either vertical or steep. The gneisses, which are usually fresh and uncrushed, consist of quartz, plagioclase, rare orthoclase, brown biotite, and green hornblende.

Graphic and micropegmatitic structures are frequently seen amongst the quartz and the plagioclase. Occasional veins of quartz are seen in the gneisses. Hypersthene bearing gneisses are also observed at certain places, similar in all respects to the charnockite of Madras, and intimately interbanded along the foliation planes of the gneisses. The thickness of the hypersthene bearing rocks varies from six metres to nine metres. They are coarse-grained and fresh, with little signs of crushing. The groundmass is chiefly composed of quartz grains and slightly decomposed plagioclase with much hypersthene scattered through it. Trap dykes are unexpectedly rare in the Mikir Hills

Milam Glacier : At Munsiyari,in Pithoragarh district of Uttaranchal,India, at an altitude of 3,872 M, mighty Milam Glacier is situated. It spread of around 37 square kms and 16 kms long. Surrounded by 52 high Himalayan peaks. So it lies at the base of the great Himalayan wall and situated on the south facing slope of the main

Himalayan range.It originates from the slope of Kohli and Trishuli peaks.The subsidiary glaciers coming off the peaks of Mangraon (6,568 m), Deo Damla (6,637 m), and Sakram (6,254 m) on the eastern rim of the Nanda Devi sanctuary flows into it.It is fed by the Nanda Devi on the west, and the Ralam Gad and the Pyunsani Gadhera emerging off the western flank of the mighty Panchachuli, Rajrambha and Chaudhara peaks and Kalabaland-Burfu Kalganga glacier system from the east.This mixed glacier system is the source of Goriganga river,which originates from the south of Milam Glacier.Munsiyari is the base for trek to Milam.

Military of Bangladesh : The Bangladesh Army, Navy, and Air Force are composed of regular military personnel. Some of the senior officers and noncommissioned officers served in the Military of Pakistan before the 1971 independence war. Senior officers include "repatriates" who were interned in Pakistan during the war, and "freedom fighters" who fought against Pakistan. In addition to traditional defense roles, the military has been called on to provide support to civil authorities for disaster relief and internal security.

The Bangladesh Air Force and Navy, with about 7,000 personnel each, perform traditional military missions. A Coast Guard has been recently formed, under the Home Ministry, to play a stronger role in the area of anti-smuggling, anti-piracy, and protection of offshore resources. Recognition of economic and fiscal constraints has led to the establishment of several paramilitary and auxiliary forces, including the 40,000-member Bangladesh Rifles; the Ansars and Village Defense Parties Organization, which claims 64 members in every village in the country; and a 5,000-member specialized police unit known as the Armed Police. The Bangladesh Rifles, under the authority of the Home Ministry, are commanded by army officers who are seconded to the organization.

In addition to in-country military training, some advanced and technical training takes place abroad, including grant-aid training in the United States. People's Republic of China, Pakistan, and eastern Europe are the major defense suppliers to Bangladesh, but military leaders are trying to find affordable alternatives to Chinese equipment. A 2,300-member Bangladesh Army contingent served with coalition forces during the 1991 Gulf war. Bangladesh is currently the leading contributor (with 9,457 members) to United Nations peacekeeping operations, with an infantry battalion in UNIKOM (Kuwait), an engineer battalion in UNTAET, (East Timor) and another infantry battalion scheduled for service in Sierra Leone in May 2000.

Milkha Singh : Milkha Singh is a Sikh athlete, who represented India in the 1960 Rome Olympics and the 1964 Summer Olympics in Tokyo. He is nicknamed "The Flying Sikh". Milkha Singh lost his parents in the Partition of India and the chaos that ensued. He reached India from Pakistan in the cross border trains carrying refugees.

Milkha Singh broke the olympic record for the 400 meter run in September 1960. He won the gold medal at the 1958 Asian Games in the 200 meter and 400 meter category. He also won the gold medal at the 1962 Asian Games.

Milkha Singh is as one of the most extraordinary athletes of our times. He was a genius and a genius is never trained. Without any formal training, without any financial reward and without any emotional support Milkha Singh took on the greatest athletes of his time and proved himself as good if not better. After retirement, Milkha Singh holds the appointment of Director of Sports in Punjab. He is a recipient of the Padma Shri.

Millat Party : The Millat Party is a political party in Pakistan, formed by Sardar Farooq Ahmad Khan Leghari, former president of Pakistan, once he was no longer the president, and needed a platform to survive politically. He had the money to start a small-scale party. Because of his support to the establishment, a number of people joined him. Millat Party is now part of the ruling coalition where it is represented by Sardar Farooq Leghari's son, Owais Leghari. At the last legislative elections, 20 october 2002, the party was part of the National Alliance, that won 4.6 % of the popular vote and 12 out of 272 elected members.

Minicoy Island : Minicoy Island or Maliku is the only inhabited island in Maliku Atoll and it is the second largest and the southern-most island of the Laccadive Archipelago north of the Maldives. The locals call the island Maliku, as do the Maldivians, while it is Minikkoy in Malayalam and it is Malik in Hindi. The nearest island is Thuraakunu in the Republic of Maldives. The island is administered by India under the Indian Union Territory of Lakshadweep. On the southern side of the island lies the uninhabited islet of Viringili.

Minicoy has a culture very different from that of any other island in the Union Territory. Dress, language, and food are similar to the non-Indian Maldive islands to the south of Minicoy. Mahl is the language spoken on the island. The language employs the unique Thaana script, written from right to left. Until the 16th century, the Laccadives appear to have been under the suzerainty of the Kolthari Raja of Chirakkal in what is now the Indian state of Kerala, until it was surrendered to the British East India Company by Ali Raja of Cannanore on December 18, 1790. However, the Rajas continued to administer Minicoy after paying a tribute to the East India Company, until the Governor General of the Presidency of Madras abolished the coir monopoly run by the Rajas from Minicoy. In 1857, suzerainty over Minicoy was transferred from the East India Company to the Indian Empire when Queen Victoria was proclaimed Empress. Finally in 1905 Ali Raja surrendered sovereignty and control over Minicoy to the Empire, and Minicoy was officially signed over to the Emperor Edward VII by Ali Raja's successor. In August 1947, Minicoy was passed to India as the Empire withdrew its control. On November 1, 1956, India formally annexed Minicoy and incorporated it into the Union Territory of Minicoy and Laccadive Islands, renamed Lakshadweep in 1973.

Mir Ashraf Ali : Mir Ashraf Ali a contemporary and courtier of Nawab Nusrat Jang (1785-1822) and Nawab shamsuddaula (1822-1831), naib nazims of Dhaka. Mir Ashraf Ali came to Dhaka from Shiraz, Iran. His father's name was Mir Ali Mahdi. Mir Ashraf Ali was the biggest landlord and as such the wealthiest person of East Bengal. His landed properties in Dhaka, Tripura (Comilla), Bakerganj (Barisal), Mymensingh and Chittagong districts. The monthly income from that property at that time was Taka twenty thousand. Hundreds of farmers used to work under him and many people in Dhaka city had been benefited by his donations.

Ashraf Ali's zamindari (estate) was in Baldakhad of Comilla district. His house at Muradnagar Upazila is in ruins now. His permanent residence was near the Ramna Racecourse (todays Suhrawardi Udyan), near Phulbaria, in between Babupura Police station and Dhaka Hall extension. He had several beautiful buildings at this place.

Ashraf Ali was a loyal subject of the east india company. In the First of Tripura wars (1824-26) he supplied provisions to the British army and went to the Tripura frontiers to join the British war effort with thousands of soldiers. When the company wanted to pay for it he refused to take anything. When they wanted to give him the title of Khan Bahadur, he declined and asked that his sons be given the title. Accordingly the company government conferred the title on his sons Syed Ali Mahdi and Syed Ali Hasan in the third decade of the nineteenth century and they were given the right to use the silver mace. Mir Asraf Ali died in Dhaka in 1829.

Mir Bahr : Mir Bahr was the head of the navy during the Sultanate and Mughal periods. Sometimes it was called nawwara. The head of the nawwara was called Mir Bahr or Admiral. In Bengal Iwaz Khalji (1212-1227 AD) first organised the navy. Since Bengal is a riverain country and the rivers are over flooded during the rains, cavalry and elephants were inactive for almost half of the year. That is why nawwara was established and Bengal's flotilla of war-boats proved to be most effective. In the Mughal period, Islam Khan strengthened the nawwara, and thus subjugated almost the whole of Bengal.

Mir Jafar Ali Khan : Mir Jafar Ali Khan (born 1691 – died February 5, 1765). He succeeded Siraj-Ud-Daulah Bengal as Nawab of Bengal. His rule is widely considered the start of British rule in India. An Arab by descent Mir Jafar came to Bengal as a penniless adventurer. He took up a job in Nawab's army and slowly promoted himself. Nawab Ali Vardi Khan later gave him the hand of his half-sister and seven thousand horses to command.

Arrogant in his position he took advantage of an Ali Vardi Khan weakened by a decade of fighting with Marathas to enter into a conspiracy with Ataullah to overthrow and murder the Nawab. The conspiracy was unearthed and he was stripped of most of his powers. He returned to Murshidabad, where he regained the trust of the Nawab's nephew, Siraj-Ud-Daulah, and slowly returned to power and prominence.

Soon after Ali Vardi Khan's natural death Siraj Ud Daulah became the Nawab of Bengal at Murshidabad. On ascending the throne, he made the controversial decision of elevating a kayasth named Mohanlal as his supreme Diwan. This elevation of a lower caste Hindu to such a prominent position caused the established nobility, and in particular Mir Jafar, great offence. He was then the bakshi or head of the armed forces, second only to the Nawab, and the elevation of Mohanlal to a post above him was taken almost as a personal insult. He became determined to overthrow Siraj-Ud-Daulah and gain the Nawabi for himself. His opportunity came when Shiraj-Ud-Daulah was distracted in his campaign against the British. Siraj-Ud-Daulah's behaviour had alienated many of his nobles, and many lent a sympathetic ear. Unfortunately, Siraj-Ud-Daulah returned victorious from Kolkata and discovered the conspiracy; he demoted Mir Jafar and appointed Mir Madan as the new bakshi.

Mir Jafar was left smarting under this new insult while Siraj-Ud-Daulah was busy with his campaign against the British. On 1st May 1757, the British Calcutta Council made a secret treaty with Mir Jafar, promising to place him on the throne of Bengal. Meanwhile, the British had recovered from initial setbacks against Siraj-Ud-Daulah. Siraj-Ud-Daulah was soon on the run, retreating to Murshidabad and attempting to win back the favor of Mir Jafar and obtain the backing of the considerable military force still under Jafar's command. Though no longer Bakshi, Mir Jafar retained a substantial number of foot soldiers and cavalry. Mir Jafar, it is recorded, was not particularly impressed by the promises of the notoriously cruel and unreliable Siraj-Ud-Daulah. He instigated the British to continue their march towards Plassey. On the day of the Battle of Plassey, Siraj-Ud-Daulah faced off against the British, apparently with overwhelming force, but at the critical time Mir Jafar's men stood watching passively while the soldiers of Siraj-Ud-Daula were decimated by the smaller but much better armed British forces. After Siraj Ud Daulah's defeat and subsequent execution, Mir Jafar achieved his long-pursued dream of gaining the throne, and was propped up by the British as puppet Nawab.

Mir Jumla : Mir Jumla (1660-1663) was a prominent subahdar of Bengal under Emperor Aurangzeb. An Iranian by birth, his original name was Mir Muhammad Said. He received various titles from the Mughal emperor such as Muazzam Khan, Khan-i-Khanan, Sipahsalar and Yar-i-Wafahdar, but he became more popular in history as Mir Jumla. Born in about 1591 AD at Ardistan in Ispahan, he was the son of a poor oil merchant. In his early age Mir Jumla acquired some knowledge of reading, writing and arithmetic through which he was able to secure the job of a clerk under a diamond merchant having connections with Golconda, which was famous for its diamond mines. He later came to India in the service of another merchant. He, however, started his own diamond business, farmed some diamond mines, engaged in maritime commercial ventures and gradually rose to be a merchant of much fame, owning many ships.

Mir Jumla, a self-made man, was one of the remarkable personalities in 17th century India. Enterprising and amiable, he started as a simple clerk and rose to be one of the greatest generals and subahdars of the Mughal Empire. A great statesman, he was intelligent and farsighted. He is remembered as a just and humane Mughal subahdar.

Mir Mosharraf Hossain : Mir Mosharraf Hossain (1847-1912) was a Bengali language novelist, playwright and essayist in 19th century Bengal: He was born in Kushtia, now in Bangladesh. He is perhaps most famous for his novel Bishad Sindhu (Ocean of Sorrow), depicting the tale of Martyrdom of Hossain or Husayn bin Ali in Karbala. He was one of the first muslim writers to emerge from colonial British India.

Mir Mosharraf Hossain was secular and promoted peace between Hindus and Muslims. His other works include Jamindar Darpan (Refelections on Zamindars), a novel on the plight of common people under the zamindars (landlords installed by the British coloniar rulers) and their struggle against them.

Mir Shakil ur Rehman : Mir Shakil ur Rehman, (b. January 8, 1957) is the Group Editor-in-Chief and Group Chief Executive of the Jang Group. He has led the group ever since the demise of the group's founder, Mir Khalil-ur-Rehman in January 1992. However when his father was dying in London and his brother was with his father he came to Lahore, instead of going to his father who was dying, to seize control over all of his father property.

Mir Sultan Khan : Mir Sultan Khan (1905 - 1966) was generally considered to have been the strongest chess master of his time from Asia. He was also the first Asian chess master since As-Suli to have been recognized in Europe. Born in a part of India, now part of Pakistan, he was brought to England by his master in 1929. There he won the British Chess Championship in 1929, 1932 and 1933 and played for England in the Chess Olympiads of 1931 and 1933. In less than four years, he rose to the top of the chess world, playing with the world's great masters, such as Alexander Alekhine, José Raúl Capablanca, Max Euwe, Aaron Nimzowitsch, and Akiba Rubinstein.

He was one of a few players who had a plus record against Capablanca. He also had a plus record against Frank Marshall and Savielly Tartakower. His most notable victory was the game he won against former world champion Capablanca at the Hastings tournament of 1930 (moves given in Algebraic chess notation): His best years were the last two years, when he was probably ranked in the top ten in the world. In 1933, just when he was beginning to improve his performance, he was taken back to India by his master, and was never heard of by the chess world again. He passed away in Sargodha, Pakistan in 1966.

Mir Zafarullah Khan Jamali : Mir Zafarullah Khan Jamali (born January 1, 1944) is a former Prime Minister of Pakistan. Born in Baluchistan, Jamali was the first Prime Minister of Pakistan to be born in that province. He completed his primary education in Baluchistan, and his secondary education in Lahore. He obtained a master's degree from the Government College of Lahore in History. In the 1970s he was a minister for the Pakistan People's Party, serving as an important minister in his home province. In the 1980s he worked in the government of General Muhammad Zia-ul-Haq as a minister of various departments. He was almost appointed to the position of Prime Minister at numerous times in the 1980s, but never succeeded. However, he was the chief minister of Baluchistan in long-time provincial ruler General Rahimuddin Khan's cabinet at various times.

In the 1990s he was an important member of the Pakistan Muslim League. However, after the removal of Nawaz Sharif, Jamali joined the new faction of that party that was formed to support General Pervez Musharraf. He was elected as Prime Minister by the Parliament of Pakistan on November 21, 2002 after the general elections of October 2002. This was the first general election to take place in Pakistan following the 1999 coup by General Musharraf. His election as Prime Minister came after weeks of political negotiations due to no party winning a majority. Jamali won the position after members of the Pakistan People's Party defected to the Pakistan Muslim League to support him.

As Prime Minister, he was seen as being close to President Musharraf, and supported the political and economic policies of Musharraf. Jamali oversaw a broad political coalition, and promised to work towards restoring democracy to Pakistan. However, he resigned on 26 June 2004. Chaudhry Shujaat Hussain replaced him as the interim Prime Minister. The reasons for his resignation are not clear, but many have speculated that it was a result of deteriorating relations with Chaudhry Shujaat.

Mira Nair : Ms Mira Nair was born in 1958 in Bhubaneshwar, Orissa. Her parents are from Punjab. At the age of 13, she attended a boarding school in Shimla, where she became a passionate student of dramatics and acted in school theatre productions. After graduating from New Delhi, she went to United States on a theater scholarship to Harvard.

Mira began her career as a documentarist and later turned to commercial films. The film titled 'India Cabaret' brought her the American Film Festival Award for the best documentary of 1985. She won her first film award, the 'Golden Camera' from the Cannes Film Festival for her renowned film 'Salaam Bombay' and this film was nominated for Oscar for Best Foreign Film in 1988. Her movies, 'Mississippi Masala' won rave reviews in Europe and 'Kamasutra - A tale of love' got world wide attention for being provocative. She won the 'Golden Lion' award for her film 'Monsoon Wedding' at the Venice Film Festival in 2001. This movie narrates the happenings of a Punjabi wedding and the bride having second thoughts about her arranged marriage. It was the first time an Indian film or particularly a woman is winning the Golden Lion award in the Venice Film Festival. Mira's future projects include a Hollywood production with a film based on Edith Wharton's novel "A Mother's Recompense".

Mirabai : Mirabai (1498-1547) (or Meera) was a female Hindu mystical poet during the Mughal period of Indian history. Disciple of guru Ravidas, she composed many prayerful songs called bhajans. They are in the bhakti tradition, and most passionately praised Lord Krishna. She was born in Merta in Rajasthan, and the extant version of her poems are in Hindi. Her father's elder brother Viram Deo who succeeded to the throne arranged her marriage with Prince Bhoj Raj, the eldest son of Rana Sanga of Chittor. This marriage raised Mirabai to a very high social status, as the ruler of Chittor was considered to be the leader of the Hindu princes of Rajputana.

However, her great devotion to Lord Krishna did not always endear her to her husband and family. Her love of Krishna was so absorbing she neglected her social and regal responsibilities. Because of this Mirabai suffered great hardship throughout her life. These physical hardships became intolerable and after praying to Krishna, she left the palace for good and went to the pilgrimage of Mathura, Vrindavana, and finally to Dwarka. Mirabai spent most of her time in prayer and worship of Krishna. She left behind a legacy of many soulful and prayerful songs, which are still sung in India today. Mirabai is widely regarded as a saint in the tradition of the Bhakti Movement. The Bhakti Movement was a cult in 16th century India that showed the path to salvation by devotion. Other saints belonging to this culture were Tukaram, Kabir, Guru Nanak, Ramananda.

Mirabai's poetry puts love for Krishna above the love for friends and family. She perceived Krishna to be her husband, lover, lord and master. The unique characteristic of Mirabai's poetry is the use of complete surrender to her love for Krishna accompanied by subtle erotic imagery. Her longing for union with Krishna is predominant in Mira's poetry who says she wants to be colored with the color of dusk (dusk being the symbolic color of Krishna). She believed that in her previous life she was one of the several gopis in Vrindavan, in love with Krishna. Much like the gopis, as mentioned in tales of Krishna, Mirabai looked upon Krishna as her lover, seeking spirtual and physical union with him. Her writings were at the same time, spiritual and sensual. Mira's songs portray a personal universe where the only existence was that of Krishna - her sole object of desire.

Miraj Khalid : Miraj Khalid (1916 - 2003) was Interim prime minister of Pakistan in 1996 and 1997. Malik Miraj Khalid was born in 1916, in a small village near Lahore. He studied law and began practice in 1948. He was elected to the Provincial Assembly in 1965. He joined the Pakistan Peoples Party soon after its inception in 1968 and was appointed President of Lahore PPP. He was re-elected to the National Assembly in 1970.

Zulfikar Ali Bhutto included Miraj Khalid in his cabinet as Minister for Food and Agriculture and Under Developed Areas in December 1971. In November 1972 he was appointed Chief of the Party's Parliamentary Affairs and in 1975 he was given the portfolios of Social Welfare, Local Government and Rural Development. Later he was elected Speaker of the National Assembly.

After the execution of Zulfikar Ali Bhutto in April 1979, he was nominated member of the PPP central committee. But he resigned from the party's central committee in January 1988. He was again appointed the Speaker of National Assembly in 1988. He lost elections in 1993 and remained aloof from politics for sometime and served as the rector of International Islamic University.

Mirani Dam : Mirani Dam is located in Gwadar District, Balochistan, Pakistan. Mirani Dam multipurpose project, is located on Dasht River, about 30 miles west of Turbat in Makran Division of Balochistan, it envisages provision of dependable irrigation supplies for the development ref irrigated agriculture on the two banks of the river.

Miranzai Valley : The Miranzai Valley, also Hangu, is a mountain valley situated in the Kohat and Hangu districts in the North-West Frontier Province of Pakistan. It is made up of two valleys, draining from the southwest into the Kunam and northeast into the Kohat Tai. It is divided into upper and lower Miranzai. It extends from the Zaimukht and Orakzai hills to the Khattaks. It is 40 miles in length and is 546 square miles in area. East of Hangu is made up of numerous smaller valleys. To the west of Hangu, consisting of all of the upper portion of the valley, is a broad and open plain, bare of trees. There are many ravines in this area. The area surrounding the valley has many inhabitants, mostly comprising the Bangash and Orakzai peoples.

Mirdha Mosque : Mirdha Mosque situated less than half a kilometre due west of the Lalbagh Fort in the Atish Khana mahalla of old Dhaka, is one of the best preserved and well protected medieval monuments in the country. Two Persian inscriptions-one over the central archway and the other over the central mihrab, speak of its construction in 1704-05 AD by one Khan Muhammad Mirdha and the name of the mosque is after its builder.

Mosques on vaulted platforms were not built in Sultanate Bengal. The idea of such Mughal mosques in Bengal must have, therefore, come from outside; perhaps directly from North India, where a number of examples are found in the Tughlaq and Lodi periods, such as Firuz Shah Tughlaq's Kotla Jami (1354) and the Bara Gumbad Mosque (1494), both at Delhi. Again the inspiration for such North Indian mosques, no doubt, came from those of early Islam. The Fatimid mosque of Salih al-Talai (1160) in Cairo, built on high vaulted terrace, provides an example

Mirpur : Mirpur is a city of Azad Kashmir. The name means city (-pur) of the mir. Its hot climate and other geographical conditions closely resemble the adjoining districts of Jhelum and Gujrat in Pakistan. Many of the people of this area are farmers. Since the 1960s, a large number of people from this district have gone abroad, especially to the United Kingdom and the Middle East, for economic reasons. As such they are today the major foreign exchange earning source for Azad Kashmir and Pakistan. Around 50,000 people were moved from this district in the mid-sixties to make way for the construction of Mangla Dam. Most of these people settled in new Mirpur whilst some moved elsewhere in Pakistan or to the UK.

Mirpurkhas : Mirpurkhas with a population of 124,371 (1981), is a south eastern Pakistani city, fourth largest in the Sindh Province. Its soil is fertile and it is very popular for its mango cultivation. There are more than 250 various kinds of mangoes found in this region.

Mirza Aslam Beg : Mirza Aslam Beg was Chief of Army Staff, Pakistan, succeeding General Muhammad Zia-ul-Haq.General Mirza Aslam Beg was vice chief of army staff in General Zia ul-Haq's military administration, and after Zia's death in a plane crash he was immediately made chief in August 1988. He was born in Azam Garh, British India. Zia's son,Ejaz ul Haq as well as son of late Director General ISI Akhtar Abdur Rahman, Humanyun Akhtar have blamed Beg in the press for being behind the crash, the cause of which was never officially established.

After Zia's death, Beg helped Pakistan to a peaceful transition of power through general elections after which the Pakistan People's Party's (PPP's) Benazir Bhutto became premier. In the meantime, Beg's then director general of the Inter-Services Intelligence, Lieutenant-General Hamid Gul, and Beg were accused of gathering all right-wing parties under the umbrella of the Islamic Democratic Alliance against the PPP. Beg remained a powerful chief of army staff until 1991, a period in which Pakistan developed nuclear weapons. After his retirement Beg remained a controversial figure, both for his alleged role in a Bank scandal and the nuclear proliferation issue.

Mirza Ghalib : Mirza Asadullah Khan, pen-name Ghalib (1797 — 1869), was a renowned classical Urdu and Persian poet of India. He is considered to be the most dominating poet of the region since Kalidas. He was born on December 27, 1797 in Agra to parents with Turkish aristocratic ancestry. He was always considered a free spirit, and the death of his father and uncle during his youth left Ghalib with no male-dominant figures. He then moved to Delhi. Although Ghalib wrote in Persian as well, he is more famous for his ghazals written in Urdu. It is believed he wrote most of his very popular ghazals by the age of nineteen.

His ghazals, unlike those of Mir Taqi Mir, a famous Urdu poet of 18th century, contain highly Persianized Urdu, and therefore not easily understood or appreciated by a vast majority of people without some extra effort. He died on February 15, 1869 in Delhi.his house in Balli Maaran in the city is a national monument, although it is not as well-kept as a national monument should be.

Mirza Ghulam Ahmad : Mirza Ghulam Ahmad (February 13, 1835–May 26, 1908), a highly controversial religious figure belonging to India, was the founder of the Ahmadiyya religious movement.

He claimed to be the "Second Coming of Christ", the promised Messiah, the Mahdi as well as the being the Mujaddid of the 14th. Islamic century. He remains a highly controversial and reviled figure among most Muslims who consider him to be an apostate. Among his followers as well, who revere him and call themselves "Ahmadi Muslims", the interpretation of his claims is controversial.

Mirza Ghulam Hafiz : Mirza Ghulam Hafiz (1920 – December 20, 2000) was a prominent statesman, politician, and philanthropist in Bangladesh. Born in Ponchagarh, North Bengal in 1920, Mirza Ghulam Hafiz was educated at the University of Dhaka and University of Kolkata. By 1948, when he first became interested in government resistance and politics, he had graduated with a B.LL and M.S. in Economics,as well as a law degree.

Hafiz was an active organizer of the Language Movement on two separate occasions—in 1952 and again in 1954—and was jailed both times. In 1954, he was elected to the Provincial Assembly in Bengal as a representative of the Ponchagarh district. He would serve in government positions until Bangladesh's independence in 1971, a revolution in which he was personally involved (as an honorary colonel in the Bengal Rifles State Guard).

In 1972, Hafiz was elected to the new parliament of Bangladesh and was appointed the Minister of Land Management. From 1978 to 1982, he served as the Speaker of the Parliament until the coup that assassinated the President, Ziaur Rahman. After the demolition of the autocratic government of Hossain Mohammad Ershad, he was reelected to the parliament in 1991. Under the BNP, he was appointed the Minister of Law and Justice. He retired from politics in 1995.

Mirza Muhammad Yusuf Ali : Mirza Muhammad Yusuf Ali was a (1858-1920) litterateur, Islamic revivalist and social reformer. He was born in 1858 at Aliabad in durgapur upazila, rajshahi, the son of Munshi Mashiatullah. He studied at Sreedharpur Madhyabanga Vidyalay and Rajshahi Normal School, but passed the Entrance (1887) as a private candidate. He sat for the FA Examination (1891) but failed. He learnt Arabic, Urdu and Persian on his own. He taught at various schools, including the Bengali School in Cooch Bihar, Loknath School and Rangpur Government Normal School, and was for some time a School Inspector. He was the founder secretary of the Rajshahi nur-al-iman samaj (1884), Anjuman-e-Hemayate Islam (1891), Rajshahi Zila Mussalman Shiksa Samiti (1918). He was closely associated with the Pradeshik Mussalman Shiksa Samiti and Bangiya Islam Samiti.

Mirzapur : Mirzapur is a city in the heart of North India, almost exactly halfway between Delhi and Kolkata, and also equidistant from Allahabad and Varanasi. Located in the huge state of Uttar Pradesh with a population of 170 million, Mirzapur has a population of a little over 200,000 and is renowned for its famous carpet industry. It is a city with several spots around it including many hills such as Rajdari, Devdari, Lakhaniyadari, and Windom fall range and Sirshi.

According to the tradition, the name of this town, after which the district itself is named, was Girzapur, which in terms derives its name from the goddess Parvati, (Girija) who sacrified herself here in a yajna. Mirza, Vindhyavasini and Lakshmi are the other names of the goddess whose temple exists at Vindhyachal. It is also locally believed that the town was founded by Raja Nanner and was known as Girijapur, but later on it came to know as Mirzapur. The earliest mention of the town is found in the writings of Tieffenthaler, who drew up his description of the country between 1760 and 1770. He mentioned it, under the name of Mirzapur specially as a great mart. In the records of Jonathan Duncan, who was resident of Varanasi, frequent mention is made of the place as Mirzapur.

Mishing Bihu : This dance is associated with the Ali-Ali Lignos festival of the Mishmi tribes of Assam. It depicts the various stages of cultivation from sowing till reaping.

Mishmi : The Mishmi of India is an ethnic tribe comprising of mainly three tribes: Idu Mishmi; Digaru (Taraon) Mishmi, and Miju Mishmi. The Idu Mishmi inhabit the Upper Dibang Valley district of Arunachal Pradesh in India which the Chinese refer to as the Autonomous council of Tibet. The Idu are also known as Yidu Lhoba in China. Many live in the Mainling and Lhunze counties of Tibet.

Mithankot : Mithankot is located on the west bank of the Indus river, only a short distance downstream from its junction with Panjnad river. The latter is formed by successive confluence of the five rivers of Punjab, namely Jhelum, Chenab, Ravi, Beas and Sutlej. Panjnad river is approximately 45 miles in length and joins the Sindhu river just above Mithankot. It is an ancient and historic town in the extreme southwest part of the state of Punjab in Pakistan; currently it is a part of the Rajanpur tahsil of the Rajanpur district. Previously Mithankot as well as Rajanpur were parts of the Dera Ghazi Khan district of Punjab, Pakistan. Sulaiman range of mountains and hills of Balochistan approach the Sindhu river near Mithankot; Giandari peak being approximately 35 miles west of the town.

Mithila : Mithila was a kingdom in ancient India. It existed in the eastern Gangetic plains in areas which is today spread over Uttar Pradesh and Bihar states of India, and parts of Nepal. The legend of Mithila extends over many centuries. Both Gautama Buddha and Vardamana Mahavira are said to have lived in Mithila. It also formed the center of Indian history during the first millennium, and has contributed to various literary and scriptural works. The dialect spoken in Mithila is Maithili. This dialect is categorised under the Bihari subset of the numerous dialects of Hindi, the most prevalently spoken language in India. The most important reference to Mithila is in the

Hindu epic, Ramayana where Lord Rama's wife Sita is said to have been the princess of the land, born to King Janaka, who ruled Mithila from Janakpuri.

Mithila Arts : Bihar boasts of an enviable wealth of rural handicrafts comprising of hand—painted wall hangings, wooden stools, miniatures in paper and leaves, stone pottery, bamboo and leather goods, and applique work. But Bihar's most famous and fascinating indigenous art forms, by far, are its Madhubani Paintings. This art is a strict monopoly of the women of Mithila. Done in primary colours of natural origin on paper and cloth, they narrate mythological and religious events. North of the river Ganges, in the state of Bihar lies a land called Mithila, shaded by old mango groves and watered by melt water rivers of Nepal and the Himalayas.

Mithun Chakraborty : Mithun Chakraborty is a leading actor in the Bollywood. He was born in Chennai and educated at the Scottish Church College, Calcutta, where he studied chemistry. He graduated from the Film and Television Institute of India. He started his film career in a Bengali film made by Mrinal Sen.

Mithun not only achieved a lot of commercial success but also tremendous critical acclaim for his performances in his first film *Mrigaya* as well as for Bengali films *Tahader Katha* and *Ramakrishna Paramhans*), Mithun's statements evidence the humility of one who has 'come up the hard way'. He has done and continues to do social service all over India.

Mitro Bahini : Mitro Bahini was a military force composed of Bangladesh Army (as part of Mukti Bahini) and the Indian Army in December 1971 during the Bangladesh Liberation War. The alliance provided the final blow to already weakened Pakistan Army which surrendered thirteen days after the formation of the alliance

Miu : In Nagaland, MIU is held in the first week of May every year. One of the main significances of this festival is to build cordial relations and to forge close-knit relations between the maternal uncle and his sister's off-springs. It is also a very special occasion of FORGIVE and FORGET. This festival is also known as dividing line between merrymaking season and the start of working season.

Mizanur Rahman Chowdhury : He (October 19, 1928-February 2, 2006) was a Bengali politician, most notable for serving as prime minister of Bangladesh from July 9, 1986, to March 27, 1988.

Chowdhury was born in Chandpur District, in what is now Bangladesh. In college, he was involved in student politics. In 1962, he was elected to the Parliament of Pakistan, of which Bangladesh was then a part, as a member of the Awami League. When Sheikh Mujibur Rahman and other leaders of the Awami League were arrested in 1966, Chowdhury served as acting general secretary of the party until his own arrest in 1967. After his release he was active during Bangladesh's successful war for independence in 1971. After Bangladesh's independence, he was a longtime member of Parliament. He became information minister in Mujibur Rahman's cabinet in 1973, and following Mujubur's assassination in 1975, he left that position and led a faction of the Awami League.

During the early 1980s, Chowdhury supported the takeover of Hossain Mohammad Ershad and joined his Jatiya Party in 1984. He served as prime minister during Ershad's presidency for two years, from 1986 until he resigned in 1988. In 1990 Ershad's presidency ended. Chodhury rejoined the Awami League in 2001 and served as an advisor to the party until his death. He died in

Bangladesh's capital Dhaka and was widely mourned by politicians of all the main parties.

Mizo : The Mizos are a scheduled tribe in northeastern India, primarily in the state of Mizoram, of which they are in the majority. Mizos are a close-knit society with no class distinction and no discrimination on grounds of sex. The entire society is knitted together by a peculiar code of ethics 'Tlawmngaihna',which makes each individual responsible for his/her actions and demands that he/she be hospitable, helpful, considerate and honest in his dealings with others. The Mizos are divided into numerous tribes/sub-tribes, which includes the Lushai, the Ralte, the Hmar, the Paite, the Mara, and the Pawi. Their languages belong to the Tibeto-Burman family, and are closely related to those of the Chin in the adjacent Chin State of Burma, as well as those of the Nagas. Kukis and others.

Mizos have long complained of political isolation and neglect from India,which was brought to a head by the Mautam (Bamboo Flowering) and these sentiments fueled aspirations for independence or greater autonomy. The Mizo National Front, took up cudgels on behalf of the Mizo people and declared independence from India,leading to a long and bloddy struggle with losses on both sides. The MNF however finally signed the Mizoram Peace Accord and gave up arms and joined the mainstream and has now become the leading political party among Mizos and is currently the strongest player in the Mizoram government. There are also smaller numbers of Mizos in Burma (chiefly in Chin State) and Bangladesh (chiefly in the Chittagong Hill Tracts).

Mizo National Front : Mizo National Front, a regional political party in Mizoram, India. MNF emerged out of the Mizo Famine Front, which was formed by Pu Laldenga to protest against the inaction of the Indian central government towards the famine situation in the Mizo areas of the Assam state in 1959.

MNF became a guerrilla force struggling for independence for Mizoram, which received support from Pakistan in its struggle against India. In 1986 a peace agreement was signed between the government of India and MNF. Mizoram was created as a separate state within India, and Pu Laldenga became Chief Minister. However in 1989, MNF lost the first elections following the peace agreement. Former guerrilla leader Pu Zoramthanga became party leader following the death of Laldenga in 1990. In 1998 and 2003 MNF won the state assembly elections, and Pu Zoramthanga is currently chief minister. In the 2003 elections MNF won 21 out of 40 seats in the state assembly, and got 132 505 votes (31,66%).

The term 'Kuki' refers to an ethnic entity that spreads out in a contiguous region in Northeast India, Northwest Burma (Myanmar), and the Chittagong Hill tracts in Bangladesh. They are most prominent in Manipur, Nagaland, Assam and Mizoram. Kuki is composed of many different entities. Aimol, Anal, Baite, Changsan, Chiru, Chongloi, Chothe, Doungel, Gangte, Guite, Haokip, Hmar, Haolai, Hangsing, Kipgen, Koireng, Kolhen, Kom, Lamkang, Lenthang, Lhouvum, Lhungdim, Lunkim, Thangeo, Lhangum, Lhanghal, Maring, Mate, Milhem, Monsang, Moyon, Paite, Purum, Simte, Singsit, Sitlhou, Tarao, Touthang, Vaiphei, Zou, etc., may loosely be put under one egalitarian ethnic entity called Kukis.

Mizoram : Mizoram is a state in northeastern India. Its population at the 2001 census stood at approximately 890,000. Mizoram boasts a literacy rate of 89 percent—the second highest among all the states of India, after Kerala.

The great majority of Mizoram's population is comprised of ethnic Mizos. The Mizos are divided into numerous tribes, the largest of which is the Lushai, which comprises almost two-thirds of the state's population. Other major Mizo tribes include the Ralte, the Hmar, the Paihte, the Poi, the Mara, and the Pawi. The Chakma, a non-Mizo tribe, is of Arakanese origin. Some 85 percent of the population (including almost all ethnic Mizos) is Christian, mostly Presbyterian and Baptist. This Christian heritage is shared by a majority in the nearby states of Nagaland and Meghalaya, and by a large minority in neighbouring Manipur.

Mizos : The Mizos are a scheduled tribe in northeastern India, primarily in the state of Mizoram, of which they are in the majority. Mizos are a close-knit society with no class distinction and no discrimination on grounds of sex. The entire society is knitted together by a peculiar code of ethics 'Tlawmngaihna',which makes each individual responsible for his/her actions and demands that he/she be hospitable, helpful, considerate and honest in his dealings with others. The Mizos are divided into numerous tribes/sub-tribes, which includes the Lushai, the Ralte, the Hmar, the Paite, the Mara, and the Pawi. Their languages (of which the largest is Lushai) belong to the Tibeto-Burman family, and are closely related to those of the Chin in the adjacent Chin State of Myanmar, as well as those of the Nagas. Kukis and others.

Mizos have long complained of political isolation and neglect from India,which was brought to a head by the Mautam (Bamboo Flowering) and these sentiments fueled aspirations for independence or greater autonomy. The Mizo National Front, took up cudgels on behalf of the Mizo people and declared independence from India,leading to a long and bloddy struggle with losses on both sides. The MNF however finally signed the Mizoram Peace Accord and gave up arms and joined the mainstream and has now become the leading political party among Mizos and is currently the strongest player in the Mizoram government.

Mlechchha Dynasty : Mlechchha dynasty ruled Kamarupa from 655 to 900 after the fall of the Varman dynasty. The rulers were aboriginals, though their lineage from Narakasura was constructed to accord legitimacy to their rule. According to historical records there were twenty one rulers in this dynasty but the line is obscure and the names of some intervening rulers are not known. The Mlechchha dynasty in Kamarupa was followed by the Pala kings. According to some historians the remnant of the Mlechchha kingdom formed the later Kachari kingdom based in Dimapur and the Chutiya kingdom based in Sadiya after being driven south and east by Brahmapala of the Pala dynasty.

Mlokom Yulo—Bangni Festival : This is one of the major festivals of Bangnis. It is the only festival which is celebrated annually in every village on a community basis in the Bangini months of Lakhang & Leehar corresponding to the English month of March & April. The festival is celebrated for five days, but occasionally the period may extend to seven days depending on the result of divination performed prior to the fixation of the date of celebration. The divination is done by a local priest (Nibu) by examining the liver of a foul and the yolk of an egg respectively. The site where the festival is celebrated is called "Mlkom-Yulo-Nyengeng". They do not have a permanent festival place. On the previous day of the festival, the villagers keep themselves busy in collecting rice beer, rice making rice powder, egg and silk cloth. Sacrificial animals such as mithun, cow, pig, goat and fowl are usually purchased either from their common village fund or by collecting money or paddy from each house hold.

The festival is started with a worship in the name of god-Doni-Yulo where rice beer, rice powder and white cock are offered. Another God called Kamio-Yulo is also worshipped in the same place by offering only rice beer. When the prayers are over, the white cock is brought down to examine its liver with a view to knowing the omen of the festival. Different worships are performed on different days in the name of different gods and goddess by offering and sacrificing different animals in accordance with the result of divination. At the end of the festival, the villagers observe taboo for five days during which period they do not go out of the village. The observance of taboo is known as Mlkom-Arina. The people of all areas both local and other including tribals and non tribals irrespective of caste clan and creed uniformly participate in the Mlokom Julo festival.

Moammer Rana : Moammer Rana aka Momi tasted super stardom early in his career with three block busters including *Deewane Tere Pyar Ke, Choorian and Nikki Jai Haan* it seemed that he had the proverbial success on the platter – but sadly enough he faced the fall soon enough. There were even times when he was written off and with Shaan back as the only sole hero on the front, Momi was facing a lot of problems. *Yeh Dil Aap Ka Huwa* gave Momi the break that he was waiting since his last success. This film has again brought Momi back into business and now he is standing above Shaan in every term.

Having given a hatrick of successes initially, his list of flops is also unending, including Jisay Da Mola, Zor, Mohlat, Chupke Chupke, Pal Do Pal, Mehndi Wale Hath, Kon Bane Ga Crore Pati and even much hyped but delayed Syed Noor film Dil Deewana Hai and Shehzad Rafique's Rukhsati. But now having tasted success in the form of Yeh Dil Aap Ka Huwa he is the main choice of all the mainstream directors and producers. His recent film Koi Tujh Sa Kahan has had a very successful theatrical run, and is now ready for its DVD release.

Moatsu : In Nagaland, among the Aos, the most important festival is Moatsu, which is celebrated after the sowing is over. The festival last six days. On the first night of the festival sexual intercourse was forbidden. Every man was required to wear a new belt, for hanging his dao. The unmarried men received belts as presents from their girl friends, the married men got from their wives. During this occasion, the restriction relating to dress and ornaments were relaxed. People could wear even the forbidden ones according to their will.

The most important role, during the festival used to be played by the youths of the bachelor's dormitory. Before the festival, the morung had to be repaired and cleansed. The dancing drums were also put to order by attaching new skins. On the first day of the festival, the boys belonging to the younger age-groups used to go to the jungle and collect six bundles of paired bamboo strips each. These they handed over to the morung elders, for use according to their discretion. On the second day, all the boys and grown-up males engaged themselves in clearing the village, particularly the main approaches to the village. That night, the cows and the pigs to be slaughtered on the occasion of this festival were tied outside the morung. On the third day, the cows and the pigs would be killed. The meat was distributed among the boys of the morung and some portion was kept apart, to be given as present.

In the evening, the boys would eat the meat outside the morung. Later some old men would come to the morung and would be entertained with meat and rice-beer. When they would eat the meat, the boys would be singing songs inside the morung. On the fourth day, the people of Mongsen Khel would dance in procession; in all the streets of the village. On the fifth day, the people of Chungli Khel would dance similarly. The women were not to take any part in these dances, but at intervals they served rice-beer to the dancers. The old men also would not dance, but follow the dancer, singing songs. A drummer always accompanied the party and the people would dance to the beatings of the drum. On the sixth day, both the Khels used to dance together.

Modak : Modak, also called modagam, is a sweet dish which originated in the Indian state of Maharashtra. Usually, modaks are made with an outer crust of rice flour, and a filling of coconut. Modaks are then steamed with turmeric leaves for aroma, and are served either hot or cold. Sometimes they are also deep-fried to increase their shelf life. It is considered to be the favorite food item of Lord Ganesh. It is customary to offer twenty-one or hundred-and-eight modaks to Lord Ganesh.

Moeenuddin Ahmad Qureshi : Moeenuddin Ahmad Qureshi, usually referred to as Moeen Qureshi, (born 1930) is a Pakistani economist and political figure. A former Vice President of the World Bank, he was the acting Prime Minister of Pakistan from July 18, 1993 until 19 October, 1993.

The continuing political crisis of 1993 in Pakistan came to an abrupt halt when the Prime Minister Nawaz Sharif and President Ghulam Ishaq Khan both resigned after two weeks of intense negotiations among the Nawaz Sharif government, Benazir Bhutto, and the army. The resolution of the crisis was unique because for the first time in the nation's history a government had voluntarily stepped down in order to avoid a possible military intervention. The negotiations had been mediated by General Wahid Kakar, the Army Chief of Staff. The resultant agreement and its implementation followed strict constitutional procedure. Ghulam Ishaq Khan was replaced by the chairman of the Senate,Wasim Sajjad, who functioned as Acting President until the elections. More important,

Moeen Qureshi, a former civil servant and senior World Bank official, agreed to serve as caretaker Prime Minister. Qureshi, a Pakistani national, had left the World Bank in 1992, obtained permanent residence status in the United States, and established his own company, Emerging Markets Corporation.

Mograpara : Mograpara is a historic village, in the Narayanganj districtof Bangladesh. It appears to be the site of the earliest Muslim settlement in Sonargaon and the centre of Islamic learning during the last quarter of the thirteenth century. Mograpada formed a suburb of the Hindu capital city of Sonargaon and the site of the later Muslim metropolis. The remains at Mograpara include the Dargahbari complex with the Dargah building, Madrasa building, Fath Shah's Mosque (1484), Nahbat Khana, grave of Sharfuddin Abu Tawwamah (d. 1300), and the tombs of Shah Ibrahim Danishmand, Shah Kamal, Shaykh Muhammad Yusuf and Munna Shah Darwesh.

Mohali : is a suburb of Chandigarh, in Punjab, India. It is officially named after the eldest son of Guru Gobind Singh, Sahibzada Ajit Singh Nagar. Mohali was built primarily to help take residential housing strain off of neighboring Chandigarh, whose population in the 2001 National Census was already nearing one million. At 900,635, Chandigarh is the 38th largest city in India, and the shared capital of both Punjab and Haryana. In 2006, Mohali's population is near 200,000, approximately 1/5 of Chandigarh's. Its value as more than a population shunt is becoming increasingly evident. Mohali has been targeted by an increasing number of outsourcing IT companies, who look to capitalize on the rich investment opportunities the city offers.

Following the success of Chandigarh's sector design, Mohali was similarly planned into identical 800 X 1200m sectors. Many have yet to be fully developed, as is the case of sector 62, which is earmarked for a future commercial City Centre. Its close proximity to the PCA Stadium, as well as unrivaled transportation links to Chandigarh make it a suitable choice.

Mohammad Ali Jinnah : Revered by Pakistanis as their Quaid-e-Azam, the Great Leader and Father of the Nation, Mohammad Ali Jinnah, alongside Mahatma Gandhi and Jawaharlal Nehru, was a pivotal figure in the Indian subcontinent's decolonisation. Ironically, the pursuit of freedom and self-determination also resulted in the partition of British India into Pakistan and India. The strategic and security repercussions of partition continue to haunt Indo-Pakistani relations.

Jinnah was born on 25 December 1876 into a prominent merchant family in Karachi. When he reached 16, his father sent him to London to be apprenticed to Graham's Trading Company. It was hoped that the young Jinnah would gain the necessary skills and experience to take over the business in the future. However, in 1893, the headstrong young man decided to pursue a career as a barrister where he would be independent. He was also inspired by how the great contemporary and past leaders of Britain had been trained in the law. Jinnah joined Lincoln's Inn and, in 1896, became the youngest Indian to be called to the Bar. Jinnah's sister later claimed that it was his varied experiences in London which caused him to become "an uncompromising enemy of all forms of colour bar and racial prejudice."

On his return to India, he set up his practice in Bombay (now Mumbai) and became a very successful lawyer. Firmly established in the legal profession, Jinnah formally joined the Indian National Congress in 1905, thus making his debut in politics. He served together with senior Indian advocates of self-government such as Gopal Krishna Gokhale and Dadabhai Noaroji. Jinnah was also the first parliamentarian to have a Private Member's Bill passed at the Imperial Legislative Council of India.

Jinnah was hailed as the leading ambassador of Hindu-Muslim unity with the conclusion of the Lucknow Pact in 1916. He had invited the All-India Muslim League to hold its annual session in Bombay simultaneously with that of the Congress. He acted as the principal conciliator between Congress and the Muslim League, bridging the differences and ensuring its successful adoption. The Pact represented a compromise between the Congress and the Muslim League on Muslim claims in a post-war democratic constitution. This allowed the two organisations to present the British with an effective united front of the Home Rule League. Thus the Lucknow Pact became the basis for the Montagu-Chelmsford Reforms, also known as the Act of 1919.

Jinnah's pragmatic stance can be seen from his speech at Lucknow when he said: "In the affairs of our common secular existence, we have to deal not with angels but with men, with passions, prejudices, personal idiosyncrasies, innumerable cross-currents of motive, of desire, hope, fear and hate. The Indian problem has all such formidable complications in its texture." He emphasised that the Muslim community must have its own self-respect, saying: "We want no favours, and crave no partial treatment. That is demoralising to the community and injurious to the State. The Muslims must learn to have self-respect. What we want is a healthy and fair impetus to be given to our aspirations and ideals as a community."

Jinnah had also been associated with gradual change through constitutional methods. He had been influential in getting the Muslim League to declare, in 1913, that its objective was: "Attainment under the aegis of the British Crown of a system of self-government suitable to India through constitutional means, by bringing about a steady reform of the existing system of administration, by promoting a steady national unity, by fostering public spirit, and by cooperation with other communities for the said purpose." Thus Jinnah was dismayed when Gandhi, who had been elected to the presidency of the Home Rule League in 1920, embarked on a path of satyagraha (civil disobedience) and invocation of Hindu religious motifs in order to secure swaraj (self-rule) within the unrealistic time frame of a year. He felt that Gandhi's methods were extra-constitutional. He also feared the injection of religion into politics was a mistake as it would distract Hindus and Muslims from their common political cause and principles. Anti-government demonstrations often turned into communal riots with many deaths in places like Malabar and Chuari Chuari. By then, Jinnah had resigned from Congress and the Home Rule League.

In the 1937 elections, the Congress came to power exclusively in seven out of 11 provinces. The predominantly Hindu program of the Congress governments caused Muslims to fear that their religion, language and culture were not safe and that they could live only at the sufferance of Hindus and as second class citizens. Jinnah seized upon this groundswell to forge the Muslim League into a truly all-India, mass-based organisation. Until then, Congress tended to see Jinnah and the Muslim League as representing only the Muslim upper middle classes - especially since Jinnah was more comfortable speaking English than the Muslim lingua franca of Urdu.

By 1940, Jinnah had become the undisputed leader of Muslims in India. He had become convinced that a partition of India along religious lines was the only way to preserve Muslim political power and culture. He declared that the Muslims of India were a separate nation and were entitled to a separate state. That year, the

Muslim League adopted the Lahore Resolution calling for a separate autonomous state in the majority-Muslim areas of northeastern and eastern India - the demand for Pakistan.

This demand was fiercely resisted by Congress. The British were opposed as well as they felt that their greatest legacy to the Indian people would be a united India. Attempts to negotiate with the Muslim League on the basis of the Cripps offer and Rajaji formula, which might have satisfied Jinnah in 1928, were rejected as offering only a "moth-eaten, mutilated" Pakistan, appended with too many conditions. Another attempt at preserving unity was made with the high level Cabinet Mission Plan of 1946. It stipulated a limited centre, having authority only over foreign affairs, defence and communications. It would consist three autonomous groups of provinces - the northeastern and eastern groups would be Muslim-controlled while the mainland would be Hindu-dominated. Jinnah was to accept this in principle, only to rescind it after perceived obstructionism and defiance from Congress, which Jinnah claimed was designed to browbeat the Muslim League into accepting Congress' dictates and interpretations of the plan. Jinnah called for demonstrations to oppose the formation of an interim Indian government and renewed his demand for partition. Communal riots erupted resulting in more than 3,000 killed and thousands wounded.

Lord Mountbatten, the new Viceroy was unable to dissuade Jinnah and partition was agreed to on 3 June 1947 by the Congress, Muslim League and Akali Dal (representing the Sikhs). The British thus handed over power to two successor states on 15 Aug 1947. Jinnah was to be Governor-General of East and West Pakistan. But to almost 100 million Pakistanis, their Quiad-e-Azam was more than a Governor-General. He worked to consolidate the new state which started without a central government, capital or organised defence force. The treasury was empty as India held its sterling balances initially. Rioting had devastated much of the Punjab and disrupted communications. The exodus of the Hindu and Sikh business and managerial classes also left the economy in an extremely difficult situation. In addition, India annexed Junagadh and war erupted over Kashmir from October 1947 to December 1948. Only Jinnah's charismatic leadership and ability played a large role in holding the fledging state together. Eventually the strain of exhaustion from over-work, poor health and tuberculosis caused Jinnah's death on 11 September 1948, only 13 months after Pakistan's creation.

Critics of Jinnah have portrayed him as a cold megalomaniac who demanded for a separate Pakistan for the sake of his own political ambition. His successors have disputed the degree to which he was committed to secular government. Two further wars over Kashmir were fought in 1965 and 1971. East Pakistan, with the help of Indian military intervention, broke away to form the independent state of Bangladesh. However one may judge Jinnah and his legacy, he remains one of the giants of the modern history of the Indian subcontinent.

Mohammad Azharuddin : Mohammad Azharuddin (born 8 February 1963, Hyderabad, Andhra Pradesh) is a former captain of the Indian cricket team. He shot into fame in 1984 when he hit three consecutive centuries in his first three Test matches, including the debut innings.

Azhar, as he was popularly known, was an elegant batsman and captain of the Indian team for most of the 1990s. He is the best captain india has ever had, in terms of total number of wins (tests and one dayers). He has won 103 matches for India, which is still unprecedented.

In Test cricket, his 14 Test wins as captain, was the best at the time, until he was overtaken by Saurav Ganguly.

He was named Wisden Cricketer of the Year in 1991, and was for long an inspirational figure in the Indian team with his athletic fielding and leadership. However, towards the end of his career Azharuddin was accused of match-fixing; South African captain Hansie Cronje in his confession for match-fixing had indicated Azharuddin also being involved. This lead the ICC to ban him from the game of cricket for life in 1999—a ban which he is now contesting.

Mohammad Haleem : Justice Haleem served as the Chief Justice of Pakistan from the period 1981 to 1989, the longest service of its kind in the history of the country. He was endorsed by successive regimes and has been celebrated as one of the foremost judicial authorities of South Asia.

Mohammad Hamidur Rahman : Mohammad Hamidur Rahman (1945-1971) was a martyr in the war of liberation. He was born in 1945 at village Dumuria in Chapra thana of the district of 24 Parganas in west bengal. After the partition of India (1947) his family migrated to East Bengal and was permanently settled at Gharoda under Khalispur in khulna district. He had his primary education at Khalispur Primary School and subsequently at a local night school. He joined East Bengal Regiment on 2 February 1971 and was posted at EBR centre in Chittagong cantonment. On the face of the attack of Pakistan army on 25 March Hamidur Rahman left the cantonment for his village home, and then joined the liberation force at Dhalai on the south-eastern border of sreemangal thana in sylhet district.

For its strategic importance the freedom fighters took a bid for capturing the Dhalai border outpost of the Pak-army. The 'C' Company of the First East Bengal Regiment was entrusted with the task with which Hamidur Rahman was enrolled. On the preceding night of 28 October three platoons of freedom fighters silently advanced towards the outpost. The platoons while approaching near to the enemy post and were on the verge of attempting a surprise, a sudden explosion of a mine alarmed the enemies who started indiscriminate firing. A battle continued for hours; but the advance of the freedom fighters was seriously obstructed by enemy firing with LMG from south-west direction.

At this critical juncture Hamidur Rahman seceded in the darkness, silently proceeded by crawling towards the LMG post, attacked and killed the two LMG operators, thereby silencing the enemy guns ; but he himself succumbed to death by an enemy bullet (28 October 1971). Thus the tide of the battle was turned and the outpost was captured by the freedom fighters. In recognition of his valour and sacrifice in the War of Liberation he was honoured with the highest state insignia of 'Bir Srestha'.

Mohammad Kaykobad : Mohammad Kaykobad is an educator, author and columnist from Bangladesh. He is a leading specialist in Information Technology in the country. Along with Muhammed Zafar Iqbal, Kaykobad started the national mathematics olympiad. He authored few books on recreational mathematics. Currently he is a professor of Computer Science and Engineering in Bangladesh University of Engineering and Technology, and a visiting professor at the North South University, Dhaka, Bangladesh.

Mohammad Mansoor Ali : Mohammad Mansoor Ali (1919-1975) was the Prime Minister of Bangladesh from 26 January 1975- 15 August 1975. He was a lawyer and politician. Captain M Mansur Ali was born in 1919 at village Kuripara in Kazipur thana of Sirajganj District. He obtained graduation from Calcutta Islamia College, MA in Economics and Law degree from Aligarh Muslim University. He joined Pabna District Court Bar in 1951.

Mansur Ali was the vice-president of Pabna District Muslim League from 1946 to 1950. He received training at Jessore Cantonment as a captain in PLG in 1948. Since then he was widely known as Captain Mansur. However, his active political life began with his joining the Awami Muslim League in 1951. He was elected member of the central executive committee of the party and was also the president of its Pabna district unit. He was arrested in 1952 while organising the Language Movement in Pabna. Mansur Ali was elected a member of the East Pakistan Provincial Assembly in 1954 as a candidate of United Front. He was the Minister of Law and Parliamentary Affairs, Food and Agriculture, Commerce and Industry in the coalition cabinet in East Pakistan headed by Ataur Rahman Khan (1956). After the promulgation of Martial Law in 1958 he was arrested under Safety Act and kept confined till 1959.

Mansur Ali played an important role in Six-point movement. He was elected a member of the Provincial Assembly from Pabna in 1970. He was the Finance Minister in the cabinet of Bangladesh Government in exile, and played vital role in organising the War of Liberation. After independence, Mansur Ali was the Minister for Communication, and then the Minister for Home Affairs and Communication in the cabinet of Bangabandhu Sheikh Mujibur Rahman. In 1973, he was elected a member of the National Assembly, and a member in the Awami League Parliamentary Party. He was made the Prime Minister after the introduction of one-party presidential form of government in 1975. He was the secretary general of Bangladesh Krishak Sramik Awami League (BAKSAL).

Captain Mansur Ali went on hiding immediately after the killing of President Sheikh Mujibur Rahman on 15 August 1975. Having captured power Khondakar Mostaq Ahmad included some of his Awami League colleagues in his cabinet. But Mansur Ali and three other national leaders refused to join the cabinet, and were thus arrested on 23 August 1975. Mansur Ali and three other leaders, Syed Nazrul Islam, Tajuddin Ahmad and Ahm Qamaruzzaman, were kept confined in the Dhaka Central Jail where they were brutally killed on 3 November 1975.

Mohammad Mostafa Kamal : Mohammad Mostafa Kamal (1947-1971) was distinguished freedom fighter and a martyr in the war of liberation of Banlgadesh. He was born at village West Hajipur under daulatkhan upazila of Bhola district. He joined the East Bengal Regiment as a soldier on 16 December 1967, and on completion of training he had his posting at the Fourth East Bengal Regiment in Comilla.

In March 1971, he was transferred to the headquarters of the Regiment at Brahmanbaria whence he joined the War of Liberation. During the War he had the status of a Lance Nayek, and was posted at village Daruin in Akhaura as a section commander. The Pak-army launched an attack on the second platoon of the Fourth East Bengal Regiment at village Daruin on 17 April.

In the encounter that followed Mostafa Kamal was killed after a heroic resistance. He lies buried at village Daruin. In recognition of his valour and sacrifice in the War of Liberation he was awarded the title of Bir Srestha by the Government of Bangladesh.

Mohammad Mushfiqur Rahim : Mohammad Mushfiqur Rahim is a cricket player from Bangladesh. He was a wildcard inclusion for Bangladesh's maiden tour of England in 2005, Mushfiqur Rahim was just 16 years old when he was selected for their daunting two-Test, six one-day international tour, having not even been named in the preliminary squad of 20. Principally selected as an understudy to the team's ever-present wicketkeeper, Khaled Mashud, Rahim's inclusion was further evidence of Bangladesh's determination to build for a better future.

Mohammad Nafees Iqbal Khan : Mohammad Nafees Iqbal Khan (better known as Nafees Iqbal; born January 31, 1985 in Chittagong) is a Bangladeshi cricketer. He is a right-handed batsman, and a right-arm medium pace bowler. He is the nephew of former Bangladesh captain Akram Khan. When approached about his century innings in Dhaka, he was disparaging toward the England bowling which he faced, dismissing their spinners as "ordinary". His comments drew more press attention than the innings in which he batted.

Mohammad Rafi : Mohammed Rafi was a famous playback singer. He was born on 25 December 1924 in Punjab. Even at a young age he was more fond of music than studies. He started learning music from the famous Hindustani singer Chotte Gulam Ali Khan. Later he became the disciple of Firoze Nizam. When Firoze was appointed as a music director in Lahore Radio Station, Rafi got an opportunity to sing in the radio. It was a turning point in his life.

He sang first for a Punjabi movie. Then in Nazeer Khan's 'Leila Majnu', Rafi began his career as a singer in the Hindi film field. But as a singer he succeeded for his songs in the film 'Gavom ke gori'. His songs in films like 'Jugnu' and 'Baiju Bavra' made him very popular. He also used to sing in various other languages. More than 26,000 songs are recorded in his name. Famous music director Naushad and Rafi had a remarkable relationship. Their team work created many hit songs.

He was very punctual and faithful to his profession. He encouraged and welcomed new comers. His famous songs are 'oh duniya ke rakwale' (Baiju Bavra), 'ghun ghuna rehe hai' (Aradhana), 'kya hua tera vaada' (Hum kise se Kum nahin), 'yaham badla vaham kya he' (Jugnu) etc. He has performed in around thirty eight musical concerts abroad. He got Padmashree Award in 1965 from India Government and National award twice. He also got Film fare Award for the best singer several times. His last recording was on May 26, 1980. He died on July 31, 1980.

Mohammad Rafiqul Islam Khan : Mohammad Rafiqul Islam Khan (born November 7, 1977, Rajshahi) is a Bangladeshi cricketer who played in one Test and one ODI in 2002.

Mohammad Ullah : Mohammad Ullah (1921-1999) President of Bangladesh, lawyer and politician. Mohammad Ullah was born at village Saicha in Raipur Thana of Luxmipur district in 1921. He passed entrance examination in 1938 from Luxmipur High School, BA (Hons) in History from the University of Dhaka in 1943, and obtained law degree from the same and also from Calcutta University. He joined Dhaka District Bar in 1950 and Dhaka High Court Bar in 1964.

Mohammad Ullah joined politics as an activist of Awami League in 1950 and was elected office secretary of the East Bengal Awarni Muslim League in 1952. He took active part in the movement for autonomy based on Six-point Programme (1966) and had to suffer imprisonment for several times. He was elected member of the East Pakistan Provincial Assembly in 1970. During the War of Liberation in 1971, Mohammad Ullah was the political adviser to the Acting President of the Mujibnagar Government. Mohammad Ullah was elected deputy speaker at the first session of the Jatiya Sangsad (1972). He was made the speaker after the death of Shah Abdul Hamid.

He was elected member of the Jatiya Sangsad in 1973 and was elected its speaker. Mohammad Ullah was elected President of the Peoples Republic of Bangladesh on 23 December 1973, a position which he held till 25 January 1975.

Mohammed Afzal Zullah : Mohammed Afzal Zullah was born on April 19, 1928, at Bijnial, Mandra (District Rawalpindi). He graduated in 1948 from Punjab University in Arts. In 1950 he received the degree in Law from Punjab University Lahore. He enrolled as a Pleader in 1950 and started practice at Sahiwal. Later on he shifted to Rawalpindi in 1951 and to Lahore in 1961. He was appointed as Additional Judge of the West Pakistan High Court in May 1968, he became permanent Judge of the High Court in March 1970. He was elevated to the Supreme Court Bench in 1979. In the same year he became member of Shariat Appellate Bench, Supreme Court of Pakistan.

He became the Chairman of the Bench in 1982. He acted as the Chief Justice from March 4 to 7, 1984. Justice Zullah remained the Chief Justice of Pakistan from January 1, 1990, to March 19, 1993. He also remained, Member Syndicate, university of Engineering and Technology Lahore, Member Board of Studies in Law University of Multan, Member Board of Trustees Islamic University Islamabad and Member Selection Board Quaid-i-Azam University Islamabad.

Mohammed Akbar Khan : Major General Akbar Khan, also known as Mohammed Akbar Khan, fought as the Brigadier-in-charge in Kashmir on the Pakistan side in Indo-Pakistan war of 1948. He also helped to stop the first Baloch insurgency of 1948. Later he served as the Chief of National Security under Zulfikar Ali Bhutto and helped quell the Balochi Insurgency during the early and mid

1970s. But he is mostly known in Pakistan as the main conspirator of the first but failed coup attempt of 1951, which came to be known as the Rawalpindi Conspiracy Case.

Mohammed Taqi : Mohammed Taqi (1723 - 1810), better known by his nom de plume of Mir Taqi Mir (sometimes also spelt as Meer Taqi Meer), was the leading Urdu poet of the eighteenth century, and one of the pioneers who gave shape to the Urdu language itself. He was one of the principal poets of Delhi school of Urdu ghazal and remains arguably the foremost name in Urdu poetry.

He was born in Agra, Uttar Pradesh, India, in 1723. He left for Delhi, at the age of 11, following his father's death.His philosophy of life was formed primarily from his father, whose emphasis on the importance of love and the value of compassion remained with him through his life and imbued his poetry. At Delhi, he finished his education and joined a group of nobility as a courtier-poet. He lived much of his life in Mughal Delhi. However, after Ahmad Shah Abdali's sack of Delhi each year starting 1748, he eventually moved to the court of Asaf-ud-Daulah in Lucknow, at the king's invitation. Distressed to witness the plundering of his beloved Delhi, he gave vent to his feelings through some of his couplets. He remained in Lucknow for the remainder of his life.

Mir's literary reputation is anchored on his ghazals, a literary style used in music, marked by brevity, suggestive imagery and musicality. His poetry is notable for a simple tone, and a voice of assured self-mockery. His style is informal, rooted in personal experience. Some of his finest poetry deals with the theme of unfulfilled love.

Mir lived at a time when Urdu language and poetry was at a formative stage - and Mir's instinctive aesthetic sense helped him strike a balance between the indigenous expression and new enrichments coming in from Persian imagery and idiom, to constitute the new elite language known as Rekhta or Hindui. Basing his language on his native Hindustani, he leavened it with a sprinkling of Persian diction and phraseology, and created a poetic language at once simple, natural and elegant, which was to guide generations of future poets.

After his move to Lucknow, his beloved daughter passed away, followed by his son, and then his wife. This, together with other earier setbacks lends a strong pathos to much of his writing - and indeed Mir is noted for his poetry of pathos and melancholy. He died in Lucknow, of a purgative overdose, on 20 September 1810

Mohammed Yaqub Ali : Mohammed Yaqub Ali born at Jallandhar in March 1912, received early education at Jallandhar, did his graduation and Law from University of Punjab in 1936. He remained active in the Freedom Movement. In 1948 he started practicing at Lahore High Court. He was elevated to the High Court Bench in 1955 and in 1965 was raised to the Supreme Court Bench. Justice Yaqub Ali was appointed the Chairman of the Karachi Airport Enquiry Commission in 1969 and in 1971 the Chairman of Special Court for Ganga Hijacking Case. In 1975 led the Pakistan Delegation to 7th World Peace Conference held at Washington. Justice Mohammed Yaqub assumed the office of Chief Justice of Pakistan on November 1, 1975. In 1976 led the Pakistani Delegation to the United Nations third Law of Sea Conference held at New York. In 1977 he was appointed as the Chairman of Indus Water Commission. He retired on July 22, 1977.

Mohammedan Sporting Club (MSC) : Mohammedan Sporting Club (MSC) is a major sporting club in Bangladesh. It is mainly located in Dhaka, Bangladesh, though there are many local branches throughout the country. Dhaka Mohammedan Sporting Club was formed in 1933. According to some people, however, the year of establishment of Dhaka Mohammedan is 1938. Although apparently, Dhaka Mohammedan was a branch of the Calcutta Mohammedan, the former was a club created through reorganisation of the Muslim Sporting Club formed at Hazaribag, Dhaka in 1927. After the Partition of Bengal in 1947, a vacuum was created in the sports arena of Dhaka. At that time, Mohammad Shahjahan, a famous football player of Calcutta Mohammedan came to Dhaka and took charge of the Dhaka Mohammedan. He reorganised it and also developed its football team as a very strong one.

The achievements of the team, however, were not significant until 1955. Dhaka's football was dominated at the time by Dhaka Wanderers' Club. Some star players and an official of the Wanderers had joined Dhaka Mohammedan in 1956. Later, the players themselves took initiatives of organising the team for increasingly better performance. In 1961, Dhaka Mohammedan played in the final match of the first division football league and in the next year, it became its champion. The club became champion also in the Independence Day Football Tournament of that year. Later, Dhaka Mohammedan Club extended their participation in other games and sports including hockey, swimming, athletics, volleyball, table tennis and badminton.

Mohan Rakesh : Mohan Rakesh (1925-1972) was one of the pioneers of the Nai Kahani (literally "new story") movement of the Hindi literature in the 1950s. He made significant contribution to novel, short story, travelogue, criticism, memoirs and drama.

Mohanlal : Mohanlal Viswanathan Nair (born May 21, 1960), simply known by the stage name Mohanlal, is an

Indian actor of mainly Malayalam movies. He is widely regarded as one of the greatest actors of his generation.

Mohanlal is enormously popular in the state of Kerala and has had striking success in both mainstream and parallel cinema.

Mohenjo-daro : Mohenjo-daro like Harappa, was a city of the Indus Valley civilization, some 80 km southwest of modern Sukkur, Sindh, Pakistan. It is a UNESCO World Heritage Site. It is somewhat better preserved than Harappa, and therefore a more informative source on its parent civilization. Mohenjo Daro was about 400 miles away from Harappa. It was probably built between four and five thousand years ago, and was abandoned around 1700 BCE, probably due to a change of course of the river which supported the civilization. It was rediscovered in the 1920s by archaeologists.

Mohenjo-daro is a remarkable construction, considering its antiquity. It has a planned layout based on a grid of streets, with structures constructed of bricks of baked mud, sun dried bricks and burned wood. At its height the city probably had around 35,000-40,000 residents. It had an advanced drainage system, a variety of buildings up to two stories high, and an elaborate bath area. The bath area was very well built and had a layer of natural tar, to keep it from leaking. Being an agricultural city, it also featured a large well, granary, and central marketplace. Perhaps most unexpected, it even had a building with an underground furnace (hypocaust), possibly for heated bathing.

Mohinder Amarnath : Mohinder Amarnath (born September 24, 1950, Patiala, India) is a former international cricketer (1969-1989) from India. His full name is Mohinder Amarnath Bhardwaj, although he is commonly known as "Jimmy". He is the son of the legendary Lala Amarnath; his brother, Surinder also played for India.

Mohinder made his debut against Australia at Chennai in December 1969. Mohinder is known as the come back man of Indian cricket. During his two decades at the top, he was dropped from the Indian side on several occasions and every time he fought his way back with sterling performances. After his debut series he had to wait until 1975 to make it into the team.

Mohinder Amarnath played 69 Tests scoring 4,378 runs at an batting average of 42.50, with 11 hundreds and 24 fifties, and claimed 32 wickets at a bowling average of 55.68 apiece. In 85 One-day internationals, he scored 1,924 runs at an average of 30.53 and a highest score of 102 n.o. and claimed 46 wickets at 42.84 apiece. He is best known for his legendary performance in the 1983 Cricket World Cup. He was awarded "Man of the Series", having led India to their first ever one-day international title.

Mohiniyattam : The Devadasi dance tradition which developed through the temple danseuses is an important form among the dance patterns of India. Mohiniyattam in Kerala took shape in the tradition of Devadasi dance which later grew and developed a classical status.

The special style of dancing developed by the Devadasis in Kerala was originally called 'Teviticci Attam'. Devadasis in Kerala were known by the general name 'Teviticci' which literally means - woman who serves at the feet of God. (Teviticci = Tevar + Ati + Acci; Tevar = God, Ati = feet; Acci = woman). Their dance was called 'Teviticci - Attam' (Attam = Dance). This later came to be known as Mohiniyattam by about 16th century AD. The word 'Mohini' literally means a maiden who excites desire or steals the heart of the on looker. It is a solo female dance in which striking features is the musical melody and rhythmical swaying of the dancer from side to side and the smooth flow of the body movement. The dance is focused essentially on feminine moods and emotions.

There is the well known Puranic story of Lord Vishnu taking on the guise of a 'Mohini' to enthrall people both in connection with the churning of the milk-ocean and with the episode of the slaying of Bhasmasura. In the Bhasmasura story, 'Mohini' towards the end of her dance, persuaded the Asura to place his own finger on his head unwittingly to his own undoing. This episode seems to be picturesquely represented in the first item of the Mohiniyatam called 'Colkkettu' which begins with a pose of the dancer showing with her right hand, the murder of 'Suchimukha' with her first finger pointing to her own head. So Vaishnava devotees could have given the name of Mohiniyattam to this art form.

Mohi-ud-Din Islamic University : Mohi-ud-Din Islamic University is located at Nerian Sharif, Azad Kashmir, Pakistan. Mohi-ud-Din Islamic University at Nerian Sharif was established under an Act of Azad Jammu and Kashmir Legislative Assembly. It is thus a chartered university and is recognized by the UGC / Higher Education Commission (HEC) and the Government of Pakistan. Mohi-ud-Din Islamic University Nerian Sharif is one similar effort of the people of Pakistan and Azad Jammu & Kashmir. The establishment of this university encourages the educational planners of Deeni circles to come forward for the promotion of the education not only for the local populace, but also for the future generations of the whole nation.

Mohiuddin Jahangir : Mohiuddin Jahangir was a Captain in the Bangladesh Army during the 1971 Liberation War. He was born in 1948 in the village of Rahimgonj under Babugonj Upazilla of Barisal district. He was killed in an attempt to break through enemy defence on the bank of the Mahananda River. His initiative seriously undermined the Pakistani Army's resistance in the area and led to the fall of the position to the Bangladesh

Army. He was awarded the highest recognition of bravery in the Bangladesh Army, Bir Sreshtho.

Mohiuddin Jahangir : Mohiuddin Jahangir was a Captain in the Bangladesh Army during the 1971 Liberation War. He was born in 1948 in the village of Rahimgonj under Babugonj Upazilla of Barisal district. He was killed in an attempt to break through enemy defence on the bank of the Mahananda River. His initiative seriously undermined the Pakistani Army's resistance in the area and led to the fall of the position to the Bangladesh Army. He was awarded the highest recognition of bravery in the Bangladesh Army, Bir Sreshtho.

Mohmand : Mohmand is one of the strongest Pashtun tribes, living in Afghanistan and western North-West Frontier Province, Pakistan. Mohmands still live under strict tribal laws, and follow the code of Pashtunwali. In Pakistan the Mohmand Agency is an abode for Mohmands, further migrations from Afghanistan and Mohmand Agency have occurred and continue down to the plains of Peshawar, Charsadda, and Mardan.

Moin Khan : Mohammad Moin Khan (born September 23, 1971) popularly known as Moin Khan is a Pakistani cricketer (wicketkeeper and batsman) and member of the Pakistani national cricket team since 1990.

He was born in Rawalpindi, Punjab. He made his international debut against West Indies cricket team at Multan. He has taken over 100 catches in Test cricket. He has scored over 3,000 ODI runs and taken over 200 catches in ODI cricket.

Moirang : Moirang is a district situated in the north east of India, 45 km from Imphal, Manipur. The Moirang C.D. Block come into existence on 4 April 1985 with its headquarters at Moirang Khunou about 1.5 km from the

Kumbi main road. It has an area of 269 km² with a population of 62,187 (BPL Survey) in 67 villages.

Loktak Lake, the biggest fresh water lake in the North East Indian region and Keibul Lamjao National Park are situated in this district. There are 12 Gram Panchayats in this block. Archeologically, the town of Moirang is famous for the ancient temple of the pre-Hindu deity, Lord Thangjing. The graceful khamba-thoibi dance also originated here at Moirang.

During World War II, Moirang was the headquarters of Azad Hind Fauz. Colonel Malik of the Indian National Army, (INA) hoisted the Tricolour for the first time on Indian soil on April 14, 1944, in Moirang with the help of Manipuris like Shri Koireng Singh and others who were members of the INA. The museum here displays some wartime relics and photographs.

Mokokchung : Mokokchung is located in Mokokchung District, Nagaland, India. Mokokchung town is the district headquarter as well as the main urban hub of Mokokchung district in Nagaland. It is a picturesque hilly town at an altitude of 1325 metres above sea level.It has a population of around 40,000. The population is predominantly Ao.Infact it is the heart and the cultural centre of the Aos. The main town Baptist church, located at the heart of the town, is one of the largest church in Asia.The town is divided into 15 wards.

National Highway No-61 passes through this town.State highways link this town with almost every corner of the state.Every village and settlement of the district is well linked to the town by district and community roads.Infact its central location has helped it to be better connected to most areas of Nagaland than Kohima and Dimapur. Mokokchung being the district headquarter of one of the most progressive as well as politically important district of Nagaland plays a very important role in every sphere of Nagaland's life.

Mokshagundam Visvesvarayya : Sir Mokshagundam Visvesvarayya (other spellings include Visweswaraiah, Vishweshwariah and Vishweshwarayya) (August 28, 1860–April 12, 1962), popularly known as "Sir M.V.", was an eminent Indian engineer and statesman.

Sir M. Visvesvarayya was given the nation's highest honour, the Bharat Ratna, in 1955.

Mollem (Bhagwan Mahavir Sanctuary) National park : Bhagwan Mahavir Sanctuary earlier known as Mollem Game Sanctuary(1969) is situated close to the Mollem village at the foot of the Western Ghats, on the eastern border of Goa. It is 60 km away from the state capital, Panaji. The sanctuary, Goa's largest wildlife preserve covers an area of 240sq.km. The core zone of the sanctuary comprising an area of 107 sq. km. was notified as a National Park during 1978 known as Mollem National Park.

Mon : Mon town is the district headquarter of Mon District and is situated at an altitude of 2,945 ft (898 m) above sea level. It is at a distance of 357 km from Kohima via Dimapur and 280 km from Dimapur, 275 km from Kohima via Mokokchung, Tamlu and Wakching. Home of the Konyaks, the town was established at the land of Chen and Mon villages. It is centrally located for the coronation of Anghs (chiefs). Mon town recorded a population of 16,119 (2001 census). The Konyaks and the Aos are the two tribes that constitute almost the entire urban population of present day Mon town.

Mongla Port : Mongla is a sea port in the Bagerhat District of south-western Bangladesh. It is located 48 km south of Khulna city. The port was developed initially about 18 km up at Chalna, which was opened to foreign vessels as an anchorage on 11 December 1950. The anchorage was shifted to Mongla in 1954 as the place could accommodate sea-going vessels with greater draughts. The port of Mongla had long retained its name Chalna. Mongla is situated on the confluence of the rivers Pasur and Mongla at Mouza Selabunia of Rampal upazila of Bagerhat district. During the Pakistan period, the administration of the port was under a port director, whose main office was at Khulna.

Sea-going vessels up to a draught of 25 feet could berth vessels here and those with a draught up to 17 feet were allowed to anchor. Although fairly small, Mongla was a busy port in the past and at times, about two dozen sea going vessels were found anchored here. Later, especially since 1980, the port often remained closed because it lost proper depth required for the ocean-going ships and every time it was reopened after dredging. At present, about 400 ships berth at the port in a year and the port annually handles about 3 million MT of imports and exports. The port has 11 jetties, 7 shades for loading and unloading of goods and 8 warehouses. It uses 12 swinging moorings or floating berthing places in deeper sections in the river. The Mongla Port Authority that now administers the port constructed a rest house for the seamen at a place named Heron Point.

The port has trade links with almost all major ports of the world, although vessels arriving here are mostly from ports of Asia, the Middle East, Australia, Europe and North America and the ships rarely come to Mongla from the countries of Latin America or Africa. In addition to promotion of imports and exports of the country, the port contributes to development of many industries and trading houses in surrounding places and along with this, of new infrastructures and job opportunities. Many local people are working in the port directly in loading and unloading vessels.

Moni Singh : Moni Singh (born 28 June 1901, Susang-Durgapur, Mymensingh district – died 31 December 1990, Dhaka) was the founder of the Communist Party of Bangladesh (CPB). Prior to the partition of India in August 1947, Singh was a successful workers' leader who led movements to abolish exploitative labour practices. He was imprisoned for long stretches on three occasions: 1930-37, 1967-69, and 1969-71. He was first elected CP head in 1951, when Bangladesh was part of Pakistan, and led it with one short interruption until his death. After the Sino-Soviet split, Singh took the side of the Soviets. Because of this, the party split in 1966. His autobiography, entitled Jiban Sangram, was first published in the Bengali language in 1983. It was translated into English with the title *Life is a Struggle* in 1988.

Monica Ali : Monica Ali (born October 20, 1967) is the author of Brick Lane, her debut novel, which was shortlisted for the Man Booker Prize for Fiction in 2003. Ali was born in Dhaka, Bangladesh to Bangladeshi and English parents, moving to England at the age of three. She grew up in Bolton, Northern England near Manchester and studied Philosophy, Politics and Economics at the University of Oxford.

Monira Rahman : Monira Rahman is co-founder of Acid Survivors Foundation, a Bangladeshi organisation dedicated to raising awareness and preventing acid attacks. She was granted the Human Rights Award of the German section of Amnesty International in 2005, as ASF was able to reduce number of acid attacs about 40% since 2003.

Monism (Advaita Vedanta) : Advaita Vedanta is probably the best known of all Vedanta schools. Advaita literally means "not two"; thus this is what we refer to as a "monistic" (or non-dualistic) system, which emphasises oneness. Its first great consolidator was Shankaracharya (788-820). Continuing the line of thought of some of the Upanishadic teachers, and also that of his own teacher Gaudapada, Shankara expounded the doctrine of Advaita - a nondualistic reality.

By analysing the three states of experience (waking, dreaming and deep sleep) he exposed the relative nature of the world and established the supreme truth of the Advaita: the non-dual reality of Brahman in which atman (the individual soul) and brahman (the ultimate reality expressed in the trimurti) are identified absolutely. Ishvara or God is seen as the manifestation of Brahman to human mind under the influence of an illusionary power called Maya. His theories were controversial from the start and some of his contemporaries accused him of teaching Buddhism while pretending to be a Hindu. However, many more see Adi Sankara as drawing from monist concepts ingrained in texts pre-dating the Buddha, like the more abstuse sections of the Vedas, as well as the older Upanishads, several of which are conservatively and thus reliably dated as far back as 1000 BCE, if not 1500 BCE.

Subsequent Vedantins debated whether the reality of Brahman was saguna (with attributes) or nirguna (without attributes). Belief in the concept of Saguna Brahman gave rise to a proliferation of devotional attitudes and more widespread worship of Vishnu and Shiva. Advaita Vedanta is strictly grounded in a belief that the ultimate truth is Nirguna Brahman. The Vishistadvaita and Dvaita schools believed in an ultimately saguna Brahman.

Monpa : The Monpa are an ethnic group in the disputed territory of Arunachal Pradesh, with a population of 50,000, centered in the districts of Tawang and West Kameng. Another 25,000 of them can be found in the district of Cuona in Tibet, where they are known as

Menba. Of the 45,000 Monpas who live in Arunachal Pradesh, about 20,000 of them live in Tawang district, where they constitute about 97% of the district's population, and almost all of the remainder can be found in the West Kameng district, where they form about 77% of the district's population. A small number of them may be found in the district of East Kameng and Bhutan (2,500).

The word "Monpa" means "People of the Mon-yul, which means land in Tibetan. They also share very close affinity with the Sharchops of Bhutan. Their language belongs to the Tibeto-Burman family, but it is significantly different from the Eastern Tibetan dialect and is written with the Tibetan script.

Monpa Hat : The Monpa tribe of Arunachal Pradesh uses a shallow conical hat to protect them from the sun and rain. The hat is made in two layers. The outer layer is woven in close diagonal twill, while the inner layer is made in an open-hexagonal weave. To make the hat waterproof, a layer from the stem of a banana tree is dried and sandwiched between the layers. The layers are held together around the edge which is sandwiched between two strips of cane, tightly bound together. A braided bamboo headband is fitted inside the hat, which is held on to the head by a strap looped below the chin.

Monpa Language : The Monpa language is spoken in Arunachal Pradesh and Tibet. It belongs to the Tibeto-Burman family, and it is mutually unintelligible to Tibetan, although it shares many similarities with the Bumthang dialect. The language uses the Tibetan script to represent its words and phonetics.

Monsoon : A monsoon is a periodic wind, especially in the Indian Ocean and southern Asia. The word is also used to label the season in which this wind blows from the southwest in India and adjacent areas that is characterized by very heavy rainfall, and specifically the rainfall that is associated with this wind.

Montagu-Chelmsford Reforms : The Montagu-Chelmsford Reforms were reforms introduced by the British Government in India to introduce self-governing institutions gradually to India. The reforms take their name from Edwin Samuel Montagu, the Secretary of State for India during the latter parts of World War I and Lord Chelmsford between 1916 and 1921. The reforms were outlined in the Montagu-Chelmsford Report prepared in 1918 and formed the basis of the Government of India Act 1919. Indian nationalists considered that the reforms did not go far enough while British conservatives were critical of the reforms.

Mopin—Adi Festival : Mopin is another popular festival of the Adis, mainly of the Gallong community of the Arunachal Pradesh. This is normally celebrated in order to get rid of natural calamities diseases, effects of evil spirits and for good harvest, health, wealth and prosperity. In this festival Mopin, the Goddess of welfare, peace, wealth, prosperity and wisdom is propitiated in grand celebration. The festival lasts for five days from the eighth of April before, sowing of paddy. The Popir dance is the most popular dance during the festival.

Moplah Rebellion : The Moplah rebellion was a British-Muslim and Hindu-Muslim conflict in Kerala that occurred in 1921. The reasons for the conflict are rooted in religious revivalism among the Muslim Moplahs (also known as Mappilas), disaffection with British governance, and resentment at the land owning Hindu Nair community. Events following the Khilafat movement helped organize Moplahs and gave impetus to their actions.

According to one view, the Moplah Rebellion was a result of dissatisfaction of Muslim Moplahs with the land-owning Hindu Nair community and the British administration that inevitably supported the latter. The rebellion had an Islamic fanatic flair to it, and had ramblings of "freedom from the foreigners."

Moradabad : Moradabad is a city in Uttar Pradesh state of India. It was established in 1600 by Murad, the son of the Mughal Emperor Akbar; as a result the city came to known as Moradabad. It is the administrative headquarters of Moradabad District. Moradabad is situated at a distance of 167 km (104 miles) from the national capital, New Delhi, at the bank of River Ram Ganga (a tributary to the great Ganges). The city is famous for its huge export of brass handicrafts to North America and Europe, and is also thus called "Brass City" or Peetal Nagri (in the local language). It has close to one million citizens of various ethnicities and religions. At present the district is divided into 6 subdivisions namely Moradabd Sadar, Billary, Kaanth, Chandausi, Thakur dwar, Sambhal.

Morarji Desai : Shri Morarji Desai was born on February 29, 1896 in Bhadeli village, now in the Bulsar district of Gujarat. His father was a school teacher and a strict disciplinarian. From his childhood, young Morarji learnt from his father the value of hard work and truthfulness under all circumstances. He was educated St. Busar High School and passed his matriculation examination. After graduating from the Wilson Civil Service of the then Bombay Province in 1918, he served as a Deputy Collector for twelve years.

In 1930, when India was in the midst of the freedom struggle launched by Mahatma Gandhi, Shri Desai, having lost his confidence in the British sense of justice, decided to resign from Government service and to plunge into the struggle. It was a hard decision to take but Shri Desai felt that 'when it was a question of the independence of the country, problems relating to family occupied a subordinate position'.

Shri Desai was imprisoned thrice during the freedom struggle. He became a Member of the All India Congress Committee in 1931 and was Secretary of the Gujarat Pradesh Congress Committee untill 1937. When the first Congress Government assumed office in 1937 Shri Desai became Minister for Revenue, Agriculture, Forest and Co-operatives in the Ministry headed by Shri B.G. Kher in the then Bombay Province. The Congress Ministries went out of office in 1939 in protest against India involvement in the World War without the consent of the people.

Shri Desai was detained in the individual Satyagraha launched by Mahatma Gandhi, released in October, 1941 and detained again in August, 1942 at the time of the Quit India Movement. He was released in 1945. After the elections to the State Assemblies in 1946, he became the Minister for Home and Revenue in Bombay. During his tenure, Shri Desai launched a number of far-reaching reforms in land revenue by providing security tenancy rights leading to the 'land to the tiller' proposition. In police administration, he pulled down the barrier between the people and the police, and the police administration was made more responsive to the needs of the people in the protection of life and property. In 1952, he became the Chief Minister of Bombay.

After the reorganisation of the States, Shri Desai joined the Union Cabinet as Minister for Commerce and Industry on November 14, 1956. Later, he took the Finance portfolio on March 22, 1958. In 1963, he resigned from the Union Cabinet under the Kamraj Plan. In 1967, Shri Desai joined Smt. Indira Gandhi's cabinet as Deputy Prime Minister and Minister in charge of Finance. In July, 1969, Smt. Gandhi took away the Finance portfolio from him.

While Shri Desai conceded that the Prime Minister has the prerogative to change the portfolios of colleagues, he felt that his self-respect had been hurt as even the common courtesy of consulting him had not shown by Smt. Gandhi. He, therefore, felt he had no alternative but to resign as Deputy Prime Minister of India.

When the Congress Party split in 1969, Shri Desai remained with the Organisation Congress. He continued to take a leading part the opposition. He was re-elected to Parliament in 1971. In 1975, he went on an indefinite fast on the question of holding elections to the Gujarat Assembly which had been dissolved. As a result of his fast, elections were held in June, 1975. The Janata Front formed by the four opposition parties and Independents supported by it, secured an absolute majority in the new House. After the judgement of the Allahabad High Court declaring Smt. Gandhi's election to the Lok Sabha null and void, Shri Desai felt that in keeping with democratic principles, Smt. Gandhi should have submitted her resignation.

Shri Desai was arrested and detained on June 26, 1975, when Emergency was declared. He was kept in solitary confinement and was released on January 18, 1977, a little before the decision to hold elections to the Lok Sabha was announced. He campaigned vigorously throughout the length and breadth of the country and was largely instrumental in achieving the re-sounding victory of the Janata Party in the General Elections held in March, 1977 for the Sixth Lok Sabha. Shri Desai was himself selected to the Lok Sabha from the Surat Constituency in Gujarat. He was later unanimously elected as Leader of the Janata Party in Parliament and was sworn in as the Prime Minister of India on March 24, 1977.

As Prime Minister, Shri Desai was keen that the people of India must be helped to become fearless to an extent where even if the highest in the land commits a wrong, the humblest should be able to point it out to him. For him, truth was an article of faith and not an expediency. He seldom allowed his principles to be subordinated to the exigencies of the situation. Even in the most trying circumstances, he stood by his convictions.

Morena District : Morena District is a district of Madhya Pradesh state in central India. The district is part of Chambal Division. The town of Morena is the district and divisional headquarters. Most of present-day Morena District formed Tonwarghar District of the erstwhile princely state of Gwalior. After India's independence in 1947, the princely states acceded to the Government of India, and Morena District acquired its present boundaries with the addition of the small princely estate of Pahargarh in the south of the district. Morena Distict became part of the new state of Madhya Bharat, which was merged into Madhya Pradesh in 1956.

Mormugao : Mormugao is Goa's main port and its district. Its appearance in the 1980 film The Sea Wolves is one of its few global advertisements, but it has a fascinating past. When the Portuguese colonised part of Goa in the sixteenth century, they based their operations in the central district of Tiswadi, notably in the international emporium City of Goa, now Old Goa. As threats to their maritime supremacy increased, they built forts on various hillocks, especially along the coast. In 1624 they began to build their fortified town on the headland overlooking Mormugao harbour.

Morni Hills : *Panchkula* district has the *Morni Hills* - the only hill station of *Haryana*. A charming and peaceful place to rest and savor the nature. During the monsoons a carpet of grass covers the hills which makes them excellent grazing ground for black buck and Neelgai (blue bull). A lone tiger or panther can be spotted on occasion, while foxes, mongooses, jackals and wild dogs are aplenty.

Morshed Khan : Morshed Khan (born August 8, 1940 in Chittagong) is the current foreign minister of Bangladesh, a post he has held since October 2001. Prior to entering politics, Khan was one of the most successful businessmen in Bangladesh. His many assets and holdings in Bangladesh include Citicell, Pacific Motors and Arab Bangladesh Bank.

Morshed Khan studied engineering at the Tokyo University of Technology and Agriculture, and graduated with a Bachelor of Engineering. Following that, he received his post-graduate diploma from Sofia University, Japan. After his return to Bangladesh, he established several industries. He became active in politics first as the chairman to the Committee of Foreign Affairs and then as a special envoy to the Prime minister of Bangladesh, during the Bangladesh Nationalist Party led government between 1991-1996. He has served several terms in the Jatiyo Sangshad, the national parliament of Bangladesh. Since October 2001, he has been serving as the Foreign Minister in the Cabinet.

Moslem Bharat : Moslem Bharat, monthly literary journal, which began publication from Kolkata in 1920. Though the name of the poet Mohammad Mozammel Huq (of Shantipur) appeared as editor, for all practical purposes its executive editor was his son, Afzalul Huq. The first issue was published in Baishakh 1327 BS (April-May, 1920) and the last one in Paus, 1328 (December-January, 1921-22). Its multicoloured cover depicted traditional Islamic art. Moslem Bharat played an important role in establishing Nazrul Islam as a poet. In March 1920, Nazrul retired from army life in Karachi and returned to Kolkata where he met Afzalul Huq. It is said that Nazrul contracted with Afzalul

Huq to contribute regularly to his journal for a fixed monthly honorarium of one hundred rupees.

M Osman Ghani : Osman Ghani (1912-1989) was a scientist, educationist and academic administrator; played a key role in the development of institutions and infrastructure of science and technology in Bengladesh. He was born in Gozadia village of Kishoreganj district. Osman Ghani received his early education at local institutions. He was the first Indian Muslim to have obtained an MSc in Biochemistry securing first class from University of Dhaka (1935) and PhD in Agricultural Chemistry from the University of London (1938).

Ghani's area of research covered soil and fertiliser, plant and animal nutrition and allied fields, fractionation of soil phosphorus, phosphate fixation in soils and its mechanism, and availability of soil phosphorus and its determination and transformation under fertiliser treatments. He has a large number of publications to his credit in the national and international scientific journals. MO Ghani was awarded the title of 'Sitara-e-Quaid-e-Azam' in 1959 and 'Sitara-e-Pakistan' in 1964 by the government of Pakistan in appreciation of his outstanding achievements. He was honoured as DSc (Honoris Causea) from Northern Colorado University, USA in 1967. He was also elected a Member of the Bangladesh Parliament as an independent candidate in 1979. M Osman Ghani died on 21 July 1989.

Mosque Ali Muhammad Khan : Another old mosque of Multan, which is still in good condition, is Mosque Ali Muhammad Khan, which is also known as Mosque Wali Muhammad Khan. It is an excellent building, situated in the busiest Chowk Bazaar of the city. It was built by Nawab Ali Muhammad Khan Khakwani in 1757 (1171 A.H.) when he was the governor of Multan in the times of Alamgir II. The mosque is provided with a reservoir for the ablutions, baths, and a large hall for prayers. During the Sikh period, the gateway of the Mosque was used as the courthouse of the Nazim, while its great hall was utilized for keeping the Granth, or the holy book of the Sikhs. The mosque was restored to the Muslims by the British Government at the commencement of the British rule.

Mosque Phool Hattan Wali : This mosque is located in the Main Bazaar (now called Chowk Bazaar) of Multan. It was named so because it was located in the midst of the flower seller's bazaar. The story recorded in a book titled "Early History of Multan" it is said that the Mughal Emperor Farrukh Sher (1713-1718 AD) on his visit to Multan, being childless, asked a Fakir to pray on his behalf, that he might be blessed with a male issue. The fakir prayed for him, and a son was born to the Empress. His Majesty, through the governor of Multan, presented the fakir with an offering of Rs. 80,000, and with this money the liberal minded fakir had this mosque built.

Mosque City of Bagerhat : Mosque City of Bagerhat is one of the three World Heritage Sites in Bangladesh.

It is located in the Bagerhat District in south-west Bangladesh. It was declared by UNESCO as a World heritage site in 1983.

Mostofa Kamal : Mostofa Kamal, better known as Shaheed Sepoy Mostafa Kamal was a Sepoy in Bangladesh Army during the Liberation War. He was born on 16 December 1947 in Hajipur village of Daulatikhan upazilla under Bhola district. His father was retired Havilder Habibur Rahman. On 18 April 1971, Mostofa Kamal was killed in a defensive battle against the occupying Pakistan Army in Daruin village of Comilla. His action inflicted heavy casualities on his enemy troops. He was awarded the highest recognition of bravery of the Bangladesh Army, Bir Sreshtho.

Mother India : Mother India is a 1957 Bollywood movie directed by Mehboob Khan, nominated for Academy Award for Best Foreign Language Film in 1957.

Mother Teresa : Mother Teresa the 'angel of mercy' dedicated herself to the service of mankind and served god amongst the poorest of the poor, sick and the dying for more than 50 years of her life. Teresa was born as Agnes Gonxha Bojaxhin on 26th August 1910 in Skopje, now the capital of Macedonia to Albanian parents. She was the youngest of three children. Exposed early to prayer and service, she was deeply religious. At the age of 18, she left home for Dublin, Ireland, to join the Loretto abbey and become a nun of the Roman Catholic church. After her training, she was given the name of Sister Teresa. Sisters of Our Lady of Loreto, were very active in India, doing missionary work. She came to India on January 6, 1929 to become a teacher and was moved at the sight of the crippled and helpless people on the pavements. She taught in St. Mary's convent school in Kolkata for 15 years later on became the headmistress. In 1937, she took her final vows as a nun, in Darjeeling.

In 1947, on a journey to Darjeeling later referred by her as the most important journey of her life she had a vision or call to leave the convent, to live among the poor and to take care of the sick and the dying, the hungry, the homeless, to be God's Love in action to the poorest of the poor, which was the beginning of the Missionaries of Charity. At first she did not get the permission to leave the convent but in 1948 she got the permission specifically from Pope Pius XIII to leave the the Loreto community and work among the city's poor. She left the convent, took basic training in nursing and went to live in the nearby slum. She wore an inexpensive and simple white sari with a blue border, which became the most recognised symbol of the Sisters of Charity.

Following one of her former student, others joined her in her mission. In 1948, she opened the first slum school. As the congregation grew she sought approval from the Pope and shifted to 54A Lower Circular Road, which became the Mother House. The Missionaries of charity was officially established as a religious congregation for the Archdiocese of Calcutta in October 1950. The organisation devoted to the working for the destitute, now have thousands of homes and members all over the country and abroad. Calcutta became the center of her humanitarian activities. Her first home was 'Nirmal Hriday' (pure heart) for the sick and the dying, and then ' Shishu Bhavan' for the disabled, orphaned and mentally retarded children, 'Shanti Nagar', a colony for lepers where they were cared for, they could learn a skill, build their own houses and could work on their own fields, AIDS hospices and so on. The first home outside India was founded in 1965 in Venezuela. Others were later opened in Italy, Tanzania, Australia, US, Communist Cuba, former Soviet Union etc.

Mother Teresa became an Indian citizen in 1962. She has received many national and international awards in recognition of her noble work for humanity. The first award being Padmashri for distinguished service (1962), then the Magsaysay Award the same year, Pope John XXIII Peace Prize (1971), Good Samaritan Award (1971), John. F. Kennedy International Award (1971), Jawaharlal Nehru Award for International peace (1972), Nobel Peace Prize (1979), Bharat Ratna (1980), Rajiv Gandhi Sadbhavana Award (1993) etc. were some of them.

In 1983, at the age of 72, Mother was diagnosed with a serious heart condition and her health steadily worsened. In 1990, Mother had decided to step down as the head due to her failing health and so called a conclave of sisters to choose a successor. But in a secret ballot, she was re-elected with one dissenting vote, that was her own. In

1991 she underwent heart surgery and in March 1997, Sister Nirmala a former Hindu converted to Roman Catholic was elected to succeed Mother Teresa as leader of Missionaries of Charity. On September 5, 1997 the 87-year old mother died of severe cardiac arrest at the Missionaries of Charity headquarters in Kolkata. The late mother taught the world the beauty in giving and left behind an enormous organisation with the will to continue her work. Mother was beatified by Pope John Paul II at St. Peters square in Vatican, on October 19th 2003, seven years after her death. Henceforth the mother will be referred to as the The Blessed Teresa of Kolkata.

Motichoor Ka Laddu : Motichoor Ka Laddu is a sweet delicacy of the central Bihar region, made from grilled gram flour flakes which are sweetened, mixed with almonds, pressed into balls and fried in ghee. Originally from Maner, a small town near Patna, it is now made and enjoyed throughout India. It is a traditional gift at weddings, engagements and births. Some of the original families who made the Laddu in Maner have now moved to Patna and sell it in the city.

Motilal Nehru : Motilal Nehru (May 6, 1861 – February 6, 1931) was an early Indian freedom fighter and leader of the Indian National Congress. He was also the patriarch of India's most powerful political family. He was born in Delhi, to a Kashmiri Brahmin family. Nehru became a barrister and settled in the city of Allahabad, Uttar Pradesh. Many of Motilal's suits involved civil cases and soon he made a mark for himself in the legal profession of Allahabad. With the success of his practice, he bought a large family home in the Civil lanes of the city and aptly christened the house as Anand Bhavan or Abode of happiness. In 1909 he got the approval to appear in the Privy Council of Great Britain.

In the 1910s, Nehru was a man of many elitist habits and attitudes, and a Westernized lifestyle, and one of the moderate, wealthy leaders of the Indian National Congress. With the ascent of Mahatma Gandhi in 1918, Nehru was one of the first to transform his life to exclude western clothes and material goods, and adopt a more native Indian lifestyle. To meet the expenses of his large family and large family homes, Nehru had to occasionally return to his practice of law.

Motilal Nehru twice served as President of the Congress Party. He was also arrested during the Non-Cooperation Movement. Although initially close to Gandhi, he openly criticized Gandhi's suspension of civil resistance in 1922 due to the murder of policemen by a nationalist mob in Chauri Chaura. Motital joined the Swaraj Party, which sought to enter the British-sponsored councils, if only in order to wreck the government. The party failed however, and Motilal returned to the Congress.

The entry of Motilal's glamorous, highly-educated young son Jawaharlal Nehru into politics in 1916, created a celebrative atmosphere, giving birth to the most powerful and influential Indian political dynasties. When in 1929, Nehru handed over the Congress presidency to Jawaharlal, it greatly pleased Motilal and Nehru family admirers to see the son take over from his father. Jawaharlal had opposed his father's favor for dominion status, and had himself not left the Congress Party when Motilal helped found the Swaraj Party.

Motilal Nehru chaired the famous Nehru Commission in 1928, that was a counter to the all-British Simon Commission. Nehru's Report, the first constitution written by Indians only, conceived a dominion status for India within the Empire, akin to Australia, New Zealand and Canada. It was endorsed by the Congress Party, but rejected by more radical Indians who sought complete independence, and by many Muslims who didn't feel their interests, concerns and rights were properly represented.

Motilal Nehru's age and declining health kept him out of the historic events of 1929-1931, when the Congress adopted complete independence as its goal and when Gandhi launched the Salt Satyagraha. He was arrested in 1930, however, after his son was arrested, but was released shortly due to his failing health. He died on February 6, 1931.

Motiya Chowdhury : Motiya Chowdhury is a prominent Bangladeshi politician. She is currently a presidium member of Awami League, a major political party, as well as a Member of Parliament. She is known all over South Asia for her fiery speeches and her adamant attitude, qualities that have earned her the nick name of Ogni Konna or Girl of Fire. Although she started her political career with the left-wing party, National Awami Party or NAP, she is one of the senior-most leader of the Awami League. She is married to Bajlur Rahman, editor of The Daily Sangbad, one of the oldest Bangla dailies in existence.

Moudud Ahmed : Barrister Moudud Ahmed was born in May 1940. He is the 6th child (4th son) of late Maulana Momtaz Uddin Ahmed and late Begum Ambia Khatun. He successfully graduated from Dhaka University and then went to Lincoln's Inn in the United Kingdom to earn his barrister-at-law degree. After completing his degree he returned to Bangladesh and started practicing in the High Court. He was also a "Freedom Fighter" for Bangladesh in the 1971 Bangladesh Liberation War against Pakistan. He had three children, two sons and a daughter, but his elder son died at a very young age.

He was Minister and Adviser to the President Ziaur Rahman from 1977-1979. In 1979 he was elected for the first time the Member of the Parliament and was made the Deputy Prime Minister. In May 1980 Ziaur Rahman was assassinated and within a year there was a military coup led by Hossain Mohammad Ershad. In 1985 an election was held and once again Moudud Ahmed was elected Member of Parliament and consequently was made the Minister of Communication. A year later in 1986 he was again made the Deputy Prime Minister. In 1988 he became the Prime Minster and the Leader of the House (Parliament). Besides being minister of different ministries he also assisted Ziaur Rahman in forming BNP. He was one of the founding members of the party. He also played a vital role in the formation of Jatiya Party which belongs to Ershad.

Mouling National Park : This park is located in West Siang District of Arunachal Pradesh. It covers an area of about 500 Sq.Km. The forest of the park is semi evergreen type. The area is famous for three varieties of goat - antelopes, locally known as takin, coral and serow. The other fauna found in the park are wild buffalo, tiger, panther, red panda, elephant, hog dear, barking deer, sambar, python etc. Besides it, the park has many birds including different types of Pheasants. Ideal for trekking, hiking and angling at river Siyom.

Mount Abu : Mount Abu is the highest peak in the Aravalli Range of Rajasthan state, in western India. It is located in Sirohi District. The mountain forms a distinct rocky plateau 22km long by 9 km wide. The highest peak on the mountain is Guru Shikhar, at 1722 meters above sea level. It is referred to as 'an oasis in the desert', as its heights are home to rivers, lakes, waterfalls and evergreen forests. The town of Mount Abu, the only hill station in Rajasthan, is located at 1220 meters elevation. Mount Abu is the highest peak in the vicinity, and is a popular retreat from the heat of Rajasthan and nearby Gujarat for centuries. Mount Abu Wildlife Sanctuary was established in 1960, and covers 290 km^2 of the mountain.

Mount Abu is home to a number of Jain temples. The Dilwara Temples are a complex of temples, carved of white marble, that were built between the eleventh and thirteenth centuries. The Vimal Vasahi temple is the oldest, built in 1031 by Vimal Shah, and dedicated to the first of the Jain Tirthankaras. The Lun Vasahi Temple, built in 1231 by the brothers Vastupal and Tejpal, who were ministers of Raja Vir Dhawal, a local ruler of Gujarat who belonged to the Porwal Jain community. Nearby Achalgarh is a fort, built in the fourteenth century by Rana Kumbha of Mewar, which encloses several beautiful Jain temples, including the Achaleswar Mahadev Temple (1412) and the Kantinath Temple (1513).

Mount Abu Wildlife Sanctuary : Mount Abu Wildlife Sanctuary is located in one of the oldest mountain ranges of India - the Aravalli range. It was declared a wildlife sanctuary in 1960. It is a popular place for nature lovers as it has a great potential of eco-tourism. It spreads out into a plateau which is about 19 km in length and 6 km in breadth. In altitude, it varies from 300 meters at the foot to 1722 meters at Guru Shikhar, the highest peak in Rajasthan. The rocks are igneous and due to the weathering effect of wind and water, large cavities are common in them. It is very rich in floral bio-diversity starting from xenomorphic sub-tropical thorn forests in the foot hills to sub-tropical evergreen forests along water courses and valleys at higher altitudes.

Mount Abu is the only place in Rajasthan where one can observe a variety of orchids. The place is also rich in bryophytes and algae. Three species of wild roses and 16 species of feras some of which are quite rare have also been reported from here. The south-west part of the sanctuary is rich in bamboo forests. A variety of fauna, including highly rare, threatened and endangered species are found in this sanctuary. The past history of Mount Abu indicates the presence of lion (last recorded in 1872) and tiger (last reported in 1970). Presently the panther is the apex predator.

Mount Harriet National Park : Located in Andaman district covering an area of 47sq.km the park was established in 1979. It is 20km away from Port Blair the capital town of Island. Port Blair is the nearest town and airport. The fauna of the park is primarily Andaman wild pig. January to March are the best months for visiting the park.

Mount Thullier : Mount Thullier is the highest point in the Nicobar Islands, located in the Indian Ocean and bordering on the Andaman Sea. The mount is located on the island of Great Nicobar, measuring 642 m above mean sea level. Its geology features intrusive igneous rock formations, such as gabbro, combined with metamorphic minerals such as serpentine. The hill is thought to have arisen due to tectonic activity in the region.

Mountain Railways of India : Still operational today, these hill passenger railways crossing regions of great beauty are outstanding examples of bold, ingenious engineering solutions for the problem of establishing an effective rail link through a rugged, mountainous terrain. The Darjeeling Himalayan Railway opened in 1881, while the Nilgiri Mountain Railway, though proposed in 1854, was begun in 1891 and completed in 1908 due to the difficulty of the mountainous location which scales an elevation of 326m to 2,203m. It was highly significant in facilitating population movement and the social-economic development in the British colonial era.

The mountain railways of India are outstanding examples of the interchange of values on developments in technology, and the impact of innovative transportation system on the social and economic development of a multicultural region, which was to serve as a model for similar developments in many parts of the world.

The development of railways in the 19th century had a profound influence on social and economic developments in many parts of the world. The Mountain Railways of India are outstanding examples of a technological ensemble, representing different phases of the development in high mountain areas.

Movement for Restoration of Democracy : Movement for Restoration of Democracy (MRD) is a multi-party political alliance in Pakistan. MRD coalition comprising of Pakistan People's Party, National Democratic Party, Tehrik-e-Istaqlal, Pakistan Muslim League, Qaumi Mahaz-e-Azadi, Pakistan Mazdoor Kissan Party, Jamiat-e-Ulema-e-Islam, National Awami Party (Pakhtoonwa); MRD demands withdrawal of martial law and immediate elections; movement elicits support of lawyers and journalists.

Mridangam : The mridangam is a percussion instrument from South India. It is the primary rhythmic accompaniment in a Carnatic music ensemble. The mridangam is a double-sided drum whose body is made using a hollowed piece of jackfruit wood about an inch thick. The two mouths or apertures of the drum are covered with a goat skin leather and laced to each other with leather straps around the circumference of drum. These straps are put into a state of high tension to stretch out the circular membranes on either side of the hull, allowing them to resonate when struck. These two membranes are dissimilar in width to allow for the production of both bass and treble sounds from the same drum.

The mridangam is played resting it parallel to the floor. A right-handed mridangam artist plays the smaller membrane with his or her right hand and the larger membrane with the left hand. This can be described in words as follows: The mridangam rests upon the right foot and ankle, the right leg being slightly extended, while the left leg is bent and rests against the hull of the drum and against the torso of the artist. For a left-handed percussionist, the legs and hands are switched.

Mrinal Miri : Mrinal Miri (born August 1, 1940) is an Indian philosopher and educationalist who is currently vice-chancellor and CEO of North Eastern Hill University (NEHU) in Shillong, Meghalaya. He was awarded a BA in Philosophy from the University of Cambridge in 1966 and gained his doctorate in 1970. From 1970 to 1974 he was a Lecturer in Philosophy at St. Stephen College under the University of Delhi, before moving to NEHU. Professor Mrinal also served as the Director of the Indian Institute of Advanced Study, Shimla, from 1993 to 1999. He has been awarded a Padma Bhushan for his contribution in the field of education and literature. He is a member of the National Advisory Council established by the Manmohan Singh government.

Mrinal Sen : Born in 1923 in Faridpur in what is now Bangladesh, Sen studied science in Calcutta before he joined the Communist Party of India. At this time he read voraciously on films and aesthetics and reviewed films. His early films were heavily influenced by Marxist ideals and his second film, Neel Akasher Neechay (Under the Blue Sky, 1958) was banned by the government for two months. His films then experimented with themes of marriage in an urban middle-class milieu. These films include BaisheyShravana (A Wedding Day, 1960), a tender love story that ends in a famine, and Punascha (Over Again, 1962), which explored the problems that arose in the Indian household when the wife went to work. In 1956 he made Akash Kusum (The Daydream), which sparked a lively debate in a national daily with Ashish Barman and Satyajit Ray. The daily grind of living in Calcutta and its social, economic and political unrest prompted Sen to make the Calcutta trilogy: Interview (1970), Calcutta 71 (1972), and Patalik (1973).

With his films Ek Din Pratidin (1979) and Kharij (The Case is Shut), Sen entered the most creative phase of his career. In Ek Din Pratidin, Sen explores the trauma induced in a middle-class Bengali home when the working daughter fails to return home on time; in Kharij, he explores the anxieties created by the accidental death of a servant from gas poisoning while he slept in the kitchen. These films are masterful explorations of the middle-class morality, the stucture of everyday life and its oppressions, the mentalite (as the French would say) of domesticity, and the urban setting of Calcutta. By the early eighties, Sen, who had now become a national figure, was beginning to show a different comtemplative side, and his films also become reflections on film-making. Akaler Sandhaney (In search of famine, 1980) is a story about a film crew that descends on a small village to recreate the conditions of the 1943 famine in Bengal. The reality they see raises disturbing questions. Khandhar (The ruins, 1983) is another movie that subtly explores guilt in class relations.

Unlike Satyajit Ray, his great contemporary with whom he is often compared, Mrinal Sen did not restrict himself to Bengali films. He made in Oriya and Telugu, as well as in Hindi. His film Bhuvan Shome, with its austere style, sardonic humor, and expressionist exploration of the politics of class, is a landmark in modern Indian cinema, and became highly influential for what used to be called the 'New Indian Cinema'. Sen's work itself shows a fusion of myriad influences ranging from Bresson to Premchand. Sen has remained active in left-wing politics, and among some in the Indian intelligentsia his work has received more accolades than the work of Satyajit Ray, who was often charged with being apolitical.

Mrugavani National Park : The Mrugavani National park covering an area of 3.60 sq. km (700 acres) was established in October, 1994 near Himayatsagar lake at a distance of 25 kms from Hyderabad. The undulating topography of the park has rocky exposures of the Deccan trap formation and the vegetation is tropical dry deciduous forest of degraded nature interspersed with woodlands and grasslands. Over 600 plant species including herbs, shrubs, climbers and trees like Teak, Rosewood, Sandalwood, Neem, Bamboo etc are found here.

M S Golwalkar : M. S. Golwalkar, known throughout India as Guruji, was the second Sarsanghchalak of Rashtriya Swayamsevak Sangh. His full name was Madhav Sadashiv Golwalkar. His was an impressive personality: dignified gait; a long flowing beard reaching down to his chest; curly locks of hair touching the shoulders; a face luminous with innate intellect and learning. His was an inspiring presence. It aroused instant reverence. Whoever saw him spontaneously folded their hands and bowed their heads. Such was Guru.

He instilled patriotism in the hearts of millions of youths of the country. He explained to them the Hindu way of life and philosophy in simple words. Like a true friend, he shared in the joys and sorrows of his countrymen. He traveled untiringly through the length and breadth of the country almost a hundred times during the 33 years of his glorious tenure as Sarsanghchalak, kindling in the society the immortal flame of enduring love for the Motherland. He had scaled the highest levels of spirituality through his intense austerity and perseverance. By constant study and reflection he had become a veritable treasure of knowledge. He was a voracious reader even as a boy. He avidly read whatever books he could lay his hands on, from childhood through youth. Several are the disciplines in which he had acquired commendable mastery—History, Art, Religion, Culture, Sciences, Sociology and Economics, to name a few; and he dedicated all his stupendous intellectual faculties to the service of the country. He vastly expanded the network of Rashtriya Swayamsevak Sangh in multipledirections, and inspired and guided thousands of efficient dedicated workers spread throughout the country.

M S Swaminathan : Prof. Monkombu Sambasivan Swaminathan (born August 7, 1925) is an Indian agricultural scientist and heads the MS Swaminathan Research Foundation. Swaminathan is known as 'Father of Indian Green Revolution' for his contributions to the Green Revolution movement in India.

He graduated from Cambridge in 1952 with a PhD in genetics. Swaminathan's contributions to the agricultural renaissance of India have led to his being widely referred to as the scientific leader of the green revolution movement. He is now widely known for his advocacy of environmentally sustainable agriculture and sustainable food security. Following the 2004 Indian Ocean earthquake, he had advised India to plant mangrove groves along the shoreline to minimise damage from future tsunamis.

Dr. Swaminathan was Chairman of the UN Science Advisory Committee set up in 1980 to take follow-up action on the Vienna Plan of Action. He has also served as Independent Chairman of the FAO Council and President of the International Union for the Conservation of Nature and Natural Resources. He is the current President of the Pugwash Conferences on Science and World Affairs (the first person from a third world country to be elected the president). He is also on the Board of Trustees of Alexandria Bibliotheca—the only non-White and non-Arab on the board.

Swaminathan is a Fellow of the Royal Society of London and the U S National Academy of Sciences. He currently holds the UNESCO Chair in Ecotechnology at the M S Swaminathan Research Foundation in Chennai (Madras), India. He is the chairman of the National Commission on Agriculture, Food and Nutrition Security of India.

M S Subbalakshmi : Madurai Shanmukhavadivu (M.S) Subbalakshmi, the great Carnatic singer was born in Madurai, Tamil Nadu on September 16, 1916 to noted Veena player Shanmukhavadivu and lawyer Subramania Iyer. Hailed as the nightingale of Carnatic music this genius of a singer is a living legend. Young Kunchamma as she was called and her siblings was brought up in a musical environment in her home close to the Madurai Meenakshi Temple. Her grand mother Akkammal was a violinist. Her mother used to play and rehearse constantly and Kunchamma used to listen and hum ragas along with the Veena and the Nadaswaram recitals frequently heard from the temple. Her first Guru was Madurai Srinivasa Iyengar but her lessons could not last long as her guru passed away soon after she finished her foundations. But she kept practicing on her own for long hours. She did her formal schooling only till class 5th and music became the world for her.

Subbalakshmi's perfect pitch whether high or low and fantastic range of voice is the result of her dedication, toil and hours of continuous practice. As a child, when she practiced she would stop playing the tambura in between to check whether she is maintaining the pitch with and without it. She also learned Hindustani music from Pandit Narayan Rao Vyas for a short while. In the 1930's she learned 'khayals' and 'thumris' from Dwijenderlal Roy in Calcutta and later from Siddheshwari Devi of Benares and bhajans and Rabindra Sangeet from Dilipkumar Roy, she incorporates bhajans in almost all her concerts. Little Kunchamma accompanied her mother in local concerts and later gave solo performances. She was the child prodigy of Madurai at one time. Her first recording was at the age of ten, when she recorded a couple of songs 'Marakat vadivu' and 'Oothukuzhiyinile' in an impossibly high pitch for HMV in Madras. In 1934, in her debut at the Madras Music Academy she was noticed and applauded by top rank musicians like Chembai Vaidyanatha Bhagavathar, Tiger Varadachariar, Karaikudi Sambavisa Iyer and the likes.

In 1940 she married Thiagaraja Sadasivam, a well known figure in the Madras Congress circle, at Thiruneermalai. They had met four years earlier and with his wide connections in the journalistic and political world, he became instrumental in the continued success of her already flourishing career. From 1938 for a period of six years she started acting in films for a short while. Her films were quite successful but later in 1944 after her big hit 'Meera' produced by her husband and released in Tamil and Hindi, she quit and concentrated solely on music. From a South Indian celebrity she went on to become a national figure. Internationally she has given concerts almost all over the world like at Edinburgh festival and at the United Nations(1970), Carnegie Hall as the inaugural concert of the festival of India in London in 1982.

Subbalakshmi has been the recipient of the highest awards and honours the nation could bestow upon an artist and significant international recognition. She has earned doctorates from famed universities and her divine voice has earned acclaim from big and famous personalities like Mahatma Gandhi, Pandit Jawarharlal Nehru, Maharana of Udaipur etc as well as top rank musicians both in the Carnatic and Hindustani sphere in the country. In 1998, she was the first musician to receive the highest civilian award 'Bharat Ratna' from the President of India. Padma Bhushan (1954), Padma Vibhushan (1975), Ramon

Magsaysay award (1974) are some of the major awards she has received. The world of fame and adoration of thousands of fans, has left Subbalakhsmi untouched. She passed away at the age of 88.

M T Vasudevan Nair : M. T. Vasudevan Nair, popularly known as MT, is a Malayalam fiction and screenplay writer and film director. He was born July 15, 1933 in Kudallur, a small village in Palakkad district, Kerala. One of the most prolific and versatile of modern Malayalam writers, his novels, short stories and screenplays speaks of the pain and anguish of the Kerala society in the post independence India.

MT was awarded the highest literary award in India, the Jnanpith in 1995. He is also the receipient of many awards including: Kerala State Sahithya Academy and Central Sahithya Academy.

Mudasarlova : Mudasarlova is a large water tank located at a distance 5 km. from Visakhapatnam. The site consists of park (for picnics) fountains, birds and peacocks in cages, water tank and a beautiful garden.

Mudumalai Wildlife sanctuary: The Mudumalai sanctuary lies on the northern and north-western side of the Nilgiri (Blue Mountains), about 80 km north-west of Coimbatore in the extreme north-western corner of Tamil Nadu, on the interstate boundaries with Karnataka and Kerala states in southern India.

Mufti Mohammad Sayeed : Mufti Mohammad Sayeed (born January 12, 1936) was the chief minister of Jammu and Kashmir till November 2005. He is from the People's Democratic Party or the PDP, a Jammu and Kashmir regional party he launched in July 1999 to "persuade the Government of India to initiate an unconditional dialogue with Kashmiris for resolution of the Kashmir problem".

He has previously been a member of the Congress party. He is said to have brought about the downfall of the Farooq Abdullah led National Conference government of Jammu and Kashmir in 1984. In 1987, he quit the Congress to join V P Singh's Janta Dal, which led to his becoming the first Muslim Home Minister of India in 1989. His daughter Rubaiya was kidnapped by militants within few days of his taking office. She was released in exchange for the release of some militants. He rejoined the Congress under P V Narasimha Rao which he left in 1999 alongwith his other daughter Mehbooba Mufti to form his own party, People's Democratic Party. He has survived several attacks on his life by militants over the years.

Mughal Empire : The Mughal Empire, was an empire that at its greatest territorial extent ruled parts of what is today Afghanistan, Baluchistan and most of the Indian Subcontinent between 1526 and 1857. The empire was founded by the Timurid leader Babur in 1526, when he defeated Ibrahim Lodi, the last of the Delhi Sultans at the First Battle of Panipat. "Mughal" is the Persian word for "Mongol". The religion of the Mughals was Islam. The teritory was largely conquered by the Afghan Sher Shah Suri during the time of Humayun, the second Mughal ruler, but under Akbar it grew considerably, and continued to grow until the end of Aurangzeb's rule. Jahangir, the son of Akbar, ruled the empire between (1605-1627). In October 1627, Shah Jahan, son of Jahangir, "succeeded to the throne", where he "inherited a vast and rich empire" in India; and "at mid-century this was perhaps the greatest empire in the world". The Mughal Emperor Shah Jahan, commissioned (between 1630 - 1653), the Taj Mahal, in Agra, India.

After Aurangzeb died in 1707, the empire started a slow and steady decline in actual power, although it maintained all the trappings of power in the Indian subcontinent for another 150 years. In 1739 it was defeated by an army from Persia led by Nadir Shah. In 1756 an army of Ahmad Shah took Delhi again. The British Empire finally dissolved it in 1857, immediately prior to which it existed only at the sufferance of the British East India Company.

To the subject of the Mughals origins, the Mughal people were created through a series of interracial marriages. When the Mongolians of north west asia took the subcontinent and middle east in its vast empire, there was much marriage between the Mongols and central asians in particular the Persians. The Mughals are derived from this unique mesh of different peoples, although they adopted the culture of their ancestral Persians, which is evident in their religious practices, customs, architecture and language; and they still retained many physical attributes from their other ancestral half, which also helped to cement new customs and traditions.

Mughal Gardens : Mughal Gardens are a group of styles in garden design which originate from the Islamic Mughal Empire. They are influenced by Persian Gardens—and have a strong structural presence in the same vein. Typical features include pools, fountains and other water features and brightly planted flowerbeds.

Mughal Painting : Mughal painting is a particular style of Indian painting, generally confined to illustrations on the book and done in miniatures, and which emerged, developed and took shape during the period of the Mughal Empire in 16th -19th centuries.

When the second Mughal emperor, Humayun was in Tabriz in the Safavid court of Shah Tahmasp II, he was exposed to Persian painting. When Humayun returned to India, he brought with him two artists well accomplished in the Persian style of painting. Their works, and during succeeding decades, assimilation of local styles, gave shape to a distinct style, which became known as Mughal painting. The Tutinama (literal meaning "Tales of a Parrot"), now in the Cleveland Museum of Art, is among the earliest examples of Mughal painting. The manuscript was made in the reign of Humayun's son, Akbar.

The Mughal painting developed and flourished during the reigns of Akbar, Jahangir and Shah Jahan. Mughal painting was rich in variety which included portraits, events and scenes from the court life, wild life and hunting scenes, and illustrations of battle fronts. The Victoria and Albert museum in London have a large and remarkable collection of Mughal paintings.

Mughal Tamasa : The 'Tamasa' is a form of opera which reminds us of the 'Mughal' administration prevalent in Orissa and is a symbol of their culture. The songs are composed in both Persian and Oriya. Dialogue is quite amusing. The 'Tamasa' is peculiar to the Bhadrak area in the district of Balasore and is not performed in any other part of Orissa.

Muhajir : Muhajir or Mohajir is a ethnic group in Pakistan. It is essentially used for Urdu speaking Muslims that migrated to Pakistan and their descendants after the partition of India in 1947. While Muhajirs form what amounts to an ethnic group within Pakistan, the group is actually comprised of people from different ethnic groups and regions in South Asia, such as Uttar Pradesh, Delhi, Aligarh, Bihar, Bhopal, and Hyderabad Deccan. They are united by many identical socio-cultural elements including speaking the Urdu language as a mother tongue. Muhajirs are spread throughout Pakistan, with large concentrations in many of the urban areas.

Muhammad Akram Khan : Muhammad Akram Khan is a Pakistani scholar of Islamic law. In 1988, while he was an audit officer for that country's government, he wrote "Commodity Exchange and Stock Exchange in Islamic Economy," for The American Journal of Islamic Social Sciences. The essay is notable because it makes a very sweeping denunciation of many contemporary western, and far eastern, practices in finance. His prescriptions amount to a more restrictive view than that of most scholars in the field.

Muhammad Ali Bogra : Muhammad Ali Bogra (1909 - 1963) was a Pakistani statesman of Bengali origin, who served as Prime Minister of Pakistan from 1953 until 1955. Born at Bogra to a family descended from the Nawabs of Bengal, he attended Calcutta University and followed his education with a career in politics. In 1937 he began to receive prominence when he was elected to the assembly of Bengal. He would move up within the government of Bengal, serving under Khawaja Nazimuddin as the Health Minister.

Upon the formation of Pakistan in 1947, Bogra was put into the foreign service, and served in Burma, Canada, and eventually as ambassador to the United States. In 1953, he was selected by Governor General of Pakistan Ghulam Muhammad to replace Khawaja Nazimuddin as the Prime Minister.Bogra was a relatively unknown personality to the national political scene of that time. As Prime Minister, he set out to form a constitution.

In order to complete this, he outlined his famous "Bogra Formula" that sought to form a bicameral legislature. An Upper House would have contained 50 seats, 10 from each province, i.e. with 10 from East Pakistan and 40 from West Pakistan. A Lower House would have contained 300 seats. The lower house seats would be determined by population of province, and East Pakistan would have 165 seats, while the four provinces of West Pakistan would have a combined 135 seats, but would be split among the provinces. A provision was also put in place that stated that if the President of Pakistan were from West Pakistan, then the Prime Minister would have to be from East Pakistan, and vice-versa. The plan was very popular, but was killed when Ghulam Muhammad dissolved the Pakistani Assembly later in 1953. Bogra was removed from office in 1955 by the new Governor General, Iskander Mirza. He returned to his post as ambassador to the United States. In 1962 he became the foreign minister of Pakistan, until his death in 1963. He was buried in his hometown of Bogra.

Muhammad Ali Shehki : Muhammad Ali Shehki, is a Pakistani pop singer. A great, loving, versatile, talented and touching star of pakistan. Along with Alamgeer or Alamgir, he set the trend of pop music not only in Pakistan but anywhere where people could undertand the great Urdu language. When he started his career, he was young energetic student of NED University at Karachi, Pakistan. He is still loved by people for his contribution to music and his charming personality. His songs delivered message of love, patriotism and sincere thoughts. A great artist who will live forever in the world of art and humanity.

Muhammad Ataul Gani Osmani : Muhammad Ataul Gani Osmani, better known by General M.A.G. Osmani (1918-16 February 1984)was the supreme commander of Mukti Bahini and Bangladesh Armed Forces during the Bangladesh Liberation War. In 1939, Osmani started his military career as a Gentleman Cadet of the Royal Armed Forces. Following the war and the Partition of India in 1947, Osmani joined the Pakistan Army on 7 October 1947, and was promoted to Lieutenant Colonel. Osmani was promoted to a Colonel in 1956 and held the post of deputy director of general staff and military operations. He retired from Pakistan Army on 16 February 1967. After his retirement, Osmani entered the politics of East Pakistan. He joined the Sheikh Mujib-led Awami League in 1970. After the commencement of Bangladesh Liberation War, Osmani became a member of the provisional government-in-exile.

With the formation of Mujib's government on 17 April 1971, Osmani was appointed commander in chief of all Bangladesh Armed Forces. Under his direct command, Osmani divided up the entire declared Bangladesh territory to 11 sectors. Each sector was under the command of a trained military officer with the title of Sector Commander. After the country's independence, Osmani was elevated to the rank of General of the Bangladesh Armed Forces with effect from the date of 16 December 1971. With the abolition of the post of Commander in Chief on 7 April, 1972, Osmany retired from service. He was then included in the cabinet of Sheikh Mujibur Rahman as Minister of Shipping, Inland Water Transport and Aviation. Osmani was elected a member of the national parliament in 1973, and was included in the new cabinet with charge of the ministries of Post, Telegraph and Telephone, Communication, Shipping, Inland Water Transport and Aviation. He resigned from the cabinet in May 1974. After the introduction of one-party system of government through the Fourth Amendment to the constitution in 1975, he resigned from Parliament and also from the primary membership of the Awami League.

Osmani launched a new political party styled as Jatiya Janata Party in September 1976 and was elected its President. He contested in the presidential elections in 1978 as a nominee of the Democratic Alliance. He contested in the presidential elections once again in 1981 as a nominee of the Jatiya Nagarik Committee. Osmani was diagnosed with cancer. He passed away in bed on 16 February, 1984 while under treatment for cancer in London, at the age of 66. He was buried in Sylhet with full millitary honours. Mohammed Ataul Ghani Osmani is currently revered as one of the greatest freedom fighters of the nation, a brave man never afraid of laying down his life. The international airport in his hometown of Sylhet has been named after him as Osmani Antorjatik Biman Bondor.

Muhammad Ayub Khan : Muhammad Ayub Khan (May 14, 1907 – April 19, 1974) was a Field Marshal during the mid-1960s, and the political leader of Pakistan from 1958 to 1969. He became Pakistan's first native Commander in Chief in 1951, and was the youngest full-rank general and self-appointed field marshall in Pakistan's military history.

Khan was born in the village of Rehana near Haripur Hazara to an ethnic Pashtun family of the Tareen clan, the first child of the second wife of Mir Dad Khan, who was a Risaldar Major in Hodson's Horse. For his basic education, he was enrolled in a school in Sarai Saleh, which was about 4 miles from his village. He used to go to school on a mule's back. Later he was shifted to a school in Haripur, where he started living with his grandmother. He enrolled at Aligarh University in 1922, but never completed his studies, as he was accepted into the Royal Military Academy Sandhurst. He did well at Sandhurst, and was given an officer's post in the British Indian Armyand then joined the 1st Battalion of the 14 Punjab regiment (Sherdils), later known as 5 Punjab Regiment.

During World War II he served as a captain and later as a major on the Burma front, from where according to Sher Ali Khan's autobiography The Story of Soldiering and Politics in India and Pakistan he was "sent back" from his post with the Assam Regiment and Sir Gilbert Laithwaite's Note on General Ayub Khan, in the UK Public Record Office "He was...a failure as a Commanding Officer on active service and had to be relieved.". Following the war, he joined the fledgling Pakistani Army as the 10th ranking senior officer. He was promoted to Brigadier and commanded a brigade in Waziristan and then was sent initially with the local rank of Major General to East Pakistan as General Officer Commanding a division that was responsible for the whole East Wing of Pakistan in 1948 from where he returned in November 1949 as Adjutant General and then briefly was named Deputy Commander-in-Chief.

Ayub Khan was made Commander-in-Chief of the Pakistan Army on January 17, 1951, succeeding General Sir Douglas Gracey, thus becoming the first native Pakistani general to hold that position. He would later go on to serve in the second cabinet of Muhammad Ali Bogra as Defence Minister, and when Iskander Mirza declared martial law on October 7, 1958, Khan was made its chief martial law administrator. This would be the first of many instances in the history of Pakistan of the military becoming directly involved in politics.

As a result of his differences with Mirza, Khan gained more and more power, and became President of Pakistan after deposing Mirza on October 27 in a bloodless coup. This was actually welcomed in Pakistan, since the nation had experienced a very unstable political climate since independence. Khan soon adopted the titles of Hilal-e-Pakistan, and the rank of Field Marshal, the only Pakistani FM to date.

Khan moved to have a constitution created, and this was done in 1961. The Constitution called for elections, which took place in 1962, when martial law was lifted. Khan's main opponent was Fatima Jinnah, the sister of Pakistan's founding father. Despite Jinnah's immense popularity, Khan won the majority of the vote; whether or not this was done without corruption is debatable.

As President, Ayub Khan allied Pakistan with the global U.S. military alliance against the Soviet Union. This in turn led to major economic aid from the U.S. and European nations, and the industrial sector of Pakistan grew very rapidly, and this in turn improved the economy, as did Khan's educational and land reforms. It was under Ayub Khan that the capital was moved from Karachi to Rawalpindi, in anticipation of the construction of a new capital: Islamabad. In 1960, Khan's government signed the Indus Water Treaty with archrival India to resolve disputes regarding the sharing of the waters of the six rivers in the Punjab doab that flow between the two countries. Khan's administration also built a major network of irrigation canals, high-water dams and thermal and hydroelectric power stations. Despite the treaty, Khan maintained icy relations with India. Khan established close political and military ties with Communist China, exploiting its differences with Soviet Russia and its 1962 war with India. To this day, China remains a strong economic, political and military ally of Pakistan.

The turning point in Khan's rule was the Indo-Pakistani War of 1965. Khan, advised by his Foreign Minister Zulfikar Ali Bhutto, attempted to flush Kashmir with militants and Pakistani soldiers. The Indian Army's response reached as close as the great city of Lahore and the bombing of the port of Karachi, and created much insecurity and resentment in the hearts of common Pakistanis. In addition, the settlement that was reached by Khan at Tashkent was seen as a loss for Pakistan. The settlement led Bhutto to resign his post and take up opposition to Khan. The war also adversely affected Pakistan's economy. Government corruption and nepotism, in addition to an environment of repression of free speech and political freedoms increased unrest. Khan began to increase censorship and his control over the nation even more. These actions only served to further agitate the

Pakistani population, which fell into disarray of protests, strikes and rioting, and required the presence of the army in the cities. Bhutto used this to his political advantage, while the Awami League also made great political gains in East Pakistan. As Khan's popularity plummetted, he decided to give up rule. In 1969 he turned over control of Pakistan to General Yahya Khan, whom he had previously appointed chief martial law administrator.

Muhammad bin Qasim : Muhammad bin Qasim (c. 695–715) was an Arab general who captured Sindh and started the Islamic era in the Indian subcontinent. Muhammad bin Qasim was born around 695. His father died when he was young, leaving Qasim's mother in charge of his education. Umayyad governor Al-Hajjaj bin Yousef was one of Qasim's close relatives, and was instrumental in teaching Qasim about warfare and governing.

With Hajjaj's patronage, Qasim was made governor of Persia, where he succeeded in putting down a rebellion. At the age of seventeen, he was sent by Caliph Al-Walid I to lead an army into India in what is today the Sindh area of Pakistan. The Umayyads claimed the attack was an attempt to rescue pilgrims that had been taken captive by pirates, though many experts regard this explanation as a pretext for invasion. Qasim was successful, rapidly taking all of Sindh and moving into southern Punjab up to Multan. The forces of Muhammad bin Qasim defeated hindu Raja Dahir, and took his daughters captive (they were sent as a gift to Caliph) On his arrival at the town of Brahminabad between six and sixteen thousand men died in the ensuing battle.

After the violence Qasim attempted to establish law and order in the newly-conquered territory by allowing a degree of religious tolerance. He was countermanded by Hajjaj, who insisted on a more hardline policy. As a whole, populations of conquered territories were treated as People of the Book and granted toleration of their Hindu religion in return for payment of the poll tax (jizya). The Brahmin caste system was tolerated and no conversion of conquered populations was attempted. Qasim also began preparations for an attack on Rajasthan. In the interim, however, Al-Hajjaj bin Yousef died, as did Caliph Al-Walid I. The new caliph, Suleiman, was a political enemy of Hajjaj and recalled Qasim, claiming that Qasim had treated Raja Dahir's daughters poorly. Qasim was wrapped in oxen hides and returned to Syria, where he was imprisoned. Muhammad bin Qasim died in jail, at the age of twenty.

Muhammad bin Tughluq : Muhammad bin Tughluq was the Sultan of Delhi from 1325 to 1351. He was the eldest son of Ghiyath al-Din Tughluq. Ghiyas ud din sent the young Muhammad to the Deccan to campaign against the Kakatiya king Pratapa-rudra of Warangal. He succeeded to the Delhi throne after Ghiyas ud din's death in 1325. Muhammad was committed to maintaining the Sultanate's expansion into the newly-conquered provinces of peninsular India. To have better administration of these southern parts of the Empire, Muhammad moved the capital from Delhi to Deogiri in the Deccan in the early part of his reign, renaming that city "Daulatabad". Instead of moving just his government offices there, he forcibily moved the entire population of Delhi to the new capital. The plan failed due to inadequate water supply arrangements in Deogiri; the capital had to be shifted back again to Delhi after two years. A vast amount of the population died during the moves due to the inadequate travel arrangements. It was said that Delhi was a ghost town for years after the move back.

Muhammad also had the idea of introducing for the first time in India token currency, modeled after the Chinese example, using brass or copper coins, backed by silver and gold kept in the treasury. However, very few people exchanged their gold/silver coins for the new copper ones and the tokens were easy to forge, which led to heavy losses. It is said that after the plan failed, there were heaps of copper coins lying around the royal offices for years. Such gradiose, unsuccessful policy experiments made Muhammad notorious in the minds of many of his contemporaries. By the end of his reign, many of the further provinces of the empire were in revolt. Due to his follies, his last name became synonymous with "wacky" in popular usage in India. Muhammad died while campaigning in Sind. He was succeeded by his cousin Firuz Shah Tughluq.

Muhammad Ghori : Muhammad of Ghor or Muhammad Ghori or Mohammad Ghauri (originally named Mu'izz-ad-din) (1162 - 1206) was a Muslim conqueror and sultan in what is today Afghanistan between 1171 and 1206. Muhammad was from the region of Ghor in what is now central Afghanistan, which lay on the western boundary of the Ghaznevid empire. Before 1160, the Ghaznevid empire covered an area running from central Afghanistan east to the Punjab, with capitals at Ghazni, a city on the banks of Ghazni river in present-day Afghanistan, and at Lahore in present-day Pakistan. In 1160, the Ghorids conquered Ghazni from the Ghaznevids, and in 1173 Muhammad was made governor of Ghazni. In 1186-7 he conquered Lahore, ending the Ghaznevid empire and bringing the last of Ghaznevid territory under his control.

Ghori attacked India many times. First time he was routed in present day Gujarat by Rajputs. Mularaja-II was not even a teen yet and his mother organized the defences of Pattan. Battle was fought at Kayadara near Mount Abu and Ghori was resoundingly defeated. After this defeat he never entered India through Gujarat. In first battle of

Taraori in 1191 Prithvi Raj Chauhan captured Ghori and Ghori begged for his life. Prithviraj allowed him to go despite his generals asking him not to do so. Following year Ghori came again. Prithvi Raj Chauhan advanced with his army and sent a letter to Ghori. In this letter ghori was asked to return as he had been beaten last year and was spared his life. Ghori replied that he was in India on the orders of his brother and he can only retreat after he gets a word from his brother. This letter was sent in the evening and Ghori moved his camp back a few kilometers. On receiving this letter and seeing Ghori move his camp back Prithviraj assumed that Ghori is not interested in fighting. Ghori also knew that Rajputs did not fight in the night and only started fighting after sun had come up. He attacked in the early morning hours when Prithviraj and his army were sleeping and was able to win this war.

In a few years Muhammad controlled northern Rajasthan and the northern part of the Ganges-Yamuna Doab. Muhammad returned east to Ghazni to deal with the threat to his western frontiers from the Turks and Mongols, but his armies, mostly under Turkish generals, continued to advance through northern India, raiding as far east as Bengal. Muhammad returned to Lahore after 1200 to deal with a revolt of the Gakhar tribe in the Punjab. He suppressed the revolt, but was killed during a Gakhar raid on his camp on the Jhelum River in 1206. Upon his death, Qutb-ud-din Aybak, Muhammad's most capable general, took control of Muhammad's Indian conquests and declared himself the first Sultan of Delhi. Muhammad's former territory in Afghanistan was conquered by the Mongols.There is a conflict about his death. It is also supposed that he was killed by khokhar on the bank of Indus river near to D.G.Khan. There is his tomb which is famous of tomb pir muhammad Ghuari

Muhammad Ilyas : Muhammad Ilyas was the founder of the Islamic movement Tablighi Jamaat of the South

Asian subcontinent. He is arguably one of the most influential, yet least well-known, figures of the twentieth century Islam. Mawlana Ilyas was born in 1885 to a family of religious scholars, and his early education was completed at home. He was then sent to study at the famous centre of Islamic learning, Darul Uloom Deoband, where he studied under several famous Ulama. After completing his studies, he taught at various madrassas. In the late 1920s, he founded the Tablighi Jamaat movement to revive Islam in teh subcontinent.

Despite his enormous contribution towards the development of a powerful grass root Islamic Dawah movement, Mawlana Ilyas has not received much attention in the literature on modern Islamic movements. Most of the Western, and even Muslim, scholarships have remain occupied with the more spectacular and dramatic manifestions of Islamic revivalist upsurge. The available literature on Maulana Ilyas and his Tablighi movement is mostly in Urdu and that too consists mainly of inspirational works by its leaders and devotional writings by its followers and supporters.

Muhammad Khan Junejo : Muhammad Khan Junejo (born August 18, 1932 Died 1992) was former Pakistani Prime Minister. He was born at Sindhri, Sind. After completing his senior Cambridge, he went to U.K. for a diploma in Agriculture. Junejo started his political career at the age of twenty one. In 1962, he was elected Member Provincial Assembly, West Pakistan from Sanghar. He was appointed Minister in the West Pakistan cabinet in July 1963 and held the portfolios of Health, Basic Democracies and Local Government, Works, Communications and Railways.

After partyless polls were held for the national and provincial assemblies in 1985, Muhammad Khan Junejo was appointed Prime Minister by General Muhammad Zia-ul-

Haq.To his credit,Junejo had stood up to Zia on several issues during his term as prime minister, including the issue of the signing of the Geneva Accords to end the fighting in Soviet-occupied Afghanistan. Zia didn't want Pakistan to sign the accords until after the Soviet troops withdrew from Afghanistan but Junejo had instructed his minister of state for foreign affairs to sign them anyway.

Zia was furious, but had bided his time before moving against Junejo. That time came soon after the Ojhri Camp blasts of April 1988. The Ojhri Camp ordnance depot in Rawalpindi was being used to supply US-financed arms and ammunition to the Afghan mujahideen to fight the Soviets. The government ordered an inquiry into the blasts. Junejo made a statement in the National Assembly promising to place the findings of the inquiry before the House. That was the last straw as far as Zia was concerned, and Junejo was dismissed on May 29, 1988 by the President using discretionary powers given under the 8th amendment. Muhammad Khan Junejo was elected member of the National Assembly in 1990, and died of serious illness in 1992.

Muhammad Mehood Alam : Squadron Leader Muhammad Mehood Alam (born July 6, 1935) also known as M.M. Alam, is a Pakistani flying ace. Pakistani sources say he had destroyed 9 enemy aircrafts and damaged 2 overall in the Indo-Pakistani War of 1965. Indians however dispute this putting his kills at 5.Whatever the correct figures, both sides agree he was Pakistan's Top Gun. He was awarded the Sitra-e-Juraat (Medal of Courage) for his wartime actions. During the 1971 war, he was not allowed to fly, as he was of Bengali origin, but after the war he preferred to stay in Pakistan (erstwhile West Pakistan). He was also involved in training and participating in the Soviet-Afghan war. Alam retired in 1982 and currently resides in Karachi.

Muhammad Munir : Muhammad Munir was born on 3 May 1895. After doing MA from Government College Lahore he joined Law College to earn his L.L.B. He started his career as a lawyer at Amritsar in 1921, later on he shifted to Lahore in 1922. He was appointed Assistant Advocate-General of Punjab in 1937, and first President of Income Tax Appellate Tribunal in 1940. He was elevated to the Bench of Judicature at Lahore in 1942. In 1948 he was made the Chairman of the Pakistan Pay Commission, next year he was made the Chief Justice of Lahore High Court.

Justice Munir was appointed as the Chief Justice of Pakistan in 1954, and in the same year as the Governor General of Pakistan. Besides being the Chief Justice he also remained the Chairman Delimitation Commission from June 1956 to July 1958. He retired as chief Justice on 2 May 1960. Justice Munir represented Pakistan at International Criminal Jurisdiction Committee in 1951 and was elected its Vice-Chairman, he also presided the Punjab Disturbances Court of Inquiry in 1953. He is also the author of "Principles and Digest of the Law of Evidence".

Muhammad Rafiq Tarar : Muhammad Rafiq Tarar (b. November 2, 1929) was President of Pakistan from January 1, 1998 until June 20, 2001.Muhammad Rafiq Tarar During Pakistan's independence in 1947, Rafiq Tarar performed voluntary duty as a relief worker in camps set up by Muslim Students Federation for refugees, migrating from India to Pakistan.

Muhammad Rafiq Tarar graduated from the Islamia College in Gujranwala, in 1949. In 1951, Mr. Tarar secured his Law Degree from Law College, Lahore. During the same year he was enrolled as a Pleader. He also was enrolled as an Advocate in the Lahore High Court during October 1955. After graduating, he established a practice in Gujranwala before rising to the position of Chairman of the Punjab Labor Court in 1970. He was appointed as the Chief Justice of Lahore High Court four years later since he started. Earlier, during his days as Judge of the Lahore High Court, he also served as member of the Pakistan Election Commission. Justice Muhammad Rafiq Tarar was elevated as a Judge of the Supreme Court in 1991, from which he retired in November 1994 on attaining the age of 65 years.

Due to his retirement in March 1997, Tarar moved from a legal career to a political career. He was elected as member of Senate on P. M. L. (N) Party and later in the same year he was elected as the President of Pakistan on December 31, 1997. During his presidency, Tarar was mostly a figurehead ruler. The Presidency of Pakistan's powers had been slowly removed over the years, culminating in 1997 Thirteenth Amendment to the Constitution of Pakistan which removed virtually all remaining reserve powers, making the office almost entirely symbolic in nature. Tarar was not removed from office when Pervez Musharraf seized control of the Pakistani government in 1999. While Prime Minister Nawaz Sharif was deposed, Tarar was allowed to remain in office until 2001, at which point Musharraf assumed the presidency in an attempt to both gain legitimacy and restructure Pakistan's model of government to a more presidential system rule.

Muhammad Sarwar : Muhammad Sarwar was an officer of the newly formed Pakistani Army. In 1947, he was part of the raiding force organised by the Pakistani Army that sneaked into the state of Jammu and Kashmir with the object of capturing the state and gaining a strategic geographical advantage over India. He was killed in one of the battles of the First Kashmir War that resulted when the Indian Army retaliated and pushed back the Pakistani forces. He was awarded the Nishan-E-Haider for his valour.

During the Kashmir Operations soon after the birth of Pakistan, as Company Commander of the 2nd Battalion of the Punjab Regiment, Captain Sarwar launched an attack causing heavy casualties against a strongly fortified enemy position in the Uri Sector under heavy machine gun, grenade and mortar fire. But on the 27th July 1948, as he moved forward with six of his men to cut their way through a barbed wire barrier, he died when his chest was riddled by a burst of heavy machine gun fire.

Major Shabbir Sharif Shaheed : Born 28 April 1943 in Kunjah, Gujrat District. Commissioned into the Frontier Force Regiment on 19 April 1964. Major Shabbir Shariff as commander of a company of 6 FF Regiment, was ordered in December 1971 to capture high ground near Sulemanki than a company of the Assam Regiment supported by a squardon of tanks.

In a wellnigh superhuman action, for the next three days and nights after crossing a minefield and massive obstacles and killing forty-three soldiers and destroying four tanks, Major Sharif and his men held two enemy battalions at bay. But after he took over an anti-tank gun from his gunner in an attack was killed by a direct hit in the afternoon of 6 December. He was 28 years old.

Muhammad Shahabuddin : Muhammad Shahabuddin was born on 13 May 1895 at Ellore in Madras. He graduated in Arts from Madras Christian College and in Law from Madras Law College. He joined Indian Civil Services in November 1921 and was posted as Sub-Collector at Madras. He later on served as Joint Magistrate and District and Session Judge till February 1943 when he was appointed Additional Judge of the Madras High Court. In September 1945 he was confirmed as a Judge of Madras High Court.

Justice Shahabuddin was appointed as a Judge of Decca High Court after Partition. He served on Indo-Pak

Boundary Disputes Tribunal in 1949-50. He became the Chief Justice of Decca High Court in February 1950. In 1953 he was appointed as a Judge of the Federal Court. From 22 December 1954 to 14 June 1955 he acted as the Governor of East Bengal (Pakistan). He became the Chief Justice of Pakistan in 1955. Justice Shahabuddin also chaired the Constitution Commission.

Muhammad Yunus : Muhammad Yunus, born 1940, is a Bangladeshi banker, economist and the developer and founder of the concept of microcredit, i.e. the extension of small loans to entrepreneurs too poor to qualify for traditional bank loans. Yunus is also the founder of Grameen Bank.

Born in Chittagong, Yunus studied in Chittagong Collegiate School and Chittagong College. He got his Ph.D. in economics from Vanderbilt University in 1969. Later, he joined Chittagong University as a professor of economics. Yunus first got into the business of fighting poverty during a 1974 famine in his Bangladesh, one of the poorest countries in the world. Yunus discovered that very small loans could make a significant difference in a poor person's ability to survive.

His first loan consisted of $27 from his own pocket which he lent to women in the village of Jobra-near Chittagong University who made bamboo furniture. They sold these items back to moneylenders to repay usurious loans that they had take out to buy the bamboo. With a net profit of 5 Bangladeshi taka (.02 USD), the women were unable to support themselves or their families. However, traditional banks were not interested in making tiny loans to poor people, who were considered poor repayment risks.

In 1976, Yunus founded the Grameen Bank to make loans to poor Bangladeshis. Since then the Grameen Bank has issued more than $3 billion in loans to approximately 2.4 million borrowers. To ensure repayment, the bank uses a system of "solidarity groups". These small informal groups apply together for loans and its members act as co-guarantors of repayment and support one another's efforts at economic self-advancement.

As it has grown, the Grameen Bank has also developed other systems of alternate credit that serve the poor. In addition to microcredit, it offers housing loans as well as financing for fisheries and irrigation projects, venture capital, textiles, and other activities, along with other banking services such as savings. The success of the Grameen model has inspired similar efforts throughout the developing world and even in industrialized nations including the United States. Many, but not all, microcredit projects also emulate its emphasis on lending specifically to women. More than 94 percent of Grameen loans have gone to women, who suffer disproportionately from poverty and who are more likely than men to devote their earnings to serving the needs of the entire family.

Muhammad Yusuf Khan Khattak : Muhammad Yusuf Khan Khattak (18 November 1917 – 29 July 1991) was a Pakistan movement activist. A scion of one of the most influential families in NWFP, he was a son of Khan Bahadur Kuli Khan Khattak, and brother to former Governor Aslam Khattak, Lt Gen Habibullah Khan and Kulsom Saifullah Khan, Yusuf Khattak was a Pakistan movement activist against the then NWFP Congress government under Dr Khan Sahib. A close confidante of Liaqat Ali Khan he became Secretary General of the Muslim League after partition. However, he fell out with Muslim League Chief Minister Abdul Qayyum Khan, who actively organised a campaign to oust him and his colleagues like Barrister Khan Saifullah Khan, from any role in provincial politics.

Frequently in the opposition, he was elected the leader of the opposition in the National Assembly and was a prominent leader in the campaign of Fatima Jinnah against Field Marshal Ayub Khan's military government. A prominent critic of Khan Abdul Ghaffar Khans Pakhtunistan policy, he also rejected the National Awami Party's claim to be the sole representative of Pashtuns. Reconciling with Qayyum Khan before the bye elections 1971 election, he joined the Pakistan Muslim League-Qayyum faction and contested and won the election from Qayyum Khan's vacated Peshawar seat. As part of Qayyum Khan's alliance with the PPP, Yusuf Khattak was appointed Federal Minister for Fuel, Power and Natural Resources in Prime Minister Zulfiqar Ali Bhutto's Cabinet. He was re-elected to his seat in the 1977 election despite the Qayyum League's rout. In 1990 the Government of Pakistan gave him a gold medal for his services to Pakistan.

Muhammad Zafrulla Khan : Sir Muhammad Zafrulla Khan (1893 1985) was a Pakistani diplomat and Ahmadiyya Community scholar. Khan was born on February 6, 1893, in Sialkot, India, the son of Nasrullah Khan. He graduated from the Government College, Lahore, in 1911. Between 1911 and 1914 he studied at King's College London and was called to the bar at Lincoln's Inn. Returning to India he practised law in Sialkot, until July 1916, and lectured in the Law College, Lahore, during 1919 to 1924, and practised law in Lahore up to 1935.

As an active Ahmadi he was the Amir of the Ahmadiyya Community in Lahore during the period 1919 to 1935. He served as Secretary to Hazrat Khalifatul Masih II, the second successor of Mirza Ghulam Ahmad at the occasion of Shura (Advisory Council) for the first time in 1924 and did so on a further seventeen occasions. He was elected a member of the Punjab Legislative Council in 1926 and presided at the Delhi Meeting of the All India Muslim

League in 1931 he advocated the cause of the Indian Muslims through his presidential address. He participated in the Round Table Conferences held in the years 1930, 1931, and 1932, and he was member of the Executive Council of the Viceroy of India, during the years 1935 to 1941.

In October 1947, represented Pakistan in United Nations General Assembly as the head of the Pakistan delegation and advocated the stand of the Muslim world on the Palestinian issue. Was appointed as Pakistan's (first) Foreign Minister a post he held for 7 years from 1947. In 1948 to 1954 he represented Pakistan at the Security Council (UN) and admirably advocated the case of liberation of the occupied Kashmir, Libya, North Ireland, Eritrea, Somalia, Sudan, Tunisia, Morocco, and Indonesia. In 1954 he became Judge of the International Court of Justice in The Hague, which he held until 1961. He became the Vice President of the International Court of Justice, the Hague, in 1958 until 1961.

Muhammed Zafar Iqbal : Muhammed Zafar Iqbal (born December 23, 1952) is a Bangladeshi academian, scientist, writer of children's books and science-fiction and columnist. He is a professor of Computer Science at the Shahjalal University of Science and Technology. Iqbal studied Physics at the University of Dhaka and graduated in 1975. He obtained his PhD from the University of Washington in 1982. He had a distinguished career at Caltech and then worked for the Bell Labs in New Jersey.

Zafar Iqbal started writing since his college days and became very popular with his teen-adventure novels, a rarity in Bangla literature in the late 1970s. His writing career was interrupted when he came to study and work in the USA. While abroad, his first two science fiction books came out, meeting great critical and popular acclaim.

He returned to Bangladesh in early 1990s, leaving his successful career in the US, and joined a Shahjalal University of Science and Technology to teach Physics and Computer Science. After his return, he took up the causes of promoting science to young children, building a first-rate science education program at the university, and promoting freedom of thought. His latter cause and his opposition to the religious fundamentalism put him in direct conflict with the religious fanatics.

Although he writes fiction and non-fiction for grown-ups, he is at his creative best with his novels for adolescents. The young people in his novels are everyday boys and girls, seek and find adventure in their otherwise unremarkable and modest lives. They go through tough times with wonderful sense of optimism and wide eyed curiosity. A couple of his novels have been made into motion pictures.

Muharram : The Muharram festival is celebrated for 10 days. For 8 days the Mullah sits besides the peeras and worship them reciting passages from Holy Koran. Many among the Hindus also offer worship at the shrine. They take a small quantity of sugar along with them and hand it over to the Mullah who after chanting scriptures returns it as prasadam to those who offered it. On the ninth day groups of young men from Muslims, Bedas, Agasas, Kurubas and other lower communities start dancing in front of the peeras till the evening of the next day to the beating of country drums. On the evening of the tenth day the peeras are ceremoniously removed and they are taken through in the main streets in a procession and later on immersed in a well. Muslim members sing in mournful tone and return home. The tombs of former Jagirdar and his wife is situated in the village Sarjapur which are held in reverence by Muslims and the annual Urs is held during Muharram.

Muhuri River : Muhuri river is one of the Trans-boundary rivers of Bangladesh. The river takes its rise on the Lushai Hill of Tripura in India and enters Bangladesh through Parshuram upazila of Feni district after flowing over the hilly regions of India. As such the river is wild in nature and often causes flash floods. At some places it demarcates the boundary between India and Bangladesh and falls into the Bay of Bengal after dividing the Feni and the Chittagong district. Before 1975, the Indian government constructed an impermeable spur on the river to save the Belonia town of Tripura State from the erosion of the river. But afterwards it has been decided in a meeting of joint river commission that none of the countries can construct spur or groyen on the river. The islands or chars formed in the Muhuri river are partly controlled by India and partly by Bangladesh.

Muhuri River : Muhuri River one of the trans-boundary rivers of Bangladesh. The river takes its rise on the Lushai Hill of Tripura in India and enters Bangladesh through Parshuram upazila of Feni district after flowing over the hilly regions of India. As such the river is wild in nature and often causes flash floods. At some places it demarcates the boundary between India and Bangladesh and falls into the Bay of Bengal after dividing the Feni and the Chittagong district.

Mujib Bahini : Mujib Bahini was formed during the War of Liberation. It was mainly composed of activists drawn from the Awami League and its student front Chhatra League. It had enlisted about 5000 members who were posted out to four sectors with a 19-member central command. Initially, the sector commanders operated from Barrackpur, Shiliguri, Agartala and Meghalaya of India. Tofail Ahmed, Sirajul Alam Khan, Abdur Razzak and Sheikh Fazlul Haq Mani were the central commanders with Moni acting as the commander-in-chief. This force was trained under the direct supervision of Major General Uban of India at Deradun hills.

Mujibnagar Government : On 10 April 1971, the Government of the People's Republic of Bangladesh was formed through a proclamation of independence issued from Mujibnagar. It confirmed the declaration of independence made earlier. Bangabandhu Sheikh Mujibur Rahmaǹ, who was then interned in Pakistan, was elected President, syed nazrul islam Vice President and Tajuddin Ahmed Prime Minister. In the absence of the President, the Vice President was empowered to exercise the powers, duties and responsibilities of the President.

Mukesh Chandra Mathur : Mukesh Chandra Mathur was a popular playback singer in Hindi Films. His smooth voice had a certain quality that won him millions of admirers. Most of his songs carved a niche in people's heart and he will be long remembered for his talent. Mukesh was introduced to the film world by actor Moti Lal. He wanted to be an actor and acted in a few films. But his fate was to become popular as a singer. In 1945, he sang for the film 'Pehli Nazar' and his song 'Dil Jalta Hai to Jalne De' brought him instantaneous popularity among the followers of film music. He gave his voice for most of the songs of Raj Kapoor and Manoj Kumar. He sang his last song for 'Satyam Shivam Sundaram'. Mukesh won international popularity and received ' Filmfare Award' four times.

Mukesh sang thousands of songs. Some of the most popular numbers among them are 'Dil Jalta Hai' (Pehli Nazar), 'Awaraa Hun' (Awara), 'Mera Joota Hai Japani' (Shri 420), 'Dost Dost na raha' (Sangam), 'Jane Kahan gaye woh din' (Mera nam Joker), 'Kayi bar yun bhi dekha hai' (Rajnigandha). His voice had a sad tone to it that touched the listener's heart. He died on August 27, 1976, while on a concert tour in the US.

Mukteswar, Siddheswar and Kedargauri Temples : Notar from the Parsuarameswar is the small 10th century Mukteswar Mandir, the Gem of Orissan architecture. The carvings of dwarfs are particularly striking. In front of the temple there is a beautiful arched architrave clearly showing a Buddhist influence. The walls are covered with figures of female warriors, erotic scenes, elephants, maidens and monkeys in various comic scenes.. The large green temple tank makes a perfect swimming pool.

Mukhtar Ahmed Ansari : Dr. Mukhtar Ahmed Ansari was an Indian nationalist and political leader, and former president of the Indian National Congress and the Muslim League during the Indian Independence Movement. He was born on December 25, 1880 in the district of Ghazipur, Uttar Pradesh. Ansari obtained a medical degree from the Madras Medical College and went to England on scholarship studies.

Dr. Ansari became involved in the Indian Independence Movement during his stay in England. He moved back to Delhi and joined both the Indian National Congress and the Muslim League. He played an important role in the negotiation of the 1916 Lucknow Pact and served as the League's president in 1918 and 1920. He was an outspoken supporter of the Khilafat movement, and worked to bring the official Khilafat body, the League and the Congress Party together on the issue against the Mustafa Kemal's decision to oust the Sultan of Turkey, who was the Caliph of Islam, and to protest the recognition of Turkey's independence by the British Empire.

Dr. Ansari served serveral terms as the AICC General Secretary, as well as the President of the Indian National Congress during its 1927 session. As a result of in-fighting and political divisions within the League in the 1920s, and later the rise of Muhammad Ali Jinnah and Muslim separatism, Dr. Ansari drew closer to Mahatma Gandhi and the Congress Party. Dr. Ansari also served as the chancellor of the Jamia Millia Islamia university in Delhi soon after the death of its founder, Dr. Hakim Ajmal Khan.

Dr. Ansari was amongst a new generation of Indian Muslim nationalists, which included Maulana Azad, Muhammad Ali Jinnah and others. He was very passionate about the issues of common Indian Muslims, but unlike Jinnah, was resolutely against separate electorates and opposed Jinnah's viewpoint that the Muslim League could be the only representative of India's Muslim communities. Dr. Ansari was very close to Mahatma Gandhi and an adherent of Gandhism, with his core teachings of ahimsa and non-violent civil resistance. He enjoyed an intimate friendship with the Mahatma. Dr. Ansari died in 1936 en route from Mussoorie to Delhi on a train due to a heart attack, and is buried in the premises of the Jamiya Milliya Islamiya in Delhi.

Mukti Bahini : Mukti Bahini (Liberation Army), was a guerrilla force which fought against the Pakistan Army during the Bangladesh War of Independence in 1971. The immediate precursor of the Mukti Bahini was Mukti Fauj (Fauj means army in the subcontinent), which was preceded denominationally by the Sangram parishads formed in the cities and villages by the student and youth leaderships in early March 1971. When and how the Mukti Fauj was created is not clear nor is the later adoption of the name Mukti Bahini. It is, however, certain that the names originated from the people who joined the liberation struggle. The Mukti Bahini obtained strength from the two main streams of fighting elements: members of armed forces of erstwhile East Pakistan and members of the urban and rural Sangram parishads.

Muktsar Fair : The Muktsar fair is held in the middle of January on the Makar Sankranti day. The festival is in commemoration of a battle fought in 1705-1706 by Guru Gobind Singh against the pursuing imperial forces which overtook him here and cut his followers to pieces. The Guru himself escaped and had the bodies of his followers disposed of with the usual rites. He declared that they had all obtained mukti and promised the same blessing to all his followers, who should thereafter, on the anniversary of that day, bathe in the Holy pool which had been filled by rain from heaven in answer to his prayer for water. On this spot a fine tank was afterwards dug by Maharaja Ranjit Singh and called Muktsar (the pool of Salvation).

It is one of the great Sikh festivals, and lasts three days. On the first day the worshippers bathe is the sacred tank. On the second day the people go in a procession (mohalla) to the three holy mounds which lie to the north-west of the town, namely, Rikab Sahib, Tibbi Sahib and Mukhwanjana Sahib. The Rikab Sahib, a mound formed out of the handfuls of earth taken from the tank by the faithful and thrown there, commemorates the spot where the Guru's stirrup broke. The procession goes up the slope to the Tibbi Sahib which, crowned with a Gurudwara, is the mound where Guru Gobind Singh stood and aimed his arrows at the imperial forces. The devotes then proceed to the Mukhwanjana Sahib where the Guru is said to have cleaned his teeth with a tooth-stick. Prayers are offered here and the devotes then return. This mound has been built in the same way as the Rikab Sahib. On their return trip people visit the Tambu Sahib where the Guru's tent was pitched before the fight started, the Shahid Ganj, which is the Samadhi of the forty martyrs and the Darbar Sahib, where the Guru held his Darbar after the cremation of the slain.

Mukut Mithi : Mukut Mithi (born 1954) is the former Chief Minister of the Indian state of Arunachal Pradesh.

He served from January 19, 1999 until August 3, 2003. He was proceeded and succeeded by Gegong Apang. For much of his political career he was a member of the Indian National Congress and then the Arunachal Congress but he broke from the Arunachal Congress in 1998 to form the Arunachal Congress-Mithi.

Mulayam Singh Yadav : Mulayam Singh Yadav (born November 21, 1939) is a politician in Uttar Pradesh, India. He has been repeatedly elected to the Uttar Pradesh legislative assembly since 1965. He first became a state minister in 1977. In 1980, he became the president of the Lok Dal (People's Party) in Uttar Pradesh which later became part of the Janata Dal (People's Party). In 1982, he was elected leader of the opposition in the Uttar Pradesh legislative council. He first became chief minister of Uttar Pradesh in 1989, serving in that position until 1991.

In 1992, he founded the breakakaway Samajwadi Party(Socialist Party). In 1993, he allied with the Bahujan Samaj Party and became chief minister of Uttar Pradesh, holding that post until his ally opted into another alliance in 1995. In 2002, following a fluid post-election situation in Uttar Pradesh, the Bharatiya Janata Party and Bahujan Samaj Party tied up to form a government under dalit leader Mayawati, considered to be Mulayam's greatest rival. After a one-and-a-half year stint, the BJP pulled out of the government, and enough rebel legislators of the Bahujan Samaj Party left to allow Mulayam to become the Chief Minister, with the support of independents and small parties.

Multan : Multan is a city in the Punjab Province of Pakistan, and capital of Multan District. It is located in the southern part of the province, and is a very historic city. It has a population of over 3.8 million (according to 1998 census), making it the sixth largest city in Pakistan. It is built just east of the Chenab River, more or less in the center of the country, and about 966 km from Karachi.

Multan is known as the 'City of Pirs and Shrines', and is a prosperous city of bazaars, mosques, shrines and superbly designed tombs. The Multan International Airport connects to flights to major cities in Pakistan and rest of the world.

Being in Punjab, the majority of Multan's residents are Siraiki, and an overwhelming majority of the people are Muslim. Most of the people speak Siraiki language with a good portion of the people knowing Urdu. English is understood by the educated. Multan is also rich in literature, there are many poets who are known country wide.

Multan District : Multan District is a district of Pakistan, capital is Multan. Multan District is surrounded by the Khanewal District on the North and North East, Vehari District on East and Lodhran District on South. The Chenab River passes on its Western side and across which lies Muzaffargarh District.

Multan Fort : Multan Fort was built on a detached, rather high mound of earth separated from the city by the bed of an old branch of River Ravi. There is no Fort now as it was destroyed by the British Garrison, which was stationed there for a long time but the entire site is known as the Fort. Nobody knows when Multan Fort came into being but it was there and it was admired and desired by kings and emperors throughout centuries.

It was considered as one of the best forts of the sub-continent from the defence as well as architectural points of view. When intact its circumference was 6,600 feet or, say, about one and a half mile. It had 46 bastions including two flanking towers at each of the four gates named as the De, Sikki, Hareri and Khizri Gate. When it was intact the Fort consisted of a hexagonal wall from forty to seventy feet high, the longest side of which faced the northwest and extended for 600 yards, and which isolated it from the town. A ditch twenty-five feet deep and forty feet wide was on the side of the wall, behind which was a glacis exhibiting a face of some eighteen feet high, and so thick as to present an almost impregnable rocky mound. Within the fort, stood the citadel. The walls were flanked by thirty towers, and enclosed numerous houses, mosques, a Hindu temple of high antiquity, and a Khan's palace, the beauty of which was severely damaged by the battering it got from the guns of Ranjeet Singh in 1818. Once this was the position of the Multan Fort, but during the British occupation everything was lost and finished forever.

Multan International Airport : The Multan International Airport is situated at 10 km away from city centre of Multan. It is not as large as the other airports in Pakistan, as it operates to cater mainly to the population of Multan.

Mumba Devi Mandir : Mumba Devi Mandir, or Mumba Devi Temple, is an old Hindu temple in the city of Mumbai (formerly Bombay) dedicated to the goddess Mumba. Mumba is the eponym of the city and a local incarnation of the Devi (Mother Goddess) conception of being. While Hindu sects devoted to the goddess Mumbadevi are attested to as far back as the 15th century, it is said that the temple was built in 1675 near the main landing site of the former Bori Bunder creek against the north wall of the English Fort Saint George by a Hindu woman also named Mumba. The creek and fort are now deteriorated to a point at which they are but derelict reminders of the city's past. The temple, on the other hand, is still active.

The goddess Mumba was patron of the agri (salt collectors) and kohli (fisherfolk), the original inhabitants of the Seven Islands of Bombay. She is depicted as a black stone sculpture in the temple. An etymology of Mumba that is popular is "Maha Amba," or "Great Mother," one of the many of India's more well-known names for the Hindu Mother Goddess (Devi). Located in Bhuleshwar area in South Mumbai, the temple is in the heart of the steel and clothing markets. It is a sacred pilgrimage spot and place of worship for Hindus and is thus visited daily by hundreds of people. It is not uncommon for visitors of Mumbai to pay their respects at the temple and is one of the popular tourist destinations in the city.

Mumbai : Mumbai is the capital of the state of Maharashtra, and the most populous city of India, with a estimated population of about 18 million (2005). Mumbai is located on Salsette Island, off the west coast of Maharashtra. Along with its neighbouring suburbs, it forms the world's 4th most populous metropolitan area, with a population exceeding 20 million. The city has a deep natural harbour, which is the largest port in western India. The port handles over half of India's passenger traffic and a significant amount of cargo.

Mumbai is the commercial and entertainment capital of India, and houses important financial institutions, such as the Reserve Bank of India (RBI), the Bombay Stock Exchange (BSE), the National Stock Exchange of India (NSE) and the corporate headquarters of many Indian companies. Mumbai has attracted migrants from all over India because of the immense business opportunities, and the relatively high standard of living, making the city a potpourri of various communities and cultures. The city is home to India's film and television industry, known as Bollywood. Mumbai is also one of the rare cities to accommodate a national park, the Sanjay Gandhi National Park, within its city limits.

Mumbai Harbour : Mumbai Harbour is the southern portion of the Ulhas River estuary, the northern (and narrower) part of which is called Thane Creek. The historical island of Elephanta is one of the six islands that lie in the harbour. Jawaharlal Nehru Port and Navi Mumbai (New Bombay) lie to the east on the mainland, and the city of Mumbai (formerly Bombay) lies to the west on Salsette Island. The harbour opens to the Arabian Sea to the south. The Gateway of India with its jetty for Elephanta is the most important tourist destination, followed by the INS Vikrant maritime Museum. Mangrove swamps line much of the northwestern and eastern shores of the harbour, and provide a rich habitat for wildlife, including thousands of migrating birds such as flamingoes.

Mumtaz Mahal : Mumtaz Mahal (from the Persian for "first lady of the palace") is the common nickname of Arjumand Banu Begum, who was born April 1593 in Agra, India. Her father was the Persian Abdul Hasan Asaf Khan, the brother of Nur Jehan, wife of Jahangir. She was married at the age of 19, on 10 May 1612, to then-Prince Khurram, who would later ascend the Peacock Throne as Mughal emperor Shah Jahan I. She was his second wife, and named Mumtaz Mahal, which means "beloved ornament of the palace" in Persian. She became his favourite wife. She died June 17, 1631 in Burhanpur in the Deccan, now in Madhya Pradesh, during childbirth of her daughter and was buried in the Taj Mahal in Agra.

Not much is known about her except that she was woman of legendary beauty and virtue, who led a very deep and loving marriage with Shah Jahan. Even during her lifetime, poets would espouse her beauty, gracefulness and compassion. It was said that even the moon would hide in shame from her beauty. Mumtaz Mahal was Shah Jahan's trusted companion, traveling with him all over the Mughal empire, and visiting the lands. He trusted her so far, that he even gave her his imperial seal, the Muhr Uzah. She was a big influence on him, apparently often intervening on behalf of the poor and destitute. But she also enjoyed watching elephant and combat fights performed for the court.

They had fourteen children, seven of whom died young. Mumtaz Mahal died during childbirth, while accompanying Shah Jahan during a war campaign against the Lodi lords in the Deccan. Legend has it that on her deathbed, her last wish to the emperor was for a symbol or a monument to their love. Inconsolable, the emperor promised immediately. Apparently after her death, Shah Jahan went into secluded mourning for a year, when he appeared again his hair had turned white, his back was bent, and his face worn out. He kept his promise and built her tomb, the Taj Mahal, in Agra. It took more than 20 years, and most of the treasury, to finish it. Today, it stands as the ultimate monument to love, and a homage to her beauty and life.

Mumtaz Mufti : Mumtaz Mufti (d. October, 1995), was a writer from Pakistan. In the beginning of his literary career, Mumtaz Mufti was considered a non-conformist writer having liberal views. Like Mumtaz Shireen he appeared influenced by Freud. As Ashfaq Ahmed, a close friend, once said before partition, Mumtaz Mufti used to read unpopular literature and even novels by a Swedish writer. he disliked the partition plan but later became a patriotic Pakistani and defender of Islam and its principles. His main transformation from a liberal to a hardline sufi came about after he came under the influence of Qudrat Ullah Shahab. All the same, he did manage to retain his individual accent and wrote on subjects which were frowned upon by the conservative elements in society.

Munda : Munda a very small group of aboriginal people living in different parts of Bangladesh. According to some estimates based on information gathered by some non-government organisations, there are 212 Munda families in the country. As counted locally, 1,163 Mundas live in scattered villages of Koyra and Dumuria upazilas of Khulna district and Shyamnagar, Debhata and Tala upazilas of Satkhira district - all falling within the Sundarbans. The ecosystem of the Sundarbans seems to suit the indigenous ways of living and cultural traits of Mundas

Munda Languages : Munda Languages are spoken in north east India. Mundari and Kolh are famous languages of this group. Munda languages are spoken by about 9,000,000 people in east-central and central India. Most linguists classify the Munda languages together with the Mon-Khmer languages of Southeast Asia into the Austroasiatic language family. The origins of the Munda languages are not firmly established; it is generally thought that the Munda languages are autochthonous languages of eastern India.

Elements of the Munda languages influenced other Indian languages like Sanskrit and the Dravidian languages. Some scholars divide the languages into two subfamilies: the North Munda (spoken in the Chota Nagpur Plateau of Jharkhand, Bengal, and Orissa) including Korku, Santali, Mundari, Bhumij, and Ho; and the South Munda (spoken in central Orissa and along the border between Andhra Pradesh and Orissa). The latter family is further split into Central Munda, including Kharia and Juang, and Koraput Munda, including Gutob, Remo, Sora (Savara), Juray, and Gorum. The classification of these languages is controversial.

Mundu : The mundu is a garment worn around the waist in Kerala and Maldives related to the Dhoti as well as the Lungi.

It is normally woven in cotton and coloured white or cream. The colour is dependent on whether the cotton is bleached. When unbleached the mundu is called a neriyathu. In modern times, two types of mundu are prevalent—the single and the double. A single mundu is draped once around the waist, while the double is folded in half before draping. A mundu is usually starched before use.

Munier Chowdhury : Munier Chowdhury (born 27 November 1925- died 14 December 1971) was a Bangladeshi educator, playwright, literary critic and political dissident. Munier Chowdhury started his career in teaching at Brojolal College in Khulna and worked there between 1947 and 1950. Later he worked for some time at the Jagannath College in Dhaka in 1950. After that, he joined the Dhaka University in 1950 and taught both in English and Bengali language departments between 1950 and 1971.

Munier Chowdhury actively participated in the Language Movement of 1952, and was imprisoned by the Pakistan government. He wrote his famous symbolic drama, Kabar (The Grave) during his imprisonment. He also fought against any type of cultural repression during the late 1950s and 1960s. In 1967, he protested against the Pakistan government's directive to ban Tagore songs on Radio and Television. In the late 1960s there was a movement in Pakistan to replace the Bengali language alphabet with the Roman alphabet. As a linguist and writer, Munier Chowdhury protested this move to undermine the native language of East Pakistan. He actively participated in the non-cooperation movement during the early part of 1971 and renounced his award Sitara-e-Imtiaz (awarded by Pakistan Govt in 1966).

Munnar : Munnar is a small town located at 10.09° North and 77.06° East in Idukki district, of the southern state of Kerala in India. The name is most often used to refer to the whole tourist area, of which the town forms a part.

It is located at the confluence of the mountain streams Mudrapuzha, Nallathanni and Kundala. It is surrounded by wild jungles and is wet and cold for most of the season.Though part of Kerala state,Tamil workers brought from Tamilnadu and their successors are now majority in Munnar

During the British rule of India, Munnar was developed to cultivate tea plants. At that time, most of the people around the area were employed as labourers for the various plantations. In the early stages of development, only Tamilians and a few Malayalis were present there.

Most of the top positions were occupied by the British, proudly called 'Managers' in Munnar. A few bungalows were built for them and these are still used. It is also believed that Munnar was a favourite place for those of the British who were in the know and it is sometimes referred to as the 'Switzerland of India' for its natural surroundings and Old World architecture. In 2000, the Government of Kerala declared Munnar as a tourist spot. This has helped in attracting more tourists to the place.

Munshi Abdur Rouf : Munshi Abdur Rouf (1943-1971) was an officer in Bangladesh Army during the Liberation War. He was born in May 1943 in the village of Salmat of Boalmari upazila under Faridpur District. Enrolled in the East Bengal Regiment on 8 May 1963, he was attached with a regular infantry unit during War of Liberation. He embraced martyrdom on 8 April 1971 at Burighat in Chittagong Hill Tracts after causing extensive damage to Pakistan Army with his MG and forcing it to retreat. He was awarded the highest recognition of bravery of the Bangladesh Armed Forces, Bir Sreshtho

Munsiyari : Munsiyari is a place situated on the northern part near the great Himalayan wall,of the Pithoragarh district, Uttaranchal state, India, at a distance of 124km.' Munsiyari, literally means the place with snow. Munsiyari is one of district's Tehsil and Sub Division. It is situated on the banks of Goriganga river. Munsiyari is a fast growing tourist destination for nature lovers and trekkers. Glacier enthusiasts and high altitude trekkers commonly use it as their base camp. Munsiyari is located on the ancient 'salt route' from Tibet. Munsiyari is at the entrance of the Johar valley which extends along the path of the Goriganga river to its source at Milam Glacier. It is inhabited mainly by the Shauka people (referred to as Bhotiya by the non-Shaukas), who are its original natives.

Muntakhab-ut-Tawarikh : Muntakhab-ut-Tawarikh a general history of the Muslim world written by Abdul Qadir Badayuni. It is a very well known history of the Muslim rule in India from the Ghaznavids to the 40th year (1595-96) of akbar's reign. Abdul Qadir, son of Muluk Shah, was born at Badayun in modern Uttar Pradesh, India in 948 AH/ 1541-42 AD. Given proper education he was well versed in various branches of Islamic learning and grew up into a bigoted Sunni Muslim. Almost of Akbar's age, he was introduced to the emperor in 1573 and was enrolled among the learned men of the court. Abdul Qadir Badayuni was a friend of Nizamuddin Ahmad Bakhshi (author of the Tabaqat-i-akbari). Shortly after the death of his friend he began to write the Muntakhab and completed it on 23rd Jamadi II, 1004 (February, 1596). Probably Badayuni died soon after that.

Murang : It is a festival of abundance and richness of wealth and is generally celebrated in the month of January every year. Although this is an individual family festival, the entire Apatani as well as others are also openly invited to take part with a liberty to eat and drink and enjoy freely. It is being celebrated for the well being of the individual family members alone, specially with a hope to be blessed with more wealth and prosperity for that individual family members in Arunachal Pradesh.

Murong : Murong is a tribe of Bangladesh. Murongs are one of the famous aborigines of Arakan and the two Murong kings, who ruled Arakan in the tenth century, were A-mya-thu (957) and Pai-phyu (964). At that time Wathaly was the capital city of Arakan. Murongs had a bloody war with the Khumis on the bank of the Koladain. The Khumi tribe defeated the Murongs and ousted them from Arakan. Murongs moved to Chittagong hill tracts sometime between the 17th and 18th centuries. Many, however, believe that this happened in the 14th century. Murongs now live in Lama, Ruma, Alikadam and Thanchi upazilas near Chimbuk Mountain of Bandarban district. In 1991, the Murong population in Bangladesh was 22,178 and constituted the fourth largest tribe in Chittagong Hill Tracts.

Murree : Murree also known as the Queen Of The Hills is a minor edition of the many classic hill stations set up by the British in the Himalayan foothills during the 19th century. This mountainous, and one of the most popular summer resorts in the country, was originally established at 7,000 feet during the British Raj. But today Murree is currently situated at an altitude of 2300 m (8000 ft) above sea level.

Murree is a thriving summer resort for the nearby capital of Pakistan and is just an hours drive from Islamabad. From the center of the Islamabad-Rawalpindi area, Murree is reachable by a well-conditioned main road in about two hours. The scenic journey, with a great view of forest clad mountains and majestic pines on densely wooded hills, is a delight for the visitors.

Murree Beer : Murree Beer is Pakistan's leading beer brand made by Murree Brewery. Recently with the arrival of General Pervez Musharraf's liberal government, prohibition laws in Pakistan have been further relaxed and Murree Beer has enjoyed tremendous sales. Murree Beer is now also being exported to Europe and the Middle East and is available in various Pakistani and Indian restaurants.

Murree Brewery : Makers of Pakistan's premiere beer brand, Murree Beer, Murree Brewery also exports to the Middle East and many European countries where it is available in Indian and Pakistani restaurants.

Murree Road : The famous Murree Road has been a hot spot for various political and social events. Nala Lai, famous for its floods, runs in the middle of the city, dividing it into city area and Cantonment area. History describes Nala Lai water pure enough to do washing clothes but now it has become polluted with the waste water from all sources including factories and houses.

Murshidabad City : The city of Murshidabad is one of the oldest cities of West Bengal, and has a rich heritage. It was the last capital of independent Nawabs of Bengal, and the first capital of Bengal under the British. However, the city has lost its prominence in modern times to bigger cities such as Calcutta. Today it is primarily a trading town for agricultural products and silk. Murshidabad is also an important educational center, with eight colleges affiliated to the University of Calcutta located here. The origins of Murshidabad are not entirely clear. According to Ghulam Hussain, author of the Riyaz-us-Salatin, a merchant named Makhsus Khan first improved the present site of Murshidabad. In 1704, Murshid Quli Khan, the Diwan of Bengal under Aurangzeb transferred the capital from Dacca (now Dhaka in Bangladesh), and renamed the city Murshidabad. In 1716, he attained the title of Nawab (ruler) of the Subah (province) of Bengal, and Murshidabad became his capital. It continued to be the capital under a succession of Nawabs, and also under the British until 1790. It was constituted as a municipality in 1869, which remains to the present day.

Murshidabad District : The district of Murshidabad—2,062 sq mi (5,341 sq km), population 5.863m (2001 census)—has its district headquarters at Baharampur. The district comprises two distinct regions separated by the Bhagirathi River. To the west lies the Rarh, a high, undulating continuation of the Chota Nagpur plateau. The eastern portion, the Bagri, is a fertile, low-lying alluvial tract, part of the Ganges Delta. The district is drained by the Bhagirathi and Jalangi rivers and their tributaries. Rice, jute, legumes, oilseeds, wheat, barley, and mangoes are the chief crops in the east; extensive mulberry cultivation is carried out in the west. The district became part of the Gaur kingdom in 1197 and passed to the British East India Company in the 18th century.

Murtaza Bhutto : Murtaza Bhutto (September 18, 1954—September 20, 1996) was a Pakistani politician. Born in Karachi he was eldest son of the former Prime Minister of Pakistan Zulfikar Ali Bhutto and Begum Nusrat Bhutto. Murtaza graduated Magna Cum Laude from Harvard University in 1976 and continued on to do graduate school at Christ College, Oxford University. In 1977, his father was removed from power and later executed in 1979. In response to the loss of power by his father, Murtaza was instrumental in the formation of Al-Zulfiqar, an organization that has been linked to various terrorist acts in Pakistan. In 1981, members of this group carried out the hijacking of a PIA airplane during which they shot a Lieutenant. He also tried to assassinate Zia-ul-Haq five times, including a SAM attack on Zia'a plane. In 1985, his brother Shahnawaz Bhutto died mysteriously in France, his wife was accused of poisoning him.

Bhutto would return to Pakistan in the 1993, a few years after his sister Benazir had become Prime Minister for the second time. Upon arrival, Murtaza was put into jail on charges built during martial law by the regime of General Zia ul Haq in the 1980s. Despite this setback, Bhutto was able to campaign for and win a seat in the provincial assembly of Sindh. Bhutto was also a critic of his sister's government, accusing it of corruption. These accusations made him a political enemy of his own sister, and split the Pakistan People's Party. The split would also affect the family, leading his mother Nusrat to publicly support him over his sister.

As the political rivalry heated up, Murtaza began to accuse police forces of targeting his group. On September 20,1996, there were close to a 100 policemen placed in sniper like positions around Bhutto's 70 Clifton residence. Bhutto and his associates were all shot in fatal positions, their injuries were not sustained in 'cross-fire' as defenders of the Karachi Police like to claim. Forensic and ballistic evidence later proved that injuries sustained by the police were in fact self inflicted.

The police left the victims to bleed for approximately 45 minutes before they were taken to hospitals, albeit hospitals that are not equipped to handle emergencies. The tribunal held later in 1997 ruled that Murtaza could not have been killed without approval from the highest echelons of government. Benazir Bhutto has not yet been able to account for her government's and police force's role in her brothers slaying. The trial is still in the courts of Pakistan.

Murud : Murud is a village in Latur district in Maharashtra, India. Murud is well known for its school education. Janta Vidya Mandir is the name of the school where disciplines are everything. Rather than being just studious, students have been made there career in

Extracarricular activities like Sports, Dramas, Dance and so on.Khokho is an improtant game in which most of students have done a great job.It has emerged as a gold standard for secondary and higher secondary education in maharashtra. Murud is an important centre of trade and commerce as it is well connected by Highway networks to Latur and Solapur as well.

Musa Khel : Musa Khel, a Pathan tribe on the Dera Ghazi Khan border of the Punjab province of India. They are of Kakar origin, numbering 4670 fighting men. They are a peaceful and united race, but at enmity with the Khetrans and the Baluch tribes to the south of their country. In 1879 the Musa Khels and other Pathan tribes to the number of 5000 made a demonstration against Vihowa, but the town was reinforced and they dispersed. In 1884 they were punished, together with the Kakars, by the Zhob Valley Expedition.

Musakhel : Musakhel (fort) is a district in the north west of Balochistan province of Pakistan. Musakhel was notified as a district on 1st January 1992 when Loralai District was divided into three districts, named Musakhel, Barkhan, and Loralai. Previously, Musakhel was one of the 4 sub-divisions of Loralai district. For administrative purposes, the whole district is one sub-division, i.e., Musakhel, and is further divided into one tehsil (Musakhel) and one sub-tehsil (Kingri). Musakhel tehsil is divided into 3 Qanungo circles, Saddar Musakhel, Toisar, and Drug which are the patwar circles as well.

Mushfiqul Alam : Mushfiqul Alam is an international Fine Art Phtographer born in Bangladesh. His photographs are also exhibited at many national & international exhibitions since 1994. He received the SAARC Youth Award 1999 for photography. Mr. Alam is also a renowned Aviation and Aerial Photographer. He is the founder of Cotheeka Stock Photo Agency that is extended to Cotheeka Group of Companies later. He also is the author of two books on hobby electronics.

Mushtaq Ahmed Yousufi : Mushtaq Ahmed Yousufi is a prominent Urdu satirical and humor writer. He received the Hilal-e-Imtiaz, the highest literary honor in Pakistan by the president in 1999.

Yousufi has also served as the president of several national and international banks.

Muslim League : The All India Muslim League was a political party in British India and was the driving force behind the creation of Pakistan as a Muslim state from British India on the Indian subcontinent. After the independence of India and Pakistan, the League continued as a minor party in India, especially in Kerala, where it is often in government within a coalition with others. In Pakistan, the League formed the country's first government, but disintegrated during the 1950s following an army coup. One or more of factions of the Muslim League have been in power in most of the civilian governments of Pakistan since 1947.

Muslim rule was established across northern India between the 7th and the 14th centuries. The Muslim Mughal Empire ruled most of India from Delhi from the early 16th century until its power was broken by the British in the 19th century. This left a disempowered and discontented Muslim minority, afraid of being swamped by the Hindu majority over whom they had previously ruled. Muslims were about 23% of the population of British India, and were the majority of the population in Baluchistan, Bengal, Kashmir, North-West Frontier Province, Punjab and the Sindh region of the Bombay Presidency.

In the late 19th century an Indian nationalist movement developed, with the Indian National Congress being founded in 1885. Although the Congress made genuine efforts to enlist the Muslim community in its struggle for Indian independence, it was inevitably a Hindu-dominated organisation, and Muslims knew that an independent united India would inevitably be ruled by Hindus. Although some Muslims were active in the Congress, the majority of Muslim leaders did not trust the Hindu majority.

A turning point came in 1900 when the British administration in the largest Indian state, the United Provinces (now Uttar Pradesh), acceded to Hindu demands and made Hindi, written in the Devanagari script, the official language, in place of Persian, which had been the court language under the Mughal Emperors. This seemed to confirm Muslim fears that the Hindu majority would seek to suppress Muslim culture and religion in an independent India. A British official, Sir Percival Griffiths, wrote of "the Muslim belief that their interest must be regarded as completely separate from those of the Hindus, and that no fusion of the two communities was possible."

During this period the unofficial leader of the Indian Muslim community was Sir Sayed Ahmed, head of the Aligarh movement (a cultural organisation based in the Muslim University at Aligarh), but following his death in 1898 a more militant leadership emerged, under the slogan "Islam is in danger." In October 1906 35 leading members of the Indian Muslim community gathered at Simla under the leadership of Sultan Mohammed Shah (the third Aga Khan), to present an address to the Viceroy, Lord Minto. They demanded proportionate representation of Muslims in all government jobs and the appointment of Muslim judges to the High Courts and members in Viceroy's Council.

In 1947, when Pakistan waas formed, Jinnah became Governor-General, and another League leader, Liaquat Ali

Khan became Prime Minister. But Jinnah died in September 1948 and Liaquat was assassinated in October 1951. Robbed of its two senior leaders, the League began to disintegrate. By 1953 dissensions within the League had led to the formation of several different political parties. Liaquat was succeeded by Khawaja Nazimuddin, a Bengali, who was forced from office in April 1953. Pakistan was racked by riots and famine, and at the first national elections in May 1955 the League was heavily defeated.

In October 1958 the Army seized power and the martial law regime of Muhammad Ayub Khan banned all political parties. This was the end of the old Muslim League. The name still held great prestige, however, and Ayub Khan later formed a new party, the Convention Muslim League. The opposition faction became known as the Council Muslim League. This latter group joined a united front with other political parties in 1967 in opposition to the regime. But when the military regime of Agha Mohammad Yahya Khan fell in December 1971, and Pakistan's first genuine free elections were held, both factions of the League were swept out of power, in West Pakistan by the Pakistan People's Party of Zulfikar Ali Bhutto and in East Pakistan by the Awami League of Sheikh Mujibur Rahman.

After the death of Pakistan's next dictator, Muhammad Zia-ul-Haq, in 1988, a new Muslim League was formed under the leadership of Nawaz Sharif, but it had no connection with the original Muslim League. Sharif was Prime Minister from 1990 to 1993 and again from 1997 to 1999, when he was ousted in Pakistan's third military coup. At the stage-managed elections held by the military regime of Pervez Musharraf in October, five different parties using the name Muslim League contested seats. The largest of these, the Pakistan Muslim League (Quaid-e-Azam), won 69 seats out of 272, and the Pakistan Muslim League (Nawaz), loyal to Nawaz Sharif, won 19 seats.

Muslim Rajputs : Rajputs were the rulings clans of India during the classical period, i.e. 8-13th century. The term Rajput is traditionally applied to 36 major clans. While a majority of the Rajputs are Hindu, many well known Rajput clans did convert to Islam from the 13th century due to Sufi missionaries which gained momentum in India after the migration of Khwaja Moinuddin Hasan Chisti of Ajmer to India. It is estimated that nearly 25 million Pakistanis belong to Rajput ancestory. Muslim Rajputs believe that being a Rajput is a matter of blood and martial upbringing, which is not exclusive to Hinduism alone. Islam's ideal of a Mujahid replaces the Hindu Kshatriya ideal and deny that it is a religious title at all. They also do not overly romanticise their ancestry which is forbidden in Islam as a sign of egoism. Many Muslim Rajputs were conferred titles by the Mughal Emperors such as Nawab (governor), Malik (Royal) and Mirza i.e. Prince of the blood. It was not uncommon for such titles to continue down the line of descendancy.

Mussoll : Mussoll is a folk-play-cum-dance in Goa played by the Kshatriyas among the Christians from the two hamlets of Chandor-Kott and Kouddi in Chandor village. Mussoll in Konkani, is an instrument used by women folk for pounding rice. It is a dance based on the legendry powers of the ancient Kshatriyas. This play must have been exhibited at the sabha-mandapa (assembly- hall) of the royal temple of Lord Chareshwar (moon god), with as many variations as circumstances of the time permitted. It is also called 'Musllam-Fell' or Khell. The dance is a war dance—a dance of a martial race or caste. From the wording of the song, the Mussoll dance commemorates the victory of King Harihara II, son of Bukka I of the Vijayanagar empire, over the Cholas at the ancient fort of Chandrapur around 1310AD. King Harihara is supposed to have claimed descent from the lunar race. Mussoll dance has a constituent symbol, i.e. a bear which is the symbol of Cholas.

Mussoorie : Mussoorie is a hill station situated in the foothills of the Himalaya ranges in north Indian state of Uttaranchal. It is also known as "Queen of Hills". Having an altitude of about 2000 meters, Mussoorie, with its green hills and varied flora and fauna, is a fascinating hill resort. Commanding snow ranges to the north-east, and glittering views of the Doon Valley and Shiwalik ranges in the south, the town presents a fairyland atmosphere to the tourists. Its history dates back to 1827 when Captain Young, an adventurous British military officer, together with a Mr Shore, the resident Superintendant of Revenues at Dehradun explored the present site and jointly constructed a shooting lodge. This laid the foundation of this holiday resort which now has few rivals. Mussoorie is famous for its scenic beauty and hectic social life. It provides all kinds of amusement and every facility for domestic and foreign tourists.

Its name is derived from a shrub "MANSOOR" behind the house of the Captain. Some believe that prerhaps that is reason behind the name of the town, which is also known as MANSOORI among the natives of the surrounding area. Mussoorie is conveniently connected by road to Delhi and major cities. It is called the "Gateway" to Yamunotri and Gangotri Shrines of Northern India. The closest rail station is Dehradun. Taxis are easily available for Mussorie as are buses at regular intervals.

Mustafa Qureshi : Mustafa Qureshi is a Pakistani film actor. He gained popularity from Punjabi films. His iconic role as the villain Noori Nat in the movie Maula Jatt became a trademark and he went on to adapt similar roles for many years to come.

He did regret being type cast as he wished to show his versatality in acting.

Mustansar Hussain Tarar : Mustansar Hussain Tarar (March 1, 1939) is one of the most famous personalities of Pakistan. He is a famous writer, compare and a media personalitiy. His first book Nikley Teri Talaash Main, a travelogue of Europe was published in 1971, he has so far over forty titles to his credit which include all genre of literature; travelogues, novels, short stories and collection of his newspaper columns and Televsion dramas.

Muttahida Majlis-e-Amal : Muttahida Majlis-e-Amal also known as the MMA is an Islamist alliance between religious-political parties in Pakistan. In the Pakistani parliament, the MMA, is a coalition opposition, formed after Pakistan became a part of the "Global War on Terror". The coalition is united against the current government of President Pervez Musharraf because of his support for the United States' fight against what they consider to be global terrorism and allegedly putting the demands of the United States above the demands of his own people.

Muttahida Qaumi Movement : Muttahida Qaumi Movement generally known as MQM, is a political party in Pakistan founded by Altaf Hussain. It originated as an ethnic student organization in 1978 from University of Karachi. The students movement later turned into an influential political party of Sindh. Later on July 26, 1997, MQM officially changed its name from Muhajir Qaumi Movement to Muttahida Quami Movement. MQM initially targeted just the Urdu speaking people, who migrated to Pakistan after the independence in 1947. Since 1997, it has started to aim downtrodden masses at the national level, with a manefesto to improve low social and economic status of the Sindh. Although it has turned into a national poitical party, working in all major cities of Pakistan, its representation in non-Urdu speaking areas remains negligible.

Muttusvami Dikshitar : Muttusvami Dikshitar (1775-1835) is the youngest of the Carnatic music composer trinity. He was born in 1775 to Ramaswami Dikshitar and Subbamma, as the eldest son, in Tiruvarur (near present day Thanjavur). Muttuswami is said to have born to the couple after they prayed for a child in the temple of Vaitheeswaran Koil. He was named after the temple deity, Muttukumaraswamy.

Muttuswami Dikshitar attained mastery over the Veena, and the influence of Veena playing is evident in his compositions. He composed his first song "Sri nathadhi guruguho" in the Raga Maya-malava-gowla, in the temple of Tiruttani (near present day Chennai). The song was in praise of his Guru, but also in praise of the Lord Subramanya, who is identified with the concept of a "teacher" or guru in the Hindu theology. His total compostions are about 450 to 500, most of which are still sung by musicians today in Carnatic music concerts. Most of his compositions are in Sanskrit and in the Krithi form i.e. poetry set to music. Muttuswami Dikshitar traveled to many holy shrines throughout his life, and composed krithis on the deities and temples he visited. Statistics on Dikshitar's Compositions

Muttuswami Dikshitar passed away on the 21st of October, 1835. Although Muttuswamy Dikshitar did not have any children of his own, his Brother Baluswami's descendents have preserved musical legacy, and his compositions have been popularised due to the efforts of people like Subbarama Dikshitar and Ambi Dikshitar.

Muzaffarabad : Muzaffarabad is the capital of the State of Azad Kashmir, located in the north of the state, which is part of the Pakistani-controlled part of the former princely state of Jammu and Kashmir, along with the Northern Areas. It is located in Muzaffarabad District. Muzafarabad district, located on the banks of the Jhelum and the Neelum rivers, is very hilly. The district is bounded to Pakistan in the west and to Kupwara and Baramulla districts of occupied Kashmir in the east while Northern Areas fall on the northeast of the district. Total area of the district is 6117 square kilometers. Total population of the district according to 1998 census stands at 725,000 and according to 1999 projection its population stands at 741,000.

Muzaffargarh : Muzaffargarh is a mostly rural district in the south of the Punjab province of Pakistan. Muzaffargarh is also the name of the principal town of the district.

Muzaffarid Dynasty : The Muzaffarid dynasty were sultans of Gujarat in western India from 1391 to 1583. The founder of the dynasty was Zafar Khan Muzaffar (later Muzaffar Shah I) who was governor of Gujarat under the Delhi Sultanate. Zafar Khan's father was a Rajput convert to Islam. When the Sultanate was weakened by the sacking of Delhi by Timur in 1398, and Zafar Khan took the opportunity to establish himself as sultan of an independent Gujarat. His son, Ahmed Shah I established the capital at Ahmedabad. The dynasty ruled for almost 200 years, until the conquest of Gujarat by the Mughal Empire. The sultanate reached its peak of expansion under Mahmud Shah I Begara, reaching east into Malwa and west to the Gulf of Kutch.

During the Muzaffarid rule, Ahmedabad grew to become one of the largest and wealthiest cities in the world, and the sultans were patrons of a distinctive architecture that blended Islamic elements with Gujarat's indigenous Hindu and Jain architectural traditions. Gujarat's Islamic architecture presages many of the architectural elements later found in Mughal architecture, including ornate mihrabs and minarets, perforated screens (jali) carved in stone, and pavilions topped with cupolas (chattri).

Muztagh Tower : The Muztagh Tower (Mustagh Tower), is a mountain of the Karakoram range in the Himalaya, and often said to be one of its most difficult to climb. The Muztagh Tower stands 7,273m high between the basins of the Baltoro and Sarpo Laggo glaciers, and also possesses a second summit that is 7,180 m high. Long thought to be unclimbable, it was first conquered in 1956 by a British expedition, consisting of John Hartog, Joe Brown, Tom Patey and Ian McNaught Davis, that came from the west side. The group just barely managed to beat a French party attempting to climb the mountain from the east, reaching the top on July 6, 1956, five days before the French did. The lower summit of 7,180m was first climbed in 1984 by the northeast ridge

Mymensingh : Mymensingh is one of the districts of Dhaka division, Bangladesh, and is bordered on the north by Meghalaya state of India and Garo Hills, on the south by Gazipur district, on the east by districts of Netrokona and Kishoreganj, and on the west by districts of Sherpur, Jamalpur and Tangail. Mymensingh town is the district headquarters. The district covers an area of around 4363 square kilometers, with several small valleys between high forests. The temperature ranges from 33 degrees to 12 degrees Celsius, and the annual rainfall averages 2174 mm.

Mymensingh district was established in 1787, which was later on reorganized into six districts, namely, Tangail, Jamalpur, Kishoreganj, Sherpur, Netrokona, and Mymensingh. Currently, Mymensingh district has 8 municipalities and 12 Upzillas. The municipalities are: Bhaluka, Gaffargaon, Gauripur, Ishwarganj, Mymensingh Sadar, Nandail, Muktagachha, and Trishal, and the 12 Upzillas are: Bhaluka, Dhobaura, Fulbaria, Gaffargaon, Gauripur, Halughat, Ishwarganj, Mymensingh Sadar,

Muktigachha, Nandail, Phulpur and Trishal. Mymensingh town, earlier known as Nasirabad, stands on the bank of Brahmaputra River.

Myokoh-Apatani Festival : It is the most highly solemnized community festival of the Apatani society in Arunachal Pradesh. It is purely a religious ceremony which is observed for the general well being of the whole Apatani society and is participated by each and every Apatani with great enthusiasm, devotion and respect. It is celebrated every year during the month of March and lasts for the whole month. For full participation, the whole Apatani villages of the plateau have been divided into three major groups-the first group consist of villages like Hija Duta, Mudangtage, Bamin and Michi. The second group consist of Hong village alone and the third group consists of Hari, Kalong, Tajang and Regu. The actual solemnization ceremony is conducted alternatively among the three major groups and then the other groups take full participation with the villages who actually perform the ceremonies.

Mysore : Mysore is the one of the larger cities of the Indian state of Karnataka, the others being Bangalore and Mangalore. Mysore is the administrative seat of Mysore District and Mysore Division, and is the former capital of the Kingdom of Mysore. Mysore is known as the Cultural Capital of Karnataka. Mysore is located at 770 m above sea level and 135 km from Bangalore at 12.18° N 76.42° E. Mysore is known for its palaces and proximity to several attractions. One of the best (some would say worst) times to visit Mysore is during the annual nine-night, ten-day Dussera or Dasara or Navaratri festival, which usually occurs in early October.

Mysore pak : Mysore pak is a sweet southern Indian dish, usually served as dessert. It is made of generous amounts of ghee (clarified butter), sugar and chick pea (besan) flour. The dish is renowned for its unrivalled richness and fantastic sweetness. Indeed, in some circles, it has become a euphemism for "fat".